"The Savage Wars of Peace"

"The Savage Wars of Peace"

Toward a New Paradigm of Peace Operations

EDITED BY

John T. Fishel

Westview Press
A Member of the Perseus Books Group

Published in 1998 in the United States of America by Westview Press, 5500 Central Avenue, Boulder, Colorado 80301-2877, and in the United Kingdom by Westview Press, 12 Hid's Copse Road, Cumnor Hill, Oxford OX2 9JJ

A CIP catalog record for this book is available from the Library of Congress.
ISBN 0-8133-8981-X

The paper used in this publication meets the requirements of the American National Standard for Permanence of Paper for Printed Library Materials Z39.48-1984.

10 9 8 7 6 5 4 3 2

Contents

Conclusion

Preface

"The savage wars of peace--
Fill full the mouth of Famine
And bid the sickness cease...
The ports ye shall not enter,
The roads ye shall not tread,
Go make them with your living,
And mark them with your dead!"

The words above, quoted from Rudyard Kipling's politically incorrect (for the 1990s) poem, "The White Man's Burden," describe far better than any modern writing, the challenge of post Cold War peace operations. When I reread the entire poem a couple of years ago, I was impressed with how well the "poet of imperialism" had captured both the challenges of this world as well as his own but also the character of the then newly emerging American world power. Today, almost a century later, the United States still has not come to terms with its super power status--as the chapters in this book attest.

Our purpose in the book, however, is not to castigate the Americans or any other national participant in modern peace operations. Rather, it is to apply theory developed from social science research to military doctrine and test it against specific cases of peace operations. These operations run the gamut from situations that developed in the 1960s, at the height of the Cold War, to the present. We have divided our nine cases into "traditional peacekeeping", "wider peacekeeping", and "peace enforcement" categories. Yet, having done so, we found that in retrospect the categories are quite arbitrary. The commonalties run through **all** the cases. And they are all unique. Nevertheless, our model informs them all and suggests that such fine distinctions are not necessary or even truly helpful.

The authors of this book are a varied group. They range from established scholars and practitioners to very junior scholars and practitioners. Without exception they have some experience in the real world of security; without exception they have some experience in the academic world. In most cases the authors are in some way affiliated with the US Army Command & General Staff College at Fort Leavenworth, Kansas. This institution, which has been called the "crossroads of the US Army" is really much more. It is the crossroads of the armies of the world (and to a lesser extent, the navies and air forces as well). More important, it is the intellectual heart of the American army and the premier military masters degree granting institution in the world. It is here that many of the authors teach or were educated. And its influence is felt by all of us. And so the book is for its students and graduates among others. Those others include all the civilian governmental and non-governmental agencies that are involved in the "savage wars of peace." Our hope is that the book is useful to them and the soldiers alike.

A last necessary word in this preface, since many of us are either civilian employees of the US government, or serving members of the US and Canadian armies, or retired from one or the other of these categories, and that is: The views expressed in this book are those of the authors and do not necessarily reflect the official policy or position of the Department of the Army, Department of Defense, Department of State, the US government, the Canadian Department of National Defence, the Canadian government, or any intergovernmental organization.

John T. Fishel, PhD

Acknowledgments

A book like this is the product of many minds, hands and computers and so the editor must proffer his thanks to all of them. First and foremost, without the efforts of the person who did all of the technical editing, none of the work of the authors or the editor would have seen the light of day. All of the technical editing was done by one of the co-authors of the book, my wife, Kimbra L. Fishel. What she did was a labor of love for the project as well as her husband. All of us thank you, Kim, for making our scribblings look professional!

To the authors: I thank each of you for the hard work, solid research, the following of format (even when you were sure you had a better way), and meeting the last--if not the first--deadline. Your expertise makes the book what it is. You are all professionals.

Thanks also to my aunt, Ruth Roman, who reviewed several chapters and suggested improvements in the writing. Thanks to the US Army Command & General Staff College for assembling the group of professionals who form the core of the authors and for the environment which encouraged this kind of effort. Thanks to Max Manwaring whose original research produced the theory that is articulated here as the "Manwaring Paradigm." Finally, thank you to the late General Maxwell R. Thurman whose question started it all.

JTF

Introduction

1

War By Other Means? The Paradigm and its Application To Peace Operations

John T. Fishel

Dag Hammarskjold, the late Secretary General of the United Nations, is said to have remarked that peacekeeping is not a soldier's job, yet only a soldier can do it. If he was correct -- and this book is premised on the assumption that he was -- then it is equally necessary for the soldier and the statesman to understand the principles on which peace operations are based and the ways in which they are applied. These "ways"are what the military calls doctrine. This chapter elaborates the relationship between principles and doctrine as well as how these principles were derived from the research that produced what we are calling the "new paradigm of peace operations."

The "new paradigm of peace operations" is hardly new in the sense that this is the first time it has ever been seen. Rather, our paradigm--known elsewhere as the SWORD Model and the Manwaring Paradigm--is new in its application to peace operations.[1] The model, as indicated by the note, was designed for and applied to insurgencies with a great deal of success. It has been used as well to address the problems posed by the "war" on drugs, particularly cocaine, with similar degrees of utility.[2] Moreover, in its initial development the model was not confined only to insurgencies.

Development of the Model

In 1984, General Maxwell R. Thurman was Vice Chief of Staff of the United States Army. Thurman, a veteran of the Vietnam War, saw in the US involvement in the ongoing insurgency in El Salvador a strategic and doctrinal problem that begged for resolution if the US Army was to avoid a quagmire in Central America as divisive as Vietnam had been. So General Thurman queried the Strategic Studies Institute of the Army War College in Carlisle Pennsylvania as to the "correlates of success in counterinsurgency."[3] Of all the analysts at the Institute, only the newly arrived Max Manwaring had the particular political science research training to undertake the kind of quantitative study that could answer the General's question. Thus it fell to Manwaring to conduct the study.

Using a "Delphic" technique, Manwaring developed a preliminary study that suggested several correlates of success. When he briefed these preliminary results to General Thurman, it was with the intent to expand the study. Thurman agreed and the original model became known as SSI 1. Manwaring now began work on the expanded study which used a similar Delphic technique to identify key variables and gather data. What was most important was that the number of cases now reached 69, or virtually all the small wars of the post World War II period which involved a Western nation as a participant.

Data analysis involved reducing the 72 identified variables into a more manageable seven dimensions by the technique of factor analysis and the elimination of all cases that could not be somehow treated as insurgencies. This reduction by 26 cases left 43 insurgencies for the full analysis. The seven dimensions then were correlated individually and collectively with success or failure of the counterinsurgency. The results produced a high degree of confidence that the model could explain the outcome of most insurgencies. Interestingly, preliminary analysis involving all 69 cases suggested that the model might be useful in explaining non-insurgency outcomes, as well.[4] This model, originally called SSI 2, has been published as the SWORD Model and the Manwaring Paradigm as noted above. As a result of an interview with Richard Halloran of the *New York Times* the nickname used by Manwaring and his associates, "the Max Factors," also became known.

The SSI 1 and 2 studies had taken the better part of two years to conduct. Even though the SSI 2 study was not yet published, Manwaring was recalled to active duty in the US Army as a Colonel to become Deputy Director of the newly formed Small Wars Operations Research Directorate of the United States Southern Command (SOUTHCOM). The directorate, called SWORD, was under the command of Colonel Robert Herrick who had spent the last year at SSI as an Army Fellow where he had worked closely with Manwaring on the studies and wanted to use the model as the intellectual foundation for what SWORD would be attempting.[5]

SWORD

The Small Wars Operations Research Directorate, first called the SOUTHCOM LIC Cell, was conceived under the watch of SOUTHCOM Commander in Chief (CINC), General Paul F. Gorman. Gorman's central focus was on technological solutions to the problems of insurgency, however, some of the action officers responsible for the LIC Cell expected it to address doctrinal and strategic issues as well. When Gorman was abruptly replaced by General John Galvin in 1985, there was also some change in the thrust of what the LIC Cell was supposed to be. This change was reinforced the next year when Galvin hired Colonel Herrick to head it and approved the name, SWORD.

Herrick, with Galvin's general support, placed emphasis on strategy, doctrine, tactics, and technology respectively. The theoretical principles under which SWORD conducted its assessments were those of the Manwaring Paradigm. Nevertheless, significant elements of the SOUTHCOM staff, as did Gorman, the former CINC, continued to believe that the appropriate answers to the problems of counterinsurgency were to be found in technology, as did Gorman. These substantive disagreements within the staff, supported by influential outsiders and coupled with internal bureaucratic political issues, resulted in the reorganization of SWORD within a year and, after only two years, its demise. In its short life, however, SWORD's impact was considerable.

The organization's accomplishments centered around the use of Manwaring's model to develop a series of assessments of ongoing insurgencies and other low intensity conflicts in SOUTHCOM's area of responsibility. A series of continuing assessments of the war in El Salvador formed the bulk of the effort. These resulted in a countermine project that, for a time, reduced Salvadoran Army casualties, an assessment of the FMLN attack on the 4th Brigade headquarters of March 31, 1987, assessments of the war as a whole, psychological operations and civil military operations. It also resulted in a major effort under the leadership of the SOUTHCOM J-3, Brigadier General Marc Cisneros, in coordination with Salvadoran Armed Forces, to assess the effectiveness of the armed forces, their conduct of the war, and US assistance.[6] This effort took place from October 1987 until the publication of the classified study on September 1, 1988.

Other assessments addressed Operation Blast Furnace, the first counterdrug operation undertaken in Bolivia in 1986, the *Sendero Luminoso* insurgency in Peru during 1987 which resulted in the creation of a SOUTHCOM Strategy Implementation Team in 1988, and some small efforts to apply the model to achieve an understanding of the US supported *contra* insurgency against the Sandinistas of Nicaragua. During its short life, SWORD produced a series of 11 papers that addressed various aspects of the model and several specific cases of insurgency. Many of those papers found their way into publication in *Military Review*, other journals, and a series of books (of which this is the latest) to be discussed below.

SWORD and the Development of LIC Doctrine

If SWORD was SOUTHCOM's response to the need to think about low intensity conflict (LIC), then the Army, the same institution that Vice Chief Max Thurman had moved to produce what became the paradigm, created a LIC proponency office at the Command and General Staff College at Fort Leavenworth. It also signed an agreement with the Air Force to establish the Army/Air Force Center for Low Intensity Conflict (CLIC) at Langley Air Force Base in Virginia. Significantly, the CLIC was located in the immediate vicinity of the Army's Training and Doctrine Command at Fort Monroe, Leavenworth's parent organization.

Together, the proponency office and the CLIC were charged to produce a new version of FM 100-20, *Military Operations in Low Intensity Conflict*, a document which for the first time would be doctrine for both the Army and Air Force. Since the doctrine writing task came at the same time as the creation of SWORD, which also had an official interest in the creation of doctrine and an organizational link with Fort Leavenworth, it was natural for the CLIC and the proponency office to consider SWORD as their field laboratory. SWORD readily encouraged this perception and soon began providing input to the draft manual. The proponents formally sent out their first draft for comment in early 1987 and SWORD responded by commenting in detail. Indeed, it contributed by rewriting major portions to have the manual conform to the findings of Manwaring's study as supported by SWORD's ongoing assessments.[7]

After a series of exchanges the new FM included most of SWORD's recommendations with special emphasis on what were then called the "LIC imperatives." In particular, two imperatives directly reflected SWORD's precise understanding and definitions. These were Legitimacy and Unity of Effort, both of which are specifically identified as dimensions in the paradigm.[8] Doctrinal development rested in a state of suspended animation for the next two years while senior leaders of the Army's Training and Doctrine Command (TRADOC) sat on the publication. Only through the efforts of newly established office of the Assistant Secretary of Defense for Special Operations and Low Intensity Conflict (ASD-SO/LIC) was the manual finally published in January 1990.[9]

FM 100-20's reflection of SWORD input, while important to this story, is less than the sum of relevant doctrinal development in the manual. Of equal importance was its division of LIC into several categories including one called "peacekeeping."[10] In so doing, the doctrine writers, for the first time, linked the LIC imperatives to peace operations. Moreover, this link would continue in all subsequent iterations of the doctrine.

The linkage, while it follows an impeccable logic path, importantly, is not supported by any empirical research other than the 26 non-insurgency cases that were dropped from the initial Manwaring research. Moreover, these cases merely suggested that such a link might exist; they provided no confirmation that it did exist. Thus the bureaucratic process that the US military uses to develop doctrine enshrined the LIC imperatives as articles of faith with respect to all categories of LIC including peacekeeping.

One problem with the new manual was its place in the doctrinal hierarchy. As conceived at the time, FM 100-20 was to be co-equal with FM 100-5, *Operations*, as keystones of Army tactical doctrine. What the drafters failed to realize at the time was that the resistance to publishing the volume that surfaced at TRADOC would also be manifest in the general lack of interest throughout the Army in what the new manual had to say. The few exceptions to this were found in the special operations community and USSOUTHCOM, the unified command whose entire existence over the decade of the eighties was predicated on LIC.

As FM 100-20 was finally being published several events converged to change the nature of the doctrinal equation in the Army. First, Operation Just Cause was undertaken in Panama from December 20, 1989 through January 31, 1990; Operation Promote Liberty began concurrently.[11] A year later Operation Desert Storm concluded with civil military operations to restore the infrastructure of Kuwait that were consciously based on the similar operations undertaken in Panama.[12] Immediately upon completion of Desert Storm US forces were engaged in military operations in northern Iraq to protect the rebellious Kurds from the oppression and repression of their Iraqi masters.[13] Concurrent with these operations the cyclone that devastated Bangladesh involved a US Joint Task Force in a humanitarian assistance mission called Operation Sea Angel. In 1992 US forces were committed to hurricane relief in Florida (Andrew) and Hawaii (Iniki) and, at the end of the year, to a US led multinational peace enforcement mission in Somalia called Operation Restore Hope. Coupled with the end of the Cold War in 1989, these events raised the visibility of LIC type operations as did the "War on Drugs" which had involved the military since 1986. This increased visibility coincided with a major revision of FM 100-5.

For our purposes the critical decision involved in the 1993 revision of FM 100-5 was that *Operations* would be the only keystone manual in the Army doctrinal inventory. This meant that FM 100-20 would, instead of being co-equal (and, incidentally, generally unread), become the capstone of a major branch of doctrine. As a result, its general thrust would have to be captured in FM 100-5.

Operations sets its schema in Chapter 2 where it posits a continuum of operations ranging from peace through conflict to war. Then, after addressing the variety of combat operations, it focuses in Chapter 13 on what it identifies as Operations Other Than War (OOTW). Although this is, in fact, just another name for LIC, the authors justify the name change in that they address activities that take place in peacetime that were not included under the LIC rubric. As the principal author of Chapter 13 has stated on numerous occasions, the activities listed are not exhaustive; they are merely illustrative. Nevertheless, the OOTW activities replace the four LIC operational categories. Similarly, the LIC imperatives are replaced by the principles of OOTW. While the activities list provides detail for what FM 100-20 included in the LIC operational categories and expands the description of what military forces may be called upon to do, the new principles represent, in some cases, real conceptual change. The first, and in the eyes of many including the principal author of 100-20, most important imperative, "political dominance" is subsumed in the principle of the Objective. Yet they are not the same; one can certainly conceive of military objectives that are nearly devoid of political content. Legitimacy, unity of effort, and perseverance are retained in their original form while adaptability is dropped. In turn, restraint and security are added.[14] We will discuss these in greater detail in conjunction with our analysis of the seven dimensions of the paradigm. Here, we are simply satisfied to show the doctrinal evolution.

That evolution, in turn, took another step in 1994 with the publication of FM 100-23, *Peace Operations*. While that volume provides numerous practical approaches to doctrine and some very useful information (such as the UN Charter and examples of Rules of Engagement and a campaign plan)[15] the particular relevance of the document for this discussion is that it accepts the principles of OOTW as if they were principles of peace operations. Although it expands on the discussion of the principles as a means of adapting them to the environment of peace operations, it makes no effort to examine rigorously their validity and otherwise leaves them intact. Thus, FM 100-23 advances little beyond FM 100-5 and, if the theory on which the principles of OOTW are based is either significantly deficient or wrong, then the current manual simply compounds the error. Hence, the next section will consider the seven dimensions of the Manwaring Paradigm and their relationship with the principles of OOTW. It will also review briefly the methodology used to derive the dimensions.

The SWORD Model/Manwaring Paradigm

The model consists of seven dimensions derived from 72 individual variables. Each of the variables was proposed by one or more of the panel of scholars and practitioners that Manwaring used in his original research.[16] The individual variables were then reduced to seven dimensions through the technique of Factor Analysis which statistically grouped most of the variables while eliminating 22 of the original 72 which could not be correlated as Factors.[17] The Factors then were termed dimensions and given names which attempted to describe in words their central tendency.[18]

The dimensions, as applied to peace operations, are: Unity of Effort, Legitimacy, Support to Belligerents, Support Actions of Peace Forces, Military Actions of Peace Forces, Military Actions of Belligerents and Peace Forces, and Actions Targeted on Ending Conflict. Each dimension, as noted, is composed of a number of individual variables. Thus, Unity of Effort involves the clarity of the mandate, the perception of coincidence of interests between the Peace Force (PF) and the belligerents, and the degree of political polarity between the belligerents and the PF.[19] Legitimacy addresses the degree of support for the peace operation and the PF as well as the public perception of PF legitimacy. These perceptions are important both in the belligerent nation(s) and the world community at large. Also important for legitimacy are the perceptions that the PF can provide security and humanitarian assistance, that it is not seen as corrupt, and that peace will provide political alternatives to endemic violence.

The Support to Belligerents dimension represents the obverse of PF legitimacy. Its component variables include the degree to which the belligerents are not isolated from their support, the time when sanctuaries became available to the belligerents and their continued availability, as well as active outside support for their cause(s). Critical variables comprising Support Actions of Peace Forces are the perceived strength of PF commitment, perceived length of PF commitment, and consistency of military support for the PF. Military Actions of Peace Forces includes as one strong variable the number of troops involved. This variable generally supports success when the numbers are either small or when they follow the British peacekeeping maxim of "maximum strength/minimum force."[20] Other key variables are the type of military activity with those addressing de-escalation of conflict leading to success, the non-use of "unconventional" (dirty war) operations, looting, vandalism, and other criminal acts.

The dimension of Military Actions-Belligerents/PF focuses primarily on the professionalism of the forces. The dimension includes both forces because, as David Last points out, belligerents must be seen as potential allies against the real enemy, conflict itself.[21] Thus key variables include aggressive patrolling, proficiency of military and paramilitary units, and the willingness to take casualties, particularly among officers. Finally, Actions Targeted on Ending Conflict address as critical variables the early initiation of population and resource control measures, intelligence operations, psychological operations, and civic action.

The Paradigm and its Relation to Current Doctrine

Current US doctrine for peace operations as found in FM 100-23 stresses the six principles of OOTW discussed above. As noted, those principles originally derived from the interaction of SWORD, the LIC Proponency Office, and the Army-Air Force Center for Low Intensity Conflict with the dimensions of the SWORD Model informing the LIC Imperatives of FM 100-20--the predecessor of the OOTW principles.

Relating the dimensions of the paradigm to the OOTW principles one finds, first, that Unity of Effort encompasses two of the principles. The first of these is Objective. As I have shown elsewhere, common objectives are necessary but insufficient conditions for Unity of Effort.[22] Second, the dimension of Unity of Effort equates to the principle of Unity of Effort with the conceptual definition of the latter taken directly from the definition of the former. The key to understanding both the dimension and the principle is that the players are independent of each other to a greater or lesser degree. Thus, Unity of Effort results not from command but from negotiation to achieve common ground.

The dimension of Legitimacy and the principle of Legitimacy, again are the same. The variables which make up the dimension clearly comprise the principle as well. However, the principle of Legitimacy also addresses the dimension we have called Support to Belligerents. The dimension focuses on the legitimacy of the belligerent parties in terms of their internal and external support. The fact of a separate dimension serves to differentiate between the legitimacy of the peace forces and the belligerents which should enhance the explanatory power of the paradigm for peace operations just as it did for the analysis of insurgency.[23] Closely related to this dimension is the perseverance of the supporters of the belligerents. What applies to the Peace Forces in the next paragraph applies here to the belligerent supporters.

Support Actions of the Peace Forces addresses the actions of the forces themselves, the international organization giving the mandate, and the governments that make up that organization. In every case one would expect to find that the actions of the Peace Forces and their organizations and governments that suggested a willingness to be committed to the operation as long as necessary contributed greatly to the success of the operation. By contrast, actions which indicated an urgency to depart or a lack of appropriate resource support would have contributed to the perceived failure of the operation. This description of the dimension clearly defines the principle of perseverance.

The several studies that have led to this volume confirmed that the Military Actions of the Peace Forces (Intervening Power in previous studies) required the exercise of restraint if success were to be achieved. This meant restraint in the quantity of troops deployed or in their employment. With respect to quantity, Manwaring and others found that generally success was more likely if fewer troops were deployed but if large numbers were needed it was essential that they be deployed "up front," in the manner the British have called with respect to peace operations, maximum strength/minimum force. Not only was the quantity of the force important, but also the ways it was used. This provides focus on the appropriateness of Rules of Engagement (ROE) as well as the behavior of the troops both with respect to the ROE and to issues not covered directly by either the law of land warfare or the ROE. US military doctrine has captured the essence of this dimension in the principle of restraint.

The principle of restraint is linked with the principle of security in the dimension called Military Actions of the Belligerents and Peace Forces. The dimension focuses on the professionalism and proficiency of the military and paramilitary forces engaged by the peace operation. The rationale for including both the belligerents and the Peace Forces lies in the need in a peace operation to see the "enemy" as conflict itself. If that is the proper perception, then the belligerents and the Peace Forces are potential allies.[24] Much anecdotal evidence lends its support to the argument that it is always easier to keep agreements if the forces involved behave professionally. Professional troops and police tend to behave in a disciplined manner with restraint thereby enhancing their security.

The last dimension, Actions Targeted on Ending Conflict, directly ties into the principle of security. Made up of population and resource controls, intelligence focused on the threats to the peace, psychological operations, and civic action, it links combat and contact related skills and ties the several types of peace operations together. What the variables used to define the dimension show is that peacebuilding is an essential component of peacekeeping and peace enforcement.

This brief discussion of the relationship of the elements of the paradigm to current doctrine suggests that there probably is reason to believe that the doctrine is likely to be valid for peace operations as well as for other types of OOTW. The strength of the doctrine is that it is grounded in serious research--research which not only produced the SWORD Model but has been subjected to continuous questioning and refinement over the years. It is the testing of the model and its continued use as the underlying assumption of doctrine that qualifies it as a paradigm. Thus, it is to the development of the paradigm over the course of the last decade in a series of publications that we now turn.

From SWORD Model to Manwaring Paradigm

The first document to appear in the series of studies making use of the Manwaring Paradigm was published as SWORD Paper # 1, *What Is to be Done? Counterinsurgency* by Robert M. Herrick and others, including Manwaring. While it appeared in several places, it is preserved in the SWORD Papers collection.[25] This document was followed by ten more SWORD Papers as of August 1988. While the Sword Papers were being published, Manwaring got his research material together and, now working again as a civilian for SWORD's contractor, BDM Management Services Company, produced, in 1987, the research report that described the SSI 2 model, (now called the SWORD Model).[26]

SWORD had focused many of its efforts on the war in El Salvador. At the urging of General John R. Galvin, the SOUTHCOM Commander in Chief, and the US Ambassador to El Salvador, Edwin Corr, Manwaring was engaged in a project that conducted numerous in depth interviews with the participants of that conflict. These were recorded in several volumes produced by BDM and turned over to SWORD.[27] They provided the grist for a book edited by Manwaring and Court Prisk, *El Salvador at War: An Oral History.*[28] A spin off of the oral history was, *The Comandante Speaks: Memors of an El Salvadoran Guerrilla Leader*, edited by Courtney Prisk.[29]

The main line of publication of the studies undertaken by SWORD was in US military publications such as *Military Review* which, beginning in 1988 and for several years thereafter, devoted a special issue to Low Intensity Conflict. Several of these articles began their life as SWORD Papers and a number were collected and published in 1991 in *Uncomfortable Wars: Toward a New Paradigm of Low Intensity Conflict.*[30] The essence of the book, however, was its explication of the SWORD Model in the context of Latin America and the insurgencies that were taking place in the SOUTHCOM Area of Responsibility.

Ambassador Edwin Corr, having retired from the US Foreign Service and accepted an endowed Chair in Political Science at the University of Oklahoma, turned his attention to expanding the focus of the SWORD Model. Corr, who had written the introduction and conclusion of *Uncomfortable Wars*, with his Oklahoma colleague, Stephen Sloan, developed a book that would apply the model to a number of insurgencies outside Latin America. Thus, of the seven insurgency cases which make up the heart of *Low Intensity Conflict: Old Threats in a New World*, four come from areas other than Latin America. Moreover, the critical contribution of the book is found in this test of the model for its explanatory power of specific cases beyond its region of principal interest and practice.[31]

The years 1989 and 1990 found SOUTHCOM intellectually engaged in the war against illegal drugs proclaimed by President George Bush. Consultant support to SOUTHCOM, of course, shifted focus and Manwaring began to adapt the SWORD Model for application to the Drug War.[32] The results of this shift of intellectual focus were published in *Gray Area Phenomena: Confronting the New World Disorder*.[33] Still, the book did not confine itself to the drug issue but also raised questions that ranged from contingency operations and their implications through conventional conflicts to organized crime as a national security threat. Nevertheless, the thrust of the book was on the application of the paradigm to the Drug War.

At the 1991 meeting of the American Political Science Association where several of the authors of *Low Intensity Conflict* presented a panel, one of them, David Scott Palmer, urged Manwaring to publish in full the SWORD Model research report in a scholarly journal so that it could be more easily accessible. He also urged that it take account of some of the more recent publications on revolution. Manwaring was, at the time, overcommmitted and asked John Fishel to undertake the revision of the study for publication. Fishel took on the task, not only developing the discussion of revolutionary theory Palmer had suggested, but also adding several appendices that had not appeared in the original work (although three of the four had been available).[34] The article was published in the Winter 1992 issue of *Small Wars and Insurgencies* thus making the paradigm fully available to the wider scholarly audience.

Ambassador David Miller's chapter in *Gray Area Phenomena*, "Beyond the Cold War: An Overview and Lessons," provided the impetus for the most recent book in this series, *Managing Contemporary Conflict: Pillars of Success*.[35] In his chapter, Miller suggested that the three pillars of success in contemporary conflict were a theory of engagement, appropriate weapons systems, and an effective Executive Branch management structure. In the new book these concepts are developed theoretically and illustrated by case studies which range from the insurgency in El Salvador through the peace enforcement operations in Somalia in 1992-93. Although the book is not constructed specifically around the dimensions of the Manwaring paradigm they permeate the discussion. For example, the two chapters on management structure explicitly address the issue in terms of the dimension of Unity of Effort.[36] Perhaps, the critical point for our discussion is that this is the first time that the SWORD Model has been applied directly, in any way, to the analysis of a peace operation. The results suggest that the application in a more general way would be fruitful.

Testing the Paradigm in Peace Operations:The Scope of the Book

This book attempts, at the same time, to be both evolutionary and revolutionary. Similarly, it seeks to address the intellectual concerns of scholars and the practical concerns of the soldiers and statesmen who must conduct peace operations. The book is clearly evolutionary in that it is a product of research supported theory that has been in use for the past decade. Indeed, this chapter has made the case that the theoretical construct of the SWORD Model has informed the doctrinal paradigm of the Principles of OOTW. Thus, Ambassador Ed Corr has been absolutely correct in labeling the model, "the Manwaring Paradigm."

Although the application of the model has evolved from its single-minded intent of explaining the correlates of success in counterinsurgency through the analysis of the drug wars to addressing the concerns of organized crime as a security threat and touching on peace operations, it never has been subjected to a real test as to its applicability in any arena but that of counterinsurgency. The original study undertaken at the Strategic Studies Institute constituted such a test; Corr and Sloan's use of seven case studies provided an excellent replication and validation of the paradigm. There, however, scientific confirmation of the model ceased. Rather, what we have in the subsequent works is the development of new hypotheses coupled with the related unquestioning reification of the paradigm as principles in US military doctrine in areas well beyond what the data can support on the basis of scientific study.

It is on the basis of this analysis of the impact of the model that the book becomes revolutionary. For the first time in the development of military doctrine, it sets out to provide a test of the intellectual premises on which that doctrine is based. The test is found in the series of nine case studies of peace operations that make up the heart of the book.

If the reader has gotten this far, he knows that the underlying premise is found in Clausewitz' dictum that war is an extension of politics by other means. As all the other books in this series suggest, the concept is neither new nor unusual. Rather, it lies at the heart of all security issues. The use of military force is a political act designed to attain political objectives. This concept embodies the one assumption made in this book; all else is subject to test.

The means of testing the Manwaring Paradigm as it applies to peace operations is to organize the case studies in three groups of three. The first such grouping consists of our cases of "traditional peacekeeping" where a neutral and impartial force of peacekeepers has been designated to keep the belligerents separated and does so with their consent. The cases that fall into this category are: UNFICYP in Cyprus, ONUSAL in El Salvador, and MOMEP on the Ecuador-Peru border.

Our second group is an intermediate category found between traditional peacekeeping and peace enforcement which, for lack of a better term (and doing some violence to it, at that), we are calling "wider peacekeeping" somewhat in the British manner. Unlike traditional peacekeeping, these cases exhibit some lack of consent by one or more parties to the conflict. Nevertheless, like traditional peacekeeping, there is some degree of consent to the role of the peacekeepers on the part of the warring parties. The three cases in this group are: ONUC in the Congo, UNTAC in Cambodia, and UNPROFOR in the former Yugoslavia.

The third group of cases is one of extreme involvement which the Secretary General of the United Nations, Boutros-Boutros Ghali, has called peace enforcement. What differentiates these operations from the others is the mandate which directs the Peace Forces to impose a truce or other settlement on the warring parties whether they consent or not. The cases representing this category are: the IAPF in the Dominican Republic, UNOSOM II in Somalia, and UNMIH in Haiti.

The cases range from the Cold War era to the present. They represent United Nations operations, UN authorized operations, an operation undertaken by a regional organization without the direct involvement of the UN, and finally an operation conducted by an *ad hoc* multinational organization created specifically for that purpose. In other words, they represent the entire range of peace operations in all their complexities and with all the difficulties of categorizing them with respect to where they might fall on a spectrum of consent.

Each case is organized and presented in the same way. Following a brief introduction to set the political context, the case authors examine the impact of the dimensions of the paradigm in the following order: Unity of Effort, Legitimacy, Support to Belligerents, Support Actions of Peace Forces, Military Actions of Peace Forces, Military Actions of Belligerents and Peace Forces, and Actions Targeted on Ending Conflict. Finally, each case concludes with a brief assessment of the degree to which it supports or denies the validity of the paradigm.

The final section of the book focuses each of its two chapters on different aspects of lessons learned in the analysis of the cases. One chapter looks at the impact of the cases on the theory, examining the degree to which the paradigm is supported, how the cases modify the theory, as well as where it is denied. The final chapter considers the paradigm and its revisions with respect to practice on the ground. It suggests modification to doctrine, tactics, techniques, and procedures as a result of the analysis of the case studies and seeks to articulate clearly useful lessons for soldiers and diplomats assigned to peace operations.

Finally, the book seeks to make a contribution to our understanding of the world we have bequeathed to the next generation of scholars, soldiers, and diplomats. In this we hope that our students at all levels, along with our peers and the decision makers, will see the utility of our endeavor.

Notes

1 See Max G. Manwaring and John T. Fishel, "Insurgency and Counterinsurgency: Toward a New Analytical Approach," *Small Wars & Insurgencies*, (Winter 1992), Frank Cass, London, pp. 272-305, and Edwin G. Corr and Stephen Sloan (eds.), *Low Intensity Conflict: Old Threats in a New World*, (Boulder CO: Westview Press, 1992).

2 Max G. Manwaring, (ed.), *Gray Area Phenomena: Confronting the New World Disorder*, (Boulder CO: Westview Press, 1993).

3 Interview with Max G. Manwaring, 1986.

4 Manwaring and Fishel, also Ibid.

5 Interview with Manwaring, 1986, and interview with Robert M. Herrick, 1986.

6 The author was a participant in all of these efforts and coordinated the assessment plan for the study of the Salvadoran Armed Forces, hereafter cited as Participant Observation.

7 Participant Observation.

8 HQDA and DAF, FM 100-20/AFP 3-20, *Military Operations in Low Intensity Conflict*, Washington, DC, 1990.

9 Interviews with members of OASD-SO/LIC.

10 HQDA, FM 100-20, *Military Operations in Low Intesity Conflict*, Washington, DC, 1990.

11 Promote Liberty continues in Panama as of this writing where it supports the development of Panama's infrastructure.

12 See John T. Fishel, *Liberation, Occupation, and Rescue: War Termination and Desert Storm*, SSI, USAWC, Carlisle, PA, 1992.

13 Ibid., Chapter 6.

14 FM 100-20/AFP 3-20, Chapter 1, and FM 100-5, Chapter 13.

15 HQDA, FM 100-23, *Peace Operations*, 1994; also informal interviews with Lt. Col. Murray Swan, Canadian Army, and "peacekeeper," 1994-95.

16 Manwaring and Fishel, Appendix III.

17 Ibid.

18 We should note here that the naming of the dimensions, in the end, was arbitrary and the names have been modified in some cases in the various published versions of the work to be discussed in the next section. In this note I will identify each dimension with its original name in the order in which they will be discussed in the text with, however, a further modification to conform to the issue of peace operations. The specific names of the dimensions are in no way critical; rather, as long as the variables which comprise them remain unchanged comparability is assured. Dimensions: Unity of Effort, Host Government Legitimacy, Degree of Outside Support to Insurgents, Support Actions of Intervening Power, Military Actions of Intervening Power, Host Government Military Actions, and Actions versus Subversion. See Manwaring and Fishel, Tables 7 and 8, p. 284.

[19] See Manwaring and Fishel, Appendix II, pp.301-304. The listing of variables in this chapter always includes the strongest within each dimension but may not include all the variables included in the Factor Analysis.

[20] Personal communication from Major David Last, Ph.D., Canadian Army, now Executive Assistant to the Deputy Force Commander, UNPROFOR.

[21] Personal communication.

[22] John T. Fishel, "Achieving the Elusive Unity of Effort," Manwaring (ed.), *Gray Area Phenomena*, p. 123.

[23] See Manwaring and Fishel.

[24] This point was impressed on me by Major David Last, Canadian Army, in numerous discussions over the past year.

[25] The SWORD Papers, although long out of print, are archived in their entirety by the private research organization, the National Security Archives, in Washington, DC.

[26] Dr. Max G. Manwaring, *A Model for the Analysis of Insurgencies*, BDM Management Services Company, Ft. Lewis, Washington, 1987. (Copies of this document are to be found in the National Security Archives. Hereafter, documents that may be consulted there will be identified by the notation NSA after the date.)

[27] These volumes have been collected by the NSA.

[28] Max G. Manwaring and Court Prisk, *El Salvador at War: An Oral History*, NDU Press, Washington, DC, 1988.

[29] Westview Press, Boulder, CO, 1991.

[30] Max G. Manwaring, ed., Westview Press, Boulder, CO, 1991.

[31] Edwin G. Corr and Stephen Sloan, *Low Intensity Conflict: Old Threats in a New World*, Westview Press, Boulder, CO, 1992.

[32] Manwaring and Prisk now were working for Booz-Allen & Hamilton, Inc. which had won the SOUTHCOM support contract.

[33] Max G. Manwaring, ed., Westview Press, Boulder, CO, 1993.

[34] Manwaring and Fishel. Only Appendix IV, "Operational Definitions," was new.

[35] Ambassador David C. Miller, Jr., "Beyond the Cold War: An Overview and Lessons," Max G. Manwaring, ed., *Gray Area Phenomena*, pp. 153-169. Also William J. Olson and Max G. Manwaring, eds., *Managing Contemporary Conflict: Pillars of Success*, Westview Press, Boulder, CO, forthcoming.

[36] John T. Fishel, "The Principle of Unity of Effort: A Strategy of Conflict Management," and "The Management Structures of Operations Just Cause and Desert Storm and UNOSOM II," in Olson and Manwaring, eds.

Traditional Peacekeeping

2

Peacekeeping In Cyprus

Murray J. M. Swan

> *The Cyprus conflict has resisted with tenacity the efforts of nations great and small to bring about a solution. It frustrates diplomats, amazes outsiders, irritates those who believe progress has been made in studying techniques of negotiation, ... has been a sore point with successive secretaries-general of the United Nations, ... and has caused sadness and bloodshed, disrupting the lives of the people who live there.*[1]
>
> -M.A. Esplin

The Cyprus problem has confounded the participants and the international community for over 30 years. Born as an independent nation on August 16, 1960 the Republic of Cyprus had a compromise constitution that was intended to balance the interests of the island's Greek Cypriot and Turkish Cypriot communities. The provisions of the constitution and the territorial integrity and sovereignty of Cyprus were further guaranteed via several treaties between nations who had interests at stake; Greece, Turkey and the United Kingdom. In practice, however, the function of governing under the constitution proved unworkable and led to a succession of political crises. Intercommunal tensions grew ever larger until in 1963 radical elements sparked violent conflict which increasingly polarized the communities and their political masters. In spite of mediation attempts by the guarantee powers, intercommunal fighting spread to include significant atrocities. Turkish Cypriot refugees especially were forced to gather in community "enclaves." It was at this stage that the governments of Cyprus and the United Kingdom asked the United Nations for assistance in the form of a military "Peacekeeping" force. In March 1964 United Nations troops began deploying to Cyprus to keep the peace for an initial three month period; they are still in place today.

Cyprus - A Geographical and Historical Overview

Recognizing that the origins of the Cyprus problem are not well known and to prepare the field for an analysis using our paradigm, a brief geographical and historical orientation is necessary. From a geographic perspective, Cyprus has a land area of 9,251 square miles and is strategically situated in the northeast corner of the Mediterranean at the meeting point of three continents: Europe, Asia and Africa. According to the 1992 census, its population is 718,000 with distribution of ethnic groupings being approximately 81.7% Greek Cypriots, Maronites, Armenians and others and 18.3% Turkish Cypriots. The climate is rated as "semi tropical" with hot summers with daytime temperatures averaging in the 90's (F) and warm winters with daytime highs averaging in the 60's(F). For a small island the terrain is varied. An east (Famagusta) - west (Xeros) central plain supports most of the island's agriculture. The Kyrenia mountain range stretches along the north coast, and the Troodos Mountains in the southwest climb to 6000 feet. Both mountain ranges contain forests made up of the ubiquitous Cyprus pine and a mix of deciduous trees. Water is scarce on Cyprus with major sources being a large underground aquifer near Morphou, springs in the Kyrenia mountains and most importantly a series of dams and reservoirs in the Troodos mountains. In all Cyprus is most pleasant human environment.

Cyprus has experienced an eventful history. While the island has been inhabited from the 7th millennium, it was the migration of the Mycenean Greeks in 1300 B.C. that established the dominance of the Greek language and culture as well as an economy based on agriculture, fishing and support of the Mediterranean shipping trade. Cyprus became part of Alexander the Great's empire until it was conquered by the Romans in 400 B.C. Under Roman rule over the next 800 years, Cyprus was prosperous and saw considerable development in infrastructure, the building of cities and most importantly the universal Christianization of its people. It is from these roots that the Cypriot Orthodox Church draws its traditions and strength even today. After several other handovers, the Ottoman Turks conquered Cyprus in 1571, dominating island life for the next 300 years. In the usual Ottoman fashion, Cypriots were allowed to continue their lifestyle although the Ottoman bureaucrats ran the administrative institutions and collected taxes for onward transmission to the Sultan. During this period, limited Turkish settlement occurred, basically from members of Ottoman military garrisons and the civilian bureaucratic establishment.

In 1878, Turkey ceded control of Cyprus to Britain in return for British support against an expansionist Tsarist Russia. With the outbreak of World War I, Cyprus was annexed into the British Empire and in 1925 became an official British Crown Colony. The British used the island as a support and staging base for military and trade purposes and, in general, were benevolent in conduct of domestic matters. After a British survey in the late 1800's, a record of land ownership was established which forms the basis for even current intercommunal land claims. A modern road infrastructure, public utilities and an airport were built and initiatives such as universal education, health care infrastructure and a legal system were introduced.

In the wake of World War II, nationalist movements occurred around the world. It sparked, in particular, the Greek Cypriot community to petition initially for more control over their political processes and administrative institutions and then later a demand that Cyprus become a part or province of Greece - called *Enosis*. Under Ottoman and British rule the Greek and Turkish Cypriot communities were generally integrated and lived in harmony. However, as the tempo of Greek Cypriot demands extended to demonstrations and then to an outright insurgency movement, Turkish Cypriots became increasingly isolated. Between 1955 and 1958 the small Greek Cypriot insurgent movement called *EOKA*,[2] conducted an effective campaign targeting British citizens, institutions and property to achieve its *enosis* goals. Turkish Cypriot leaders had no desire to live under a Greek controlled government and so countered the *Enosis* concept with a concept called *Taksim* which envisioned partition of the island into Turkish and Greek Cypriot zones. A military arm called the TMT was then formed to defend and advance these interests.

In the face of increasing violence, a deteriorating political situation and considerable pressure from Greece and Turkey, the British government attempted to defeat the insurgency using military means and, on a parallel path, conducted negotiations with all parties to determine the best formula for moving Cyprus towards non aligned self government. In 1959 Britain, Greece and Turkey developed the Zurich - London Accords and later in 1960, with Cypriot representation, concluded the Treaties of Alliance, Establishment and Guarantee which formed the basis for the constitution of the Republic of Cyprus.

There were a number of key provisions in these agreements involving the guarantee powers which reflected their national interests and their commitment to the two Cypriot communities. In 1963 Britain was in the process of shedding its former colonies in Africa and the Middle East and therefore needed secure support bases to ensure effective military presence in the region. In these treaties, Britain maintained control over several areas of Cyprus; two Sovereign Base Areas (SBA) at Akrotiri and Dhekelia and several other military installations such as Mount Olympus as radar facility, the RAF facility at Nicosia airport and a strategic communications installation at Ayios Nicolios. Both Turkey and Greece established embassies on Cyprus and were allowed to permanently position selected military forces to assist in the development of an integrated Cypriot military and provide a measure of security and confidence in their aligned communities: Greece and Turkey were allowed 950 and 550 soldiers respectively. In fact, these arrangements actually ensured the direct involvement of the guarantee powers in the political life and military actions which ensued in Cyprus.

This overview has provided a geographical and historical context and outlined some of the interests, key players and parties to the Cyprus problem. With this as background, the remainder of this chapter will examine the various aspects of the Cyprus problem using key headings of the SWORD model.

> A story goes that a group of Cypriot leaders got together to devise a plan to become the world's greatest superpower. After considerable discussion their assessment was that Cyprus simply did not have the population, resources and money to achieve this particular dream. Not to be thwarted however, they considered a variety of other options for world leadership, in the end deciding to become the world's biggest nuisance!
>
> -An anonymous UN diplomat

Unity of Effort

As with all protracted social conflicts, resolution of political problems is the key to success of any peacekeeping mission. Cyprus has been the focus of inordinate and enormous international effort with the firm objective of resolving the political aspects of this conflict. A plethora of initiatives were undertaken by the United States, the United Nations and the guarantee powers in order to find a fair and workable solution to the "so called" Cyprus problem. Some examples include the Acheson Plan of July 1964, developed in consultation with Turkey and Greece, which proposed the granting of local autonomy to the Turkish Cypriot community within the context of a unitary state: it was roundly rejected by the Greek Cypriots. A 1965 UN initiative by Galo Plaza Lasso, the Special Representative of the UN Secretary-General (SRSG), emphasized preservation of the unity of Cyprus with guaranteed minority rights: it was rejected so strongly that UN mediation efforts had to be suspended for some time.

After intercommunal fighting flared again in 1967, threatening open conflict between Turkey and Greece, Cyrus Vance of the United States successfully defused the crisis and precipitated a process of direct negotiations between the leaders of the two communities, Rauf Denktash and President Makarios. These direct talks lasted seven years and were close to success, when in 1974, the attempted coup against President Makarios and following Turkish intervention smashed contact between the communities. Another effort was made in 1977 with the American, British and Canadian (ABC) Group developing a set of principles for constitutional agreement accompanied by supporting financial incentives: it too was rejected. Anon over the next 16 years, the United Nations and the international community sponsored, in consultation with the parties, no less than ten full proposals all of which were rejected by one or both communities.

From these many initiatives, there must be no question that there has been an extraordinary international diplomatic "unity of effort" focused on the objective of resolving the political problems between the two Cypriot communities. It is significant that a Special Representative of the Secretary General (SRSG) was appointed as the head of mission to lead international and intercommunal diplomatic efforts to resolve the political issues. These United Nation's efforts were strongly supported by the UN Security Council, in particular by the United States and the United Kingdom, who individually offered considerable financial and political carrots. Yet in spite of these efforts, the Cyprus problem continues unresolved to today.

The special concerns and positions of Greece and Turkey have had mixed effect on the resolution and mediation processes. Long historical ties, cultural affinities, close religious links and regional concerns regarding Turkey, have obliged Greece to provide strong and consistent support to the Greek Cypriot community and its institutions; the government, the Greek Cypriot National Guard (GCNG) and the Orthodox church. From 1960 to 1974, Greece was an aggressive player in Cypriot politics, often at odds with President Makarios. With the failed Greek led coup against Makarios and subsequent fall of the military regime in Greece in 1974, successive Greek governments have taken a most systemic approach to political issues in Cyprus. Greece has supported international mediation attempts. However, when crisis or open conflict occurred, Greece was always first in with diplomatic backing in international fora then military assistance to the Greek Cypriot National Guard (GCNG). Since day one of the conflict, Greece has consistently provided officers and NCO's to manage the training and the equipping of the GCNG and perhaps more importantly, the commander of the GCNG has always been an officer from the Greek Army. Turkey has a plethora of strategic, regional and historical interests in Cyprus. Confronted on three sides by potential adversaries, Turkey sees Cyprus at 50 miles off her southern coast as covering an exposed flank. It is important for Turkey that Cyprus remain at least a neutral nation and never a Greek possession. As a growing regional power with strong historical and cultural ties to several regional nations, Turkey had to demonstrate its political and military strength in support of Turkish minorities anywhere. For the Turkish public and legislature, the feisty Turkish Cypriot minority that took up arms to fight a majority Greek entity and that continues to stymie the world's premier diplomats, is a positive symbol of the Turkish ethnic character and the stuff of "folk" heroes. Turkey has reluctantly supported the negotiation process but practically is drawn towards the *Taksim* or partition platform developed by Turkish Cypriot leaders in the 1950's. From the Turkish military intervention in 1974, Turkey has permanently positioned some 35,000 well armed troops in northern Cyprus to support the *de facto* partition of the island. Since 1974, command of all Turkish and Turkish Cypriot military forces has been managed by a Turkish national military officer operating under direction of the General Staff in Ankara. Diplomatically, Turkey is one of only three nations that has recognized the 1983 self declared "Turkish Republic of Northern Cyprus" (TRNC) as an independent sovereign state. In spite of significant pressures from the United States, the UN Security Council, the European Union and many other fora, Turkey continues to support and advance the Turkish Cypriot positions supporting the partition option.

The United Kingdom has been a strong third party actor in the Cyprus problem. A former colonial master, a leader of the British Commonwealth, a member of the European community, a NATO member, a guarantee power, a permanent UN Security Council member, a resident in the sovereign base areas and a contributor of the largest contingent in UNFICYP, Britain's prestige and actions bear on every aspect of the Cyprus problem. British support for a fair and lasting solution is related to their many national interests thus they have been vigorous, constant and positive in every forum. Inevitably in times of greatest crisis, it has been the United Kingdom who has been called upon to take diplomatic and military actions subsequently instrumental in de-escalating conflict. As such the United Kingdom has been the most significant, effective and beneficial third party actor in diplomatic and military circles involved with the Cyprus problem.

In attempts to resolve the Cyprus political problem, there have been notable and long term efforts by the international community. The United Nations has been a leader in encouraging and supporting negotiation and mediation processes which have defused serious crises and generally de-escalated the conflict. Mediation efforts by the major powers which included healthy incentives have met, at best, with stop gap successes. Both Greece and Turkey have been supportive of negotiation processes; however, crises have always polarized them to support their aligned communities. Each has close visceral connections to the Cypriot communities which, over 32 years, have obliged them to take positions or actions, in many cases injurious to their own international standing. The failure of the parties to resolve these contradictory interests and positions has stalemated efforts to achieve a political reconciliation. The political reality has been an acceptance of the political and military *status quo* as the lowest acceptable common denominator.

Legitimacy

The introduction of United Nations "peacekeeping" forces into Cyprus was the result of in-depth negotiations among the UN Secretary-General, the guarantee powers and both Cypriot communities. Each party expressed concerns which were factored into the mandate then reflected in the terms of reference for the Force: its method of operation, force composition, administrative arrangements and special rights and privileges. The Secretary-General noted "that UNFICYP was a UN force, operating exclusively under the mandate given to it by the Security Council and, within that mandate, under the instructions given by the Secretary-General. It was an impartial, objective body which had no responsibility for political solutions and would not try to influence them one way or the other."[3] Based on this process and agreements, the governments and parties involved in the conflict formally participated in the building of the mandate and authorized (thus made legitimate) UNFICYP's peacekeeping role in Cyprus.

For the Cypriot communities, the introduction of UNFICYP represented a tangible demonstration of international support in resolving their national political problems. Initially, community leaders and the island's media gave strong vocal support to UNFICYP, in fact encouraging perhaps unreasonable expectations for a quick improvement of the security situation and resolution of political problems. In a practical sense, the sudden introduction of 6,000 new residents and accompanying U.N. money had a tangible effect in stimulating the Cypriot economy and generating new employment across the island. A combination of expectations and impact of force deployment certainly made UNFICYP legitimate in the eyes of the majority in the Cypriot public.

As time passed, the United Nations and UNFICYP became part of the military and political landscape for the communities in Cyprus. The many efforts by the United Nations (New York) to lead the negotiation process on the political issues and UNFICYP's constant involvement in defusing military crises strengthened UN legitimacy, perhaps to the point of absurdity. The public perception, quietly nurtured by political leaders, actually transferred a large part of the responsibility for resolution of both security and political issues to the United Nations. This situation provided a convenient foil for politically adroit community leaders to take credit for any successes and shift blame for any failures to the United Nations. It may well be that Cyprus represents a situation where a third party force can have too much legitimacy!

The Mandate

On March 4th, 1964 the UN Security Council passed SCR 186 (1964) which approved the deployment of a military peacekeeping force to Cyprus with a mandate to "use its best efforts to prevent a recurrence of fighting, and as necessary, to contribute to the maintenance and restoration of law and order and the return to normal conditions"[4]. Following the hostilities of 1974, the Security Council also charged UNFICYP with additional functions: the maintenance of the "Cease-fire" and a variety of humanitarian functions such as encouraging farming in the United Nations Buffer Zone (UNBZ), assisting the communities with the supply of electricity and water across the UNBZ and facilitating emergency medical services and the transport of mail across the lines. In 1964 UNFICYP was a new type of UN undertaking thus the Security Council mandate was kept deliberately ambiguous to allow maximum flexibility to parties, the diplomats and supposedly the UN peacekeepers. Unfortunately, this lack of precision worked against resolution of the political problem and has in many ways impaired UNFICYP's potential effectiveness, both in term of its legitimacy and its ability to achieve Unity of Effort.

The initial authorized period of UNFICYP's deployment was three months; then it was extended to six months. Over the 32 years of UNFICYP's existence, the Security Council has continued to extend this mandate in only six month increments. This practice has had several negative implications which have impacted on the effectiveness of the Force. First, it has constrained UNFICYP's ability to develop and implement a long term "Campaign Plan" aimed appropriately at progressively de-escalating the conflict and supporting diplomatic efforts towards political reconciliation. Out of necessity then, the Force was obliged to focus on short term projects and the maintenance of a sketchy status quo; a limited military objective with no real chance of long term success. Secondly, it spawned a short term perspective and commitment by troop contributing nations as evidenced in a troop rotation policy where the majority of individuals and units were replaced every six months. This procedure saw the loss of valuable continuity, on-the-ground experience and critical interpersonal relationships with opposing military forces and civilian agencies. Each new unit or even individuals thus had a "spool up" period during which they were "tested" by the more knowledgeable, experienced and politically savvy opposing forces. Those who failed lost hard won UN credibility and often that advantageous bargaining position.

Thirdly, opposing forces took advantage of the non specific nature of the mandate by constantly challenging UNFICYP's authority. Because all participants approved political agreements establishing UNFICYP, opposing forces generally albeit begrudgingly, acknowledged UNFICYP's legitimate role in dealing with issues of a military nature. However, the lack of a definitive mandate resulted in escalation of many easily resolved issues to the operational then political level in the hope that UNFICYP would either give in or mismanage the process. In many cases that was exactly what happened. Even after the cease-fire agreement of August 1974 which detailed specific responsibilities for UNFICYP and was supported by all parties, minor issues continued to be argued at the political level.

The devil is in the details. Thus, over 25 years, UNFICYP addressed the non specific nature of their authority through painstaking efforts to conclude local verbal arrangements and even global written agreements. Finally, in 1989, a compendium of these commitments was documented to form a United Nations interpretation of the *status quo*. This document was forwarded to military and political leaders of all parties for comment but, not surprisingly, no official response was ever received. Nonetheless this *status quo* forms the baseline *modus operandi* under which military forces are working today.

The UNFICYP mandate, established in 1964, has been the baseline for UN military operations in Cyprus for over 32 years. In spite of this ambiguous mandate, UNFICYP has progressively established a goodly measure of agreement and support for its authority. The product speaks for itself; UNFICYP as a peacekeeping mission has successfully kept the peace. There have been Unity of Effort problems as a fallout of the UNSC practice of renewing mandates in six month increments; long term planning has been severely restricted and the financial and political commitments of troop contributing nations have been denigrated. It has been an uphill fight to establish UN military authority as situations best handled soldier to soldier were unnecessarily escalated to the political level. However UNFICYP has been successful overall because it has engendered the real support of opposing military forces thus in fact established its legitimacy as a common ally to defeat the mutual conflict.

Support to Belligerents

Long term external military and political support to each of the Cypriot communities has been a key factor in prolonging the conflict and the avoidance of a final political solution. As recorded earlier, the London - Zurich Accords and the treaties of Establishment and Guarantee were concluded with the direct involvement of the key outside actors who had real interests and commitments in Cyprus. By these treaties, both Turkey and Greece were allowed to position limited military forces on the island and, more importantly, each country was obliged to safeguard the rights and security of their aligned communities. The governments of both Turkey and Greece had long-standing bilateral grievances over other territorial and political issues. These embedded and often opposing commitments to Cyprus served only to aggravate their relationship. Even a locally undistinguished incident in Cyprus was often interpreted by these countries as an attempt to gain an advantage in other bilateral areas. Conversely, regional events involving Greece and Turkey, such as Presidential elections, were interpreted for their political impact on Cyprus. As such, for Greece and Turkey, Cyprus became a "two way" lightening rod for issues between the Cypriot communities and their larger bilateral relationship.

The tangible result of Greek and Turkish support was a quantitative and qualitative improvement in the military capability of the Cypriot communities. At an early stage in the conflict, both undertook to limit the introduction of arms and equipment to Cyprus. However, as crises occurred, each side channeled additional arms and munitions to the Cypriot communities. As the military capability improved, the military option for response became more appealing.

In addition to these equipment improvements, Greece and Turkey provided military contingents resident in Cyprus which assisted in the training and upgrading of the military forces of each side. Both Greece and Turkey seconded officers and NCO's to lead units, staff HQ and operate technical equipment. Over time both Greece and Turkey became increasingly embedded within the military forces of their aligned community and became part of the military problem for UNFICYP and international diplomats.

Perhaps of more significance however was the financial, moral and political support given by the governments and the publics of Greece and Turkey to the associated Cypriot communities. Particularly in the early days of the conflict, this financial support helped underwrite the development of military forces and fund political agendas. In periods of crisis, moral and political support from these nations kept the cause and perspectives of their community on the agenda of outside fora such as the United Nations, the European Community (Greece) and even NATO. For Greece and Turkey, Cyprus became a two edged sword. For example, when intercommunal talks were building to a positive level, an incident instigated by a Cypriot faction would engender public support in Cyprus and the supporting nation. The result for the aligned nation would be an obligation to support the position or actions of their community, aggravating rather than de-escalating the situation.

In summary, from the very processes and agreements that established Cyprus as a nation, Greece and Turkey have been obligated players in the Cyprus problem. The nature of their opposing interests in Cyprus and their strained bilateral relations have had an adverse effect on the resolution of Cypriot political problems. Each has provided significant financial, military and diplomatic support for their aligned communities over the long term. On the military side, the provision of national military forces, equipment and training has served to extend the military option for both Cypriot communities; an option exercised all too often particularly in the early years of the UNFICYP.

Support Actions of the Peace Forces

UNFICYP initially deployed to Cyprus with a robust military force of approximately 6000 personnel with military contingents from Austria, Canada, Denmark, Finland, Ireland, Sweden and the United Kingdom and Civilian Police contingents from Australia, Austria, Denmark, New Zealand and Sweden. Infantry and reconnaissance units brought their full range of equipment including mortars, anti-tank weapons, machine guns and armored vehicles. A strong logistic/ service support capability was also deployed by force contingents or supplied via local arrangements with the British sovereign bases. This tangible demonstration of international interest and, for Cypriots, not an inconsiderable military capability, had a positive effect on the Cypriot public and a salutary effect on the irregular military forces. It is fair to say that the force started off on the right foot.

Once UNFICYP began its regular six month rotations and the belligerent forces determined the strengths and weaknesses of the force, the situation gradually changed. Using tactics gleaned from the insurgency period, the irregular forces of both sides commenced "hit and run" raids away from areas of UNFICYP observation posts and patrol routes. When it became apparent that the peacekeepers had extremely limited "Rules of Engagement" and were generally confined to interpositioning tactics, the game was up and UNFICYP was in a defensive "firefighting" mode. This particular situation existed through the period 1964 to 1974.

Civilian Police Activities

Civilian police contingents have been included in virtually every UN mission and as such brought a considerable capability to UNFICYP. Their duties as summarized in the Secretary-General's report of September 10, 1964 were "to establish liaison with Cypriot police, accompany Cypriot police patrols ..... man UN police posts in areas of tension ....and investigate incidents where Greek and Turkish Cypriots were involved with the opposite community, including searches for persons reported missing". Although vested with **no** authority to arrest, detain, or even legally question, these experienced and unarmed policemen effectively acted as honest brokers for all sides. They were absolutely instrumental in raising the standards of policing and instilling a modicum of professional values in the fledgling Cyprus Police (CYPOL) as well as the Turkish Cypriot Police Element (TCPE).

In a small country with an economy based on rural agriculture and a citizenry imbued with a village mentality, it was extremely difficult for foreign military contingents to be professionally or socially accepted by the general Cypriot public. For the civilian police however, professional contacts in the Cypriot police allowed them access to usually "close hold" police type information. Phone in information from the public or casual tips from CYPOL and TCPE associates were of tremendous benefit to a Force banned from intelligence collecting activities. In literally hundreds of cases, such information was the key to UNFICYP's military actions to deter or stop major confrontations. The small contingents of UN Civilian police enhanced the effectiveness of the Force far above their numbers.

The Greek Cypriot Coup and Turkish Army Intervention - July 1974

During operationally quiet periods between 1968 to 1974, UNFICYP gradually reduced its strength to approximately 3100 soldiers and civilian police. With the coup attempt of 1974 against President Makarios, in which Nicos Sampson[5] was temporarily installed as the President, Greek Cypriots began to even old scores - akin to a civil war. This coup and subsequent attacks on Turkish Cypriot enclaves infuriated Turkey who then landed a large military force on the North coast of Cyprus. Using air support from Turkey and parachuting airborne troops into key terrain, the Turkish Army achieved an overwhelming military victory over the GCNG in six weeks.

During these frenetic events and in the face of an overwhelming force, UNFICYP troops focused on protecting innocent civilians and moderating combat activities of the opposing military forces through negotiations. It should be noted that some contingents did better than others. Reinforced from participating nations and British forces from the sovereign bases, UN posts provided sanctuary to civilians while many UN soldiers remained in villages overrun by the battle to ensure responsible conduct by the militaries of both sides. The UN was successful in many areas during this period: UN units fought both sides to defend the Nicosia International airport; many refugees were spared as a result of the individual bravery of UN soldiers and, after the cease-fire, the UN assisted in transporting some 250,000 refugees to their majority community across the lines. This effort, which saw three UNFICYP soldiers killed and many wounded, brought great credibility and respect from the international community, Cypriot civilian officials, the involved militaries and the publics of both communities. It was in no small measure that UNFICYP helped mitigate this conflict: the saving of civilian lives, drafting workable cease-fire agreements and, in the longer term, the continued de-escalation of military activity since 1974.

With the development of the cross island UNBZ in 1974, UNFICYP focused its efforts on maintaining the cease-fire and a variety of humanitarian activities to assist both Cypriot communities. The seriousness of violations has diminished over the last 22 years; however, everything from unauthorized entry into the UNBZ to directed rifle shootings continue to this day.

Military Actions of the Peace Forces

Although UNFICYP has been operating in Cyprus for over 32 years, it is important to understand that there have been two distinct circumstances, each requiring different approaches by the Force. From 1964 to 1974, UNFICYP was operating against essentially mobile irregular forces with UN troop deployments based on the Cypriot Administrative Districts and covering the whole island. The prime missions were monitoring key terrain, protecting enclaves and interpositioning between combatants when fighting occurred.

From August 1974 and the conclusion of the Turkish Army intervention operation to the present, UNFICYP has been dealing with formed military forces defensively positioned and led by professional Greek and Turkish officers. In 1974 the island was cut into two parts separated by a UNBZ with the Turkish Army and the Turkish Cypriot Security Forces in the North and contingents of the Greek Army and the GCNG located in the Republic of Cyprus in the South. In this latter situation, UN operations were essentially confined to the UNBZ to monitor violations, maintain a cease-fire and foster intercommunal relations via humanitarian activities.

In March 1964, the United Nations Forces in Cyprus (UNFICYP) established its headquarters and support base at the Royal Air Force portion of the international airport in Nicosia, the capital and seat of government. Over the next three months Force units were deployed into the theater and assigned to areas roughly aligned to Cyprus administrative districts. Unit HQ were located close to local District Officers and subunits deployed to dominate key terrain, to protect enclaves and to monitor cease-fire provisions. A liaison system was established that allowed direct radio or telephone communications with both belligerents' military forces. UNFICYP then developed the tried and proven UN technique of conducting regular meetings at all levels of opposing military forces to de-escalate conflict. These meetings developed initiatives to deal with current disputes and concluded longer term arrangements or agreements.

The introduction of the United Nations force into Cyprus did **not** stop the intercommunal violence.[6] In spite of UNFICYP's 6000+ man presence, sporadic violence punctuated by outbreaks of severe fighting often caught UNFICYP troops in crossfires requiring them to return fire. Major fighting in April/May and again in August 1964 resulted in the deaths of several UN soldiers. Only the personal intervention of the UN Secretary-General with pressure on the Cyprus, Greek and Turkish governments stopped the fighting and established a cease-fire. Again in early 1967 General George Grivas[7], the commander of Cyprus National Guard, deployed formed units to sensitive areas which precipitated direct conflict with Turkish Cypriot fighters. In several cases, UNFICYP outposts were overrun and UN troops were manhandled thus causing real friction between Force units and both belligerents. The crisis continued until December when the Secretary-General again personally interceded with Greece and Turkey to conclude a cease-fire and a partial disarmament agreement.

UNFICYP managed to contain serious conflict through its presence, active patrolling and impartiality until July 1974 when there was an attempted Greek Cypriot coup. Corollary activities against the Turkish Cypriot community prompted Turkey to intervene; landing some 10,000 troops on the northern coast and eventually advancing to positions which absorbed approximately 40% of the Cyprus land mass. In August 1974, a cease-fire agreement was concluded between the United Nations and each belligerent (separately). This agreement resulted in the establishment of a 180 Km "Buffer Zone" (UNBZ) across the island which varied in width; 5 kilometers in open country to a few meters along the "Green Line" of Nicosia. UNFICYP then assisted the United Nations High Commissioner for Refugees (UNHCR) and the International Committee of the Red Cross/Red Crescent (ICRC) in the movement of in excess of 250,000 refugees across the UNBZ in both directions; one third of the nation's population being effectively displaced. In 1983 the Turkish Cypriot community declared its independence under the still internationally unrecognized name of the "Turkish Republic of Northern Cyprus" (TRNC). This *de facto* situation continues today.

While in most cases UNFICYP was made aware of selected aspects of political negotiations, as implied in the discussion of "Unity of Effort", there was little correlation between those diplomatic actions and the Force's operational activities. At no time was a strategic plan formulated which would allow coordinated and complimentary actions by UNFICYP at the operational or tactical levels. As such the Force has been confined to limited tactical objectives aligned with maintaining the separation of forces and attempting to enforce cease-fires, purely defensive measures.

Humanitarian Activities

Perhaps the only area where UNFICYP has achieved significant praise with all entities has been in the humanitarian sphere. UNFICYP has placed prime importance on the protection of innocent Cypriot civilians, an effort which in many cases caused UN soldiers to unreasonably risk personal injury or even death in rescuing or shielding minorities. Modest programs to initiate farming in the UNBZ, to arrange the transport of mail and medical emergencies across cease-fire lines, to facilitate repair and transport of electricity and water in the UNBZ and a host of self help projects in schools and orphanages have reaped tremendous public and opposing forces praise. It is from these functions that the Force has received universal respect and credibility which has been leveraged it to attain certain operational, tactical and even political concessions.

Military Actions of the Belligerents and the Peace Forces

In the initial years of UNFICYP's operations (1964 - 74), relations with the opposing forces could be classified as "strained" but workable. There were many reasons for this condition but the clash of military cultures was perhaps the most important one. The majority of UN units and staff came from western armies with professional officers and NCO's specifically trained for conventional operations in a "Cold War" Europe. Except for British units, most soldiers lacked training and experience in low intensity operations and had little knowledge of the conflict, the issues or techniques required in peacekeeping. By contrast, the opposing forces were largely irregular in nature, experienced in insurgency warfare and, as is usual, extremely political in nature. This clash of military cultures made understanding, personal relationships and, perhaps more importantly, mutual respect extremely difficult.

With the key advantage of "home turf", opposing forces quickly became aware of UNFICYP's many cultural and political limitations and took full military advantage. With at least tacit support of their community leaders, indigenous forces initiated military actions for many reasons: to maintain their public and often external support, to compliment political actions of community leaders, to maintain the military initiative and the profile of the struggle, to harass the UN and finally even to encourage continuance of a UN military commitment for their real financial and political benefits. As such their military actions were deliberate and well targeted to achieve the desired outcome at minimum risk of casualties for themselves.

Another key UN limitation which adversely affected credibility with opposing forces was the modest and defensive "Rules of Engagement" (ROE) given to UNFICYP. Essentially, UN forces could not use lethal force except in "self defense" to protect soldiers or UN property. Such ROE, compared by UN soldiers to those of a British Bobbie, virtually removed the threat of lethal offensive response for opposing forces violating the cease-fire. An example of this limitation was a 1966 GCNG operation north of Limmasol where British soldiers were ordered by the UN to lay down their weapons in the face of that attack against Turkish Cypriot fighters. For a professional soldier there was no worse humility; for the opposing forces it was confirmation of the UN's military ineffectiveness.

Since the 1974 cease-fire agreements, relations with the opposing forces have steadily improved and UNFICYP's role changed. This transpired primarily because the operational situation changed significantly. Rather than policing scattered enclaves and military forces all over the island, the situation moved to one of complete separation of communities and military forces with a UN monitored buffer zone in between. This separation significantly reduced the ability of opposing forces to maneuver and placed UNFICYP in a clear position to monitor and adjudicate violations in the UNBZ. Relations with the opposing forces also improved because UNFICYP's units mastered peacekeeping techniques. This was possible because essentially the same nations continued to provide troops to UNFICYP. Lessons learned were captured and, perhaps more importantly, the same officers and NCO's returned to the theater for subsequent tours. After 32 years, many UN personnel have more military experience in Cyprus than even the most experienced opposing forces officers and NCO's.

Perhaps the most important reason for an improvement of relations between UNFICYP and opposing military forces has been the significant organizational changes instituted in these forces since 1974. The GCNG and the Turkish Cypriot Security Forces (TCSF) have transitioned from their initial irregular character to semi-professional militaries. Both became conscript armies trained and led by professional military officers from Greece and Turkey respectively. As these senior military leaders were accountable to home governments sensitive to the negative impacts of conflict in Cyprus, they have adopted a "defensive" operational posture and actively relied on UNFICYP's third party position to negotiate issues rather than fight. UNFICYP has thus become a cooperative ally to opposing forces by providing instrumental third party assistance in dealing with disputes and violations. UNFICYP relationships with these professional officers have been improved over time to great effect via close and constant contact on both a professional and social basis.

Actions Targeted on Ending Conflict

The *modus operandi* of international efforts in Cyprus was to use a third party military force to stop intercommunal fighting and create a stable security situation thus allowing diplomats to work with the community leaders to resolve the root political problems. The concept was simple but the actual implementation, particularly developing the formulae for political reconciliation, proved very difficult. Although the full range of international instruments of power (diplomatic, economic, military and informational) were brought to bear in the Cyprus problem, it has continued to defy resolution.

The military aspect of this effort, coined as "peacekeeping", was largely successful for most of UNFICYP's 32 year tenure. The initial UN deployment, with troops positioned on dominating terrain and between opposing irregular forces all over the island, was effective in monitoring and even controlling most military movements on key roads and in the larger cities. However, the Force did not have the manpower to monitor small roads and tracks in remote areas, and no naval resources to monitor let alone control the many (and oft used) sea approaches to the island. As noted previously, these limitations were well exploited by opposing irregular forces. After 1974 and the establishment of the UNBZ, UNFICYP focused on maintaining the cease-fire and reestablishing normal activities in this given area. The Turkish forces severely restricted UNFICYP's freedom of movement in the North to point to point administrative travel and support for UN camps positioned in the North - Famagusta and

Xeros. In the South, UNFICYP was also limited to main routes away from GCNG military facilities. Since 1974, the net effect for UNFICYP has been no real ability or responsibility to monitor and control military or civilian activities outside of the UNBZ.

Dearth of Intelligence

A serious problem which restricted UNFICYP's operations was the prohibition on the collection of anything but overt "open source" intelligence. Since UNFICYP was "invited" into Cyprus in a status likened to a "guest", both UN New York and the government of Cyprus considered covert efforts to collect intelligence as akin to treason. Even the word intelligence was dropped from UNFICYP's lexicon and replaced by the less intrusive label of "information". Another reality was that information gleaned from UN sources was accessible to UN delegations in New York and therefore was available to players in the conflict. This restriction on intelligence collection limited official information collection to reports from newspapers, UN and selected opposing forces tactical military sources and filtered information from the diplomatic community. Unofficially, however, a number of other sources were used based on the Force's national contingent's intelligence and diplomatic chains. The effect however was a serious limitation in this key decision making tool which restricted timely and accurate planning. Every military, police or government agency knows that you must have great intelligence to be effective.

Civic Actions Programs

As noted earlier, modest humanitarian and civic action programs were initiated early in the mission and had a beneficial effect in terms of engendering public respect and leveraging the resolution of operational problems. In large measure these programs were initiated, managed and funded by national contingents with HQ UNFICYP providing a modicum of management and coordination. It should be noted that UNFICYP never had formal funding for civic action programs but it took advantage of funding and status of other UN agencies such as the United Nations High Commissioner for Refugees (UNHCR) and the United Nations Development Program (UNDP). An example of a major bicommunal project involving all UN agencies was the Nicosia Sewerage Project which saw the building of a modern and integrated sewer system serving both parts of the capital, Nicosia.

The 1974 division of Cyprus caused serious difficulties in the provision of scarce public utilities to both communities. The Morphou aquifer, located in the North provided water via pumps and a pipeline for both parts of Nicosia and the surrounding area. On the other hand, the main electric power generating station at Dhekelia (near Larnaca) in the South provided the bulk of the island's electric power. UN mediators took action and negotiated a "*quid pro quo*" whereby electric power was supplied free of charge to the entire North based on the requirement to power the pumps to provide a given amount of water to Nicosia. Over the last 22 years, UNFICYP has continuously fielded community complaints on compliance with this arrangement and has facilitated efforts to repair pumps and pipeline infrastructure. This example demonstrates UNFICYP's effectiveness in this project and many other civil action areas.

Conclusion

For most of us who are focused on the challenges of complex threats and concerns as represented by militarily capable and strategically important nations like Russia and Iraq, then Cyprus, with a minute population of 750,000 citizens on a small island in the Mediterranean must be a curious anomaly. This chapter has used that seemingly minor Cyprus conflict as a case study, applying the dimensions of our paradigm and focusing on the operation of the United Nation's Forces in Cyprus; one of the first and now a longstanding "Peacekeeping" mission. There has been an inordinate effort over 32 years by nations great and small to settle this conflict. The diplomats of the international community have shown extraordinary Unity of Effort, patience and perseverance in working with the Cypriot, Greek and Turkish political leaders to find that elusive formula acceptable to all involved parties. The military component of this long term effort, UNFICYP, has played an important role in stabilizing the security situation thus providing an environment of opportunity for political leaders to negotiate and build a political settlement. However, over time, the responsibility for the security situation, the negotiation process and the settlement formula has been shifted to the UN and the international community; perhaps the ultimate form of "Legitimacy" for third party intervenors.

UNFICYP itself has a remarkable record of success considering its many limitations in terms of physical resources and political mandate. It has stopped intercommunal fighting, saved countless lives and property and provided a stable security environment for most of its 32 years in Cyprus. Over time, it has developed a cooperative arrangement with the opposing military forces which focuses on maintaining a *status quo*; a military position equivalent to a "no mans land. The future of the force seems fixed and inconclusive, particularly as the responsible political leaders continue to procrastinate in their efforts to reach a settlement.

Notes

[1] M.A. Esplin, `Efforts to resolve the Cyprus dispute', in D.B. Bendahmane and J.W. McDonald, eds, *Perspectives on Negotiation* (Washington: Foreign Service Institute, Department of State, 1986).

[2] EOKA is the Greek acronym for the armed guerrilla movement for union with Greece.

[3] *The Blue Helmets, A Review of United Nations Peacekeeping*, Second Edition, United Nations, August 1990, pp. 287. The peacekeeping force was called the United Nations Force in Cyprus and known by the acronym of UNFICYP.

[4] United Nations Security Council Resolutions, World Wide Web.United Nations organization/ Departments/DPKO/Missions/UNFICYP.html, November 1994

[5] Nicos Sampson was a Cypriot and former "EOKA" fighter. Basically banished from Cyprus in the late 1969, he was selected to replace Makarios by the architects of the coup as he had a hero's reputation with the general Greek Cypriot public. After the coup he was arrested and successfully tried for treason. Although given a life sentence, he served 20 years then was pardoned and released by decree of the President with strong support of the legislature and the Greek Cypriot public.

[6] "The Blue Helmets", pp. 290 - 300

[7] General George Grivas was a Greek national who led the armed element of the EOKA insurgency against the British 1954 - 1959. A veteran of guerrilla fighting in World War II and the following "Greek Civil War", he was a skilled and charismatic commander. Nicknamed Denghanias, he is a Greek Cypriot national hero of a stature only rivaled by Arch-Bishop Makarios, leader of the Cyprus Orthodox Church and first President of Cyprus. His efforts in the insurgency struggle and his significant public stature won him the post as the first commander of the fledgling Greek Cypriot National Guard.

3

UN Peace Operations In El Salvador: The Manwaring Paradigm In A Traditional Setting

Kimbra L. Fishel and Edwin G. Corr

On May 20th, 1991 Security Council Resolution 693 established the United Nations Observer Mission In El Salvador (ONUSAL). ONUSAL created several divisions, including a human rights division, an electoral division, and a military and police division as part of a peace keeping operation designed to monitor agreements between the government of El Salvador and the Farabundo Marti National Liberation Front (FMLN). This operation resulted from a 1989 negotiation process between the Salvadoran government and the FMLN, conducted under the auspices of the UN Secretary General, in which the objective was to "achieve a series of political agreements aimed at resolving the prolonged armed conflict in El Salvador by political means as speedily as possible, promoting democratization in the country, guaranteeing unrestricted respect for human rights and reunifying Salvadoran society."[1] In January 1992, the government of El Salvador and the FMLN signed an historic peace agreement, and into the mid 1990s the country continues to build a delicate though precarious peace. This chapter introduces the political and military context that the UN entered when it joined the peace process and examines the role of the United Nations in the Salvadoran peace process. United Nations involvement in El Salvador is analyzed through use of the seven dimensions of the Manwaring paradigm illustrating the application of the paradigm to a traditional peacekeeping operation and emphasizing again the centrality of the role of legitimacy.

Before the UN: The Political and Military Context

Organized Salvadoran insurgent groups first surfaced in the early 1970s, claiming to act on behalf of the poor. Initially, these groups sprang out of radical student organizations and the working classes. Formation of guerrilla groups occurred in response to excessive abuses from successive Salvadoran governments, social and economic injustices, and the repressive nature of a sometimes conflictive power elite composed of economic and social oligarchs as well as the military officer corps which controlled the government. The Salvadoran Communist Party (PCES) successfully converted the National University into a center for "agitation and change" and set about a campaign designed to prepare the people for revolution, subvert political parties, and undermine the institutions and functions of the Salvadoran government.[2] The methods employed by these groups were relatively nonviolent until the 1972 presidential election occurred and a coalition of the PCES, the National Revolutionary Movement (MNR), and the Christian Democratic Party (PDC) was denied its rightful seat as victor due to fraud and corruption. As a result, radical extremists began to espouse violent revolution and armed confrontation.[3] What ensued was the inevitable cycle of violence, increased government repression, further violence, and further government repression characteristic of revolutionary systems.

In July of 1979, the Sandinista Revolution occurred in Nicaragua. This Marxist revolution ended with the overthrow of the government of Anastasio Somoza and the Sandinista National Liberation Front's (FSLN) rise to power. The Nicaraguan revolution's impact on El Salvador was immediate and fanned the flames of El Salvador's own revolutionary movements already strongly backed by Cuban and Soviet support.

Sensing the need for radical reform, young military officers staged a coup d'état in October of 1979, removing Colonel Carlos Humberto Romero from power. This reform minded junta government hoped to offset a Marxist revolution through revolutionary violence by initiating a democratic revolution through evolutionary change. The officers' intent was to install a junta government, abolish organizations which violated human rights, control inflation, and implement a land reform program.[4] These officers' broad sweeping aims sought a fundamental transformation of Salvadoran society and greater justice but in an orderly and peaceful manner.[5] Nevertheless, domestic chaos and internal struggle within the junta followed the coup d'état as army officers fought among themselves. A power vacuum was created as the army, the security forces, the ministries, and the leftists all attempted to grab power and control the government.[6] Within three months this junta dissolved and was replaced by a second junta composed of both Christian Democrats and military officers. This second junta also dissolved and, finally, in December of 1980,

Jose Napoleon Duarte assumed the junta presidency as the final hope for a centrist coalition.[7]

The insurgents were also highly fragmented. Cuba's Fidel Castro conditioned his support of the guerrillas on the insurgents forming a "Unity," a unified organization that would provide coordination. In December of 1979 the National Forces of Armed Resistance (FARN), the People's Revolutionary Army (ERP), and the Popular Armed Forces of Liberation (FAPL) met in Havana, Cuba and determined to unite, taking the name Farabundo Marti National Liberation Front (FMLN). The Armed Forces of Liberation (FAL) and the Popular Liberation Revolutionary Armed Forces (FARLP) joined the FMLN shortly thereafter. In 1980, an official alliance was signed by the FMLN in which the FMLN formally determined to wage a guerrilla war against the Salvadoran government. In 1981, the FMLN was joined by the Democratic Revolutionary Front (FDR), three social democratic political organizations consisting of the National Revolutionary Movement (MNR), the Popular Social Christian Movement (MPSC) and the Independent Movement of Salvadoran Professionals (MIPTES), which became the supposed political wing of the organization.

From the time of the initial 1979 coup d'état, plans for reform and reincorporation of the radical left into Salvadoran society were underway. The idea was to take action against the general insurgency while simultaneously guaranteeing a democratic process which would allow for political openness and pave the way for all parties involved to participate in a legitimate, democratic system.[8] The guerrillas remained adamant in their demand for a Marxist revolution. Duarte acknowledged the possibility that the guerrillas may indeed have had good reasons for initially taking up arms when there was no hope of "economic reform, social justice, or free elections under the tyranny of the oligarchy allied with the armed forces."[9] However, once reforms were instituted by the new government, the guerrillas, through violent revolution, hindered progress toward those very reforms they supposedly avowed.

After 1979 successive Salvadoran governments sought national reconciliation at several levels. Programs were designed to attract individuals and families fighting for or supportive of the FMLN to reincorporate themselves into Salvadoran society. These programs were a byproduct of political, economic and social reforms and also sought through specific incentive projects to entice defectors to reintegrate into the life of the national community. During certain periods the Salvadoran Government had a relative degree of unpublicized success in persuading small groups of disenchanted families to abandon their guerrilla cause and resume more normal lives. These reconciliation programs enjoyed a modicum of success in that the size of the FMLN combatant forces actually declined from about 12,000 to about 6,000 from the end of 1983 to 1986, and the FMLN-FDR's political base shrunk significantly from the level achieved in the early eighties.

The Salvadoran governments also continually attempted to split off democratic elements of the FMLN and the FDR by convincing them to abandon violence and participate in the evolving democratic process, especially elections. Always there were hopes that the FDR, or most of it, would, as a political organization distinct from the FMLN, opt for strictly peaceful political action and abandon violence as a means to power and/or the attainment of its programmatic goals.

The events of the reconciliation effort that received greatest public attention were the formal and informal attempts of Salvadoran governments and the FMLN-FDR to negotiate a peace agreement. The governments' efforts in this area took place within the context of the declared purposes of the 1979 Armed Forces coup and the 1983 Constitution, drafted and adopted by an Assembly elected by the majority of the Salvadoran people. Until 1989, the FMLN-FDR often negotiated upon the basis that changes ensuing from the 1979 coup actually altered little in the political and economic system. They argued that despite the reforms there still existed an unjust society at the service of a rightist oligarchy; and that because the far Left did not participate in the drafting of the 1983 Constitution it was an invalid document, even though the Constituent Assembly was elected by the largest number of citizens ever to participate in a Salvadoran election.

Joaquin Villalobos, the leading FMLN military commander, told reporters in September 1989, that the FMLN had made mistakes, including a failure to negotiate a peace agreement in 1980.[10] What a tragedy to understand and admit this following a decade of destruction and bloodshed. Villalobos' comment, however, was perhaps just one more in a decade of propagandistic statements aimed at garnering international support and sympathy needed for the guerrillas' goal of becoming the dominant political power in El Salvador. The FMLN launched its November 1989 offensive less than six weeks later and continued a war of destruction and killing until the January 1992 Peace Accords.

Unity of Effort

Successful peacekeeping operations are highly dependent upon the degree to which the major actors involved are united with a common objective. By 1992, the government of El Salvador, the FMLN, the "four friends plus one" (Venezuela, Mexico, Colombia, Spain and the United States) and ONUSAL were in agreement on the most important conditions - a desire and commitment for peace. Both the government of El Salvador and the FMLN exhibited a purposeful willingness and firm commitment to achieve a peace settlement. This willingness on both the part of the Salvadoran government and the FMLN was central to the success of the United Nation's mission but occurred due to a specific set of conditions. The government of El Salvador wanted what it had hoped to achieve since the 1979 coup - peaceful democratization and reunification within the context of the structure set forth by the 1983 constitution. The FMLN found itself politically and militarily pressed into abandoning its revolutionary role for a more favorable political role within the system. In general, Unity of Effort to achieve peace was maintained among the major players. Specifically, Unity of Effort between the Salvadoran government and the FMLN was articulated through a series of initial UN sponsored meetings. In actuality, Unity of Effort was intricately connected to the concept of legitimacy that was reinforced by external pressures and developments.

On March 29, 1990, the government of El Salvador and the FMLN met in Mexico City under the auspices of the United Nations. On March 30, the United Nations announced that the two sides would meet again on April 4 in Geneva and that Secretary General Perez de Cuellar would participate. In Geneva, the Salvadoran government and the FMLN set a general agenda for the conduct of negotiations and pledged to embark upon a process of continuous negotiation for a peaceful settlement. The Geneva Agreement, signed April 4, 1990 states that the purpose of the negotiation process is to "end the armed conflict by political means as speedily as possible, promote democratization of the country, guarantee unrestricted respect for human rights and reunify Salvadoran society."[11] On May 16, 1990 another meeting was held in Caracas at which time the agenda of the negotiating process was divided into two parts: first, negotiation and agreements on institutional and political reforms of the armed forces, human rights, the judicial and electoral systems, constitutional, economic and social issues; and second, negotiation on a cease fire and demobilization of the guerrillas.[12] The aim of the United Nations mediator, Alvaro de Soto, on behalf of the United Nations Secretary General Javier Perez de Cuellar was to keep the Salvadoran government and the FMLN in continuous talks in order to build an atmosphere of trust.[13] Thus, the framework for Unity of Effort between the Salvadoran government and the FMLN was established with the UN acting as a facilitator to maintain the effort.

Unity of Effort is not easy to maintain among conflicting parties. In June of 1990 talks stalled with disagreement between the Salvadoran government and the FMLN over reform of the armed forces. In response to FMLN demands, the Salvadoran government put forth a 33-point proposal on the armed forces. The government indicated it would bring to trial among others, four cases suggested by the FMLN, create a permanent armed forces honor tribunal to handle unresolved cases, and grant general amnesty to guerrillas and members of the military for most cases. In addition the government proposed the regulation of private security forces, various measures to ensure submission of the armed forces to civilian authority and declared support for the Central American regional negotiations on issues of demilitarization.[14] The FMLN rejected these proposals.

By de Soto's ability to skillfully refocus negotiations from areas of conflict into areas where agreements might be reached such as human rights, the UN was able to maintain a degree of unity between the parties. As a result, the San Jose Agreement on Human Rights was signed on July 26, 1990 and called for a UN observer mission to monitor the human rights situation in El Salvador. This marked the first time that the United Nations carried out such an extensive oversight role.[15] It also marked the fragility of the peace process, as areas of conflict can only be avoided temporarily. In November of 1990 the FMLN launched its most significant and disruptive offensive against primarily military targets since the 1989 "final offensive." For the FMLN, the purpose of the 1990 offensive was to demonstrate that the guerrillas remained a viable force with which to be reckoned. Conversely, it helped create both a political and a military situation in which it no longer appeared viable to the FMLN to pursue full scale military operations. The FMLN was losing legitimacy both within and without Salvadoran society. Thus, Unity of Effort was maintained in part due to the perceived loss of legitimacy by the FMLN and the gain in the legitimacy of the government.

Nevertheless, the San Jose Agreement helped lay the groundwork for more substantive agreements aimed at ending armed conflict. These agreements included those reached on April 27 and September 25, 1991, respectively, as well as the cliff hanging negotiations of December 31, 1991 that had to be completed prior to Perez de Cuellar's departure as Secretary General. In addition, the parties agreed that the final peace agreement would be signed at Mexico City, January 16, 1992. Thus, when ONUSAL was officially established in July 1991, the foundation had been created among the parties for a legitimate peacekeeping operation which could maintain Unity of Effort. ONUSAL's task was to secure that unity and maintain legitimacy.

Legitimacy

The legitimacy of the peacekeeping process depends upon the degree of agreement among the conflicting parties on the common objectives which conjoin them in a Unity of Effort. Both de jure legitimacy and de facto legitimacy are relevant with the former being straight forward and legalistic and the latter being less tangible but even more highly salient. The Security Council Resolutions which define the terms of the peace accords provide juridical legitimacy to the mission. The degree of compliance with the accords and the will to carry out the accords provide de facto legitimacy. More specifically, de facto legitimacy of the mission or the lack thereof was determined by the behavior of ONUSAL and the perception of the other parties involved as to how ONUSAL carries out its mission. In addition, the actions of the government of El Salvador, the Salvadoran Armed forces and the FMLN also determined de facto legitimacy of the peace process and again rested on the groups' commitment to achieve the common objective - peace. The key to de facto legitimacy is perception.

The November 1990 offensive, launched by the FMLN under the name of the "National Army For Democracy," suffered a major political setback. This attempt to invalidate the peace process was perceived by the Salvadoran government as well as regional and international states to be illegitimate. In mid-December the Central American presidents issued the "Declaration on El Salvador" in Puntarenas, Costa Rica. This declaration underlined the support of the Central American presidents for President Alfredo Cristiani's peace efforts and condemned the violent actions of the FMLN! The FMLN condemned the declaration, stating that agreements on reform issues, including military reforms, were to be concluded prior to a cease fire.[16] Nonetheless, the FMLN agreed to negotiations with the government of El Salvador, and from January 1991 to February 1991 a series of meetings took place in which the two sides once again began to move slowly toward agreement on sensitive issues such as military reform.

Simultaneously, the government's perceived legitimacy increased as it continued the democratization process. On March 10, 1991, legislative and municipal elections were held. Ambassador Edwin G. Corr, one of the authors of this chapter, served as an official observer. Despite some minor incidents, the elections marked the continuous opening of the political process to more groups in society. The Nationalist Democratic Union, a Communist organization and explicit supporter of the guerrilla forces actually won one seat,[17] and Democratic Convergence (CD), a FDR group running for the second time, also won seats.

Problems with perception occurred as the government of El Salvador, the El Salvadoran Armed Forces, and parts of the US government perceived favoritism on the part of ONUSAL toward the FMLN. A case in point is the Report of the UN Truth Commission in which the Truth Commission used an entirely different set of standards in evaluating the FMLN and the Salvadoran armed forces.[18] In addition, the Truth Commission overstepped its bounds from investigating and reporting the truth to recommending actions be taken contrary to the peace accords and antithetical to national reconciliation. For example, Miguel A Salaverria, the Salvadoran Ambassador to the United States, stated in a letter to the US Congress that "the Truth Commission recommended some changes which either conflict with the reforms adopted by the peace negotiators or are beyond the powers of our government's executive branch."[19] Furthermore, states Salaverria, "The core objective of the peace negotiations was to persuade the FMLN to change from an armed group to a political party... But the Truth Commission has called for key FMLN leaders to be barred from office for ten years. This recommendation goes against what the peace negotiations sought to achieve...."[20] Fortunately, the parties involved were able to overcome this potential impasse by simply ignoring the Truth Commission and forging ahead with the peace accords.

Support to Belligerents

This dimension examines outside support to the FMLN belligerents. Prior to 1989, the FMLN enjoyed support from Cuba, the Soviet Union and the ruling Sandinista government in Nicaragua. Beginning in 1989, support to the FMLN by its Communist allies was drastically cut. The fall of the Soviet Union and communism in Eastern Europe dealt a major blow to the insurgency. Without the backing of the Soviet Union, Cuba was forced to diminish support for foreign insurgents because of the increasing vulnerability of Cuba itself. Therefore, Cuba could no longer afford to support the FMLN. In addition, the February 1990 elections in Nicaragua signaled Nicaragua's own move toward democratic government. The victory of the United Nicaraguan Opposition over the Sandinistas signaled a change in the Central American environment. The FMLN's lack of outside support created a situation in which FMLN participation in civil society continually became more attractive than armed insurrection. This was especially true after the November 1989 offensive.

While the FMLN was losing the support of its former allies, it was simultaneously gaining the support of ONUSAL, the government of El Salvador and the United States government. Thus, the "support to belligerents" dimension shifts from FMLN supporters seeking to reinforce a revolution to FMLN supporters seeking compliance with a negotiated, peace settlement. In addition to the direct support it received from ONUSAL, the FMLN received indirect support from the Cristiani government. By abiding by the peace accords, the Cristiani government gave the FMLN incentives to participate in civil society. As for the United States, US government officials began to meet with FMLN leaders, something the US had previously refused to do, further fostering the benefits to the FMLN of participating in and complying with the peace accords.

United States support to the government of El Salvador and the El Salvadoran Armed Forces did not fall significantly up to and immediately following the peace accords. The US Congress, with Executive Branch cooperation, enacted foreign assistance legislation that held out financial incentives and disincentives to both the Salvadoran Armed Forces and the FMLN for progress in the peace talks and their implementation. US support provided a sounding board for the FMLN through use of the US embassy and the Military Group. The key point is that as support for the war continuation died, US military assistance to the Salvadoran armed forces declined at a rate such that the armed forces could adjust. Thus, confidence in US support to both the government and the armed forces remained high.

The role of the United Nations was to reinforce support for the parties to the extent to which they were in compliance with the accords. The UN role was particularly important in demonstrating that what at times appeared to be non compliance by one party really was not non compliance, thereby contributing to the perception of legitimacy of the process among all parties which was essential for the process to continue.

Support Actions of Peace Forces

Support actions of the peace forces refers to the degree to which the governments of the United Nations Security Council members and force providers were committed to the mission. The end of the Cold War allowed for cooperation among the Security Council members. The United States government in particular had been long committed to peace in El Salvador, and its warming relationship with the Soviet Union allowed for a joint effort of the superpowers.

From 1979 until the early 1990s, the United States recognized Central America as a primary security interest. Throughout the 1979 - 1992 period, the US task included aiding "our neighbors not only to secure their freedom from aggression and violence, but also to set in place the policies, processes and institutions that will make them both prosperous and free."[21] When one of the authors of this chapter became chief of mission to El Salvador in August 1985, he was given clear and simple instructions from President Reagan: "Go down there and help Salvadoran leaders consolidate constitutional democracy, attain peace, and improve the standard of living for their people."[22] Reagan's statement is reflective of overall US policy throughout the time period.

The support of the US government for Salvadoran efforts to establish a viable constitutional democracy fell into five major interrelated areas. The primary security interests and ideals of the United States were best served by helping Salvadorans to consolidate and expand a functioning constitutional democracy and to create a more just and prosperous society. The United States would support Salvadoran efforts to (1) create the political institutions and attitudes necessary for a lasting constitutional democracy; (2) reduce human rights abuses and improve the justice system; (3) foster economic growth and development, generate employment, and distribute more fairly the nation's wealth; (4) seek peace through effective efforts and dialogue, negotiation, and national conciliation while successfully conducting the war; and (5) help establish peace and democracy in all of Central America.

After the January 31, 1990 New York meeting between President Cristiani and United Nations General Secretary Perez de Cuellar, Cristiani called on

President George Bush at the White House. Bush supported Cristiani's latest initiatives aimed at using the good offices of the United Nations Secretary General. Bush stressed to Cristiani the need to press forward for a negotiated settlement and the wish of the United States to be supportive of his efforts.[23] Warmed relations between the two superpowers allowed for joint support of the peace process. Following a February 7-9, 1990 meeting in Moscow, Secretary of State James Baker and Soviet Foreign Minister Eduard Shevardnadze declared in a joint statement "support for the UN Secretary General's efforts to secure a permanent cease-fire and renewed negotiations in El Salvador, and for the more vigorous and effective use of UN machinery to supervise compliance with existing and future agreements in Central America." On January 17, 1992, the day after the Salvadoran government and the FMLN formally signed the Peace Agreement in Mexico City, Secretary Baker proclaimed the support of the United States government for the peace agreement and his hope for a hemisphere in which "democracy is the only legitimate form of government, the rule of law is respected, and human rights are secure."[24]

US policy and new US-Soviet relations were an important background element to the support actions of peace forces dimension in that it allowed for an international environment conducive to the UN peace process. Commitments by other actors were equally important, however, and were reflected in the parties' support for a number of increased UN mandates.

On January 14, 1992, Security Council Resolution 729 authorized the enlargement of ONUSAL's mandate. This was the first in a series of enlargements that would take place throughout the early to mid 1990s. ONUSAL would verify all aspects of the cease-fire and the separation of forces as well as maintain public order during the transitional period in which the new National Civil Police would be established.[25] Two new divisions were added to the Human Rights Division: Military and Police.

By the end of 1992, cease-fire violations had significantly diminished, 60% of FMLN ex-combatants had been demobilized, reductions in the armed forces continued per agreement, and human rights conditions greatly improved. On December 1, 1992, President Cristiani reported to the United Nations that "he had taken the administrative decisions to implement the recommendation of the Ad Hoc Commission on Purification of the Armed Forces." In addition, destruction of the FMLN's cache of weapons was well underway, and on December 14, 1992 the FMLN was established as a legal, political party.[26]

On January 8, 1993, ONUSAL's mandate was expanded again when the Salvadoran Government formally requested that the United Nations monitor the upcoming March 1994 general elections in which a President, Legislative Assembly, representatives to the Central American Parliament and mayors would be selected by the voters.[27] ONUSAL took on this expanded role, and despite challenges to both the peace and the democratic processes, Salvadorans elected the Arena candidate, Armando Calderon Sol over the CD/FMLN/MNR candidate, Ruben Zamora, as the next president of El Salvador.[28] Because the situation in El Salvador was exceedingly fragile, the role of the United Nations continued through verification processes, the use of good offices and human rights monitoring beyond its originally scheduled mandate.

/

Military Actions of Peace Forces

The UN operation was a traditional peacekeeping mission. Military actions were undertaken in an environment in which there was not only an agreement to peace but a commitment to peace. Military actions were well integrated with the overall political goal of achieving national reconciliation under constitutional government.

Traditional military operations require a sufficient size force to complete the objective. In the case of El Salvador, the small size in number of troops was sufficient for the mission. Legitimacy is again the key concept as the accords were sufficiently legitimate that there was no need for a larger number of troops. ONUSAL's military division initially consisted of 380 observers from ten different countries: Brazil, Canada, Colombia, Ecuador, India, Ireland, Norway, Spain, Sweden and Venezuela. Spain provided approximately 80% of the force as well as the military division commander.[29] The large Spanish contingent is especially relevant in relation to the role played by Spain which helped to maintain the integrity and legitimacy of ONUSAL's military division. Spain provided a special leadership role because the Spanish presence helped offset the perception in the Salvadoran Armed Forces that ONUSAL was biased toward the FMLN. Cooperative relations between the Spanish observers and the Salvadoran armed forces had existed for many years prior to ONUSAL's military operation and provided a basis for trust, thus contributing to the continued perceived legitimacy of the mission.

ONUSAL's military officers functioned as liaisons between the military leaders of the conflicting parties and, in conjunction with the United Nations Observer Mission in Central America, enabled FMLN field commanders to be escorted from conflict zones to negotiation meetings. On July 20, 1992, when the peace agreement was signed, 380 military observers in the Military Division were responsible for verifying the cease fire, redeployment of the Armed Forces of El Salvador, and the concentration of FMLN forces in agreed upon "designated locations." The military division provided for 15 Designated Assembly Zones (DAZs) for demobilization of the FMLN, each zone with two UN observers and a small liaison team to work in conjunction with the Salvadoran Armed Force in the region. ONUSAL military observers had to be perceived by the FMLN as "trusted friends" if the demobilization was to be successful, and ONUSAL was often lenient toward the FMLN ex-combatants in resolving minor disputes, such as former FMLN members leaving the DAZ safe haven to visit family and friends. This leniency, in turn, was perceived by many in the Salvadoran Armed Forces and in the Salvadoran government as pro-FMLN.[30] Thus, the Spanish presence was particularly helpful in defusing potentially volatile situations.

ONUSAL's military division was quite willing to take the initiative to prevent conflicts from erupting and to keep the demobilization process on track. For example, ONUSAL's military division created a Rapid Reaction Force consisting of a five man mediation team. This force was devised for zones of friction, such as the 16 zones outside those designated in the peace agreements which remained occupied by the Salvadoran Armed Forces on the basis of national security. The Rapid Reaction Force had a general directive to prevent military actions perpetrated by either side and could arrive quickly by helicopter to any area of dispute and "talk it to death."[31] In response to the initial difficulties of treaty implementation, ONUSAL produced a compliance report in May 1992 that blamed all sides, most significantly the Salvadoran government, for non compliance. This resulted in a temporary hold placed on US aid to the government and influenced all parties concerned into more attentive compliance with the accords.[32]

Military Actions of the Belligerents and the Peace Forces

This dimension treats the FMLN belligerents, the Salvadoran Armed Forces and the ONUSAL peace forces as allies and refers to the degree of professionalism of the military and paramilitary groups on all sides. For the ESAF, this included the military and police sections. The new National Civil Police was formed and composed of 20 % FMLN, 20% old National Police, and 60% new recruits. These three groups were integrated with the support of the police section of ONUSAL, worked well initially and, according to the former US Military Group Commander in El Salvador Colonel Steve Fee, continues to work well four years into the program.

ONUSAL's police division was supported by the service of police officials from Spain France and Italy. The police division served to monitor National Police activities during the transitional period from armed conflict to national reconciliation. From October 1992 to July 1993, the police division provided instruction to the Auxiliary Transitory Police which was responsible for maintaining public order and security in the former conflict zones.[33] The functions of the police division later increased to include, in March 1992, the territorial deployment of the National Civil Police and a follow on evaluation of the new police force. The police division assisted in locating illegal arms caches, provided security measures for the FMLN and supported the electoral division established in September 1993.

Actions Targeted on Ending Conflict

From its inception, the ONUSAL mission focused on specific actions targeted at ending the conflict. ONUSAL's mandate was established upon a decade of efforts by the Salvadoran government to end the conflict and reincorporate the FMLN back into civil society, a changed regional and international environment conducive to Salvadoran national reunification, and exhaustion of the parties involved. Nevertheless, ONUSAL focused its actions on particular "sticking points" of internal conflict, such as land redistribution and the Salvadoran economy as well as the demobilization of the FMLN and ESAF, which continually threatened the fragile peace.

One of the most important elements involved in ending the conflict was the realization by the major actors that "ending the conflict" would be a protracted undertaking requiring a continued, long term commitment to the peace process. The US commitment is witnessed by the February 1996 signed agreement between Secretary of State Warren Christopher and the Salvadoran Government to provide $10 million to complete El Salvador's land transfer program. Secretary Christopher reiterated US support for the peace accords and the fostering of hemispheric conditions for development and free trade.[34] The successes or failures of the Salvadoran government to complete its economic reform and insure growth is highly dependent upon the full implementation of the peace accords which is in turn dependent upon international support.

From the beginning of its mission ONUSAL helped maintain an environment in which political, societal and economic reforms could be conducted under the initiative of the Salvadorans. This was a key action targeted at ending the conflict. The primary role played by the Salvadorans continues today and was and is essential for insuring legitimacy of the peace process. The 1992 Peace Agreement called for the reinsertion of demobilized persons into a productive society, the strengthening of democratic institutions, and the reconstruction of conflict torn areas.[35] El Salvador's current National Reconstruction Program (NRP) was designed specifically to implement the accords, help consolidate peace, resolve social injustices and inequalities, and provide a foundation for further democratic development. The NRP targets approximately 30,000 demobilized persons from the FMLN, the Armed Forces and other security agencies; 60,000 displaced persons; 26,000 persons who formerly left the country only to return under UN sponsorship; and 1.6 million people inhabiting conflict ridden areas.[36]

In its quest to aid the Salvadoran peace process, ONUSAL was not unrealistic in what it believed it could or could not accomplish. This fact is important as ONUSAL not only assisted with the monitoring of the treaty but also assisted with the implementation of the treaty.[37] There was a willingness by the major actors involved to accept a "60%" solution, and this willingness to accept a less than perfect solution kept the peace process on track.[38]

The United Nations and the United States also acted to end the conflict by assuming the necessary role of scapegoat on behalf of the government of El Salvador or the FMLN. Acts such as the purge of the Salvadoran Armed forces and the demobilization of the FMLN were required but were nonetheless politically difficult to undertake. This is an important issue because it allowed both sides a way out in that each could claim outside pressure for controversial actions[39] and therefore helped to maintain the overall legitimacy of the mission.

Conclusion

The Manwaring Paradigm applies well to a traditional peacekeeping operation, which is not surprising if one understands the dimensions of the paradigm. The key factors to ONUSAL's success were the commitments of the parties to peace which in turn influenced the legitimacy of the mission. In the Salvadoran case, all dimensions of the paradigm overlap with each other and revolve around the central concept of Legitimacy which leads to a Unity of Effort. It is important to note that the United Nations did not enter the Salvadoran situation without a firm basis on which to work. This basis had been established through the efforts of successive Salvadoran governments, beginning with President Duarte, and solidified under changed international and regional conditions. El Salvador presented the United Nations with a traditional operation, tailor made for peace keeping and peace building. Thus, the United Nations did not enter the environment attempting to create a Unity of Effort or a de facto Legitimacy among the parties. These two critical dimensions of the paradigm were already present and allowed the other five dimensions to be created and maintained. This analysis is by no means meant to imply that the UN mission in El Salvador is either simple or guaranteed to succeed. What the Salvadoran case does suggest is that having de facto Legitimacy and Unity of Effort going into a peace keeping operation allows for a greater degree of ambiguity, mistakes, and less than perfect outcomes to occur during the mission without causing an entire derailment of the peace process. A case in point is the UN Truth Commission mentioned earlier in this chapter and the ability of the parties involved to overcome the Commission's faults and move forward in their quest for peace.

El Salvador's future prospects at continued democratization, economic reform, social, political and institutional reform is by no means secured. The Salvadorans are on the right track, but much will depend on their continued ability to integrate economic, social, institutional and political reform policies within the context of the peace accords. It is up to the Salvadorans themselves as well as to the international community to determine if the precarious peace so craftily established will be able to withstand social, political and financial pressures in order to ensure continued development and democratization.

Notes

[1] "United Nations Observer Mission In El Salvador," Program on Peacekeeping policy, The Institute of Public Policy, George Mason University on-line, June 1997.

[2] Max Manwaring and Court Prisk, "A Strategic View Of Insurgencies: Insights From El Salvador," McNair Paper No. 8, Washington DC, The Institute For National and Strategic Studies, 1990.

[3] Ibid.

[4] Thomas M. Leonard, *Central America And The Search For Stability*, Athens, University of Georgia Press, 1991.

[5] For a more indepth discussion of reformist goals, see Edwin G. Corr, "Including the Excluded in El Salvador: Prospects for Democracy And Development," in *Institutions of Democracy And Development*, Peter L. Berger, editor, San Francisco, Sequoia Institute, 1993.

[6] Jose Napoleon Duarte with Diana Page, *My Story*, New York, G.P. Putnam's Sons, 1986.

[7] Linda Robinson, *Intervention Or Neglect*, New York, Council on Foreign Relations, 1991.

[8] General Jaime Abdul Gutierrez, "We Had To Administer Reform, But We Had No Resources," in *El Salvador At War An Oral History*, Max G. Manwaring and Court Prisk, editors, Washington, D.C., The Institute For National Strategic Studies, 1986.

[9] Duarte, *My Story*.

[10] "El Salvador Conversations With Two Foes," *Time*, October 2, 1989, p. 26.

[11] Letter dated 8 October 1991 from El Salvador transmitting the text of the Geneva Agreement signed on 4 April 1990 by the Government of El Salvador and the FMLN. In *The United Nations and El Salvador, 1990-1995*, New York, United Nations Department of Public Information, February 28, 1995, p. 164.

[12] *The United Nations and El Salvador, 1990-1995*, p. 12.

[13] Laraman C. Wilson and Raul Gonzalen Diaz, "The Central American Peace Process, 1983-1993; Nicaragua and El Salvador--Transitions From US Opposition to Support And From OAS-UN to UN Peacekeeping," School of International Service, The American University, Washington D.C., p. 33.

[14] K. Larry Storrs, *CRS Report for Congress El Salvador: Status Of U.N. -Mediated Government-Guerrilla Peace Talks*, Congressional Research Service, The Library of Congress, March 26, 1991, pp. CRS-8, CRS-9.

[15] *The United Nations And El Salvador, 1990-1995*, p. 14.

[16] Storrs, p. CRS-12.

[17] IBID, CRS-15.

[18] For a full analysis of the Truth Commission Report, see John T. Fishel, "The Partial Truths of the UN Truth Commission," *Low Intensity Conflict And Law Enforcement*, 3/2, Autumn 1994, pp. 378-383.

[19] Quoted in John T. Fishel, "The Partial Truths of the UN Truth Commission," p. 379.
[20] Ibid.
[21] National Bipartisan Commission on Central America, *Report of the National Bipartisan Commission on Central America*, January 1984, pp. 126-127.
[22] See Edwin G. Corr, "Societal Transformation For Peace In El Salvador," ANNALS, *AAPSS*, 541, September, 1995.
[23] "Bush Seeks a Rise in Aid to El Salvador," *The New York Times*, February 2, 1990, p. A-10.
[24] James Baker, "The Hemisphere's Hopes For Peace," Address before the Salvadoran National Assembly, San Salvador, El Salvador, January 17, 1992, US Department Of State Dispatch, January 20, 1992, pp. 33-34.
[25] United Nations Observer Mission In El Salvador.
[26] *The United Nations and El Salvador, 1990-1995*, pp. 33-34.
[27] Ibid, p. 36.
[28] Ambassador Corr was also an observer at both rounds of this election.
[29] Thomas K. Adams, "Disengage, Disarm, Demobilize: The Success of ONUSAL in Implementing the 1992 El Salvador Peace Accords," in *Low Intensity Conflict and Law Enforcement*, 3/2, Autumn 1994, pp. 290-299.
[30] Ibid.
[31] Ibid., p. 295.
[32] Ibid.
[33] Ibid.
[34] El Salvador background notes. March 1997. Released by the Bureau of Inter-American Affairs, US State Department.
[35] Ministry of Planning And Coordination Of Economic And Social Development and The National Reconstruction Secretariat. "El Salvador Financing Needs To Conclude The Peace Agreements." *Report to the Consultative Group Meeting on El Salvador*, Paris, France, June 22, 1995.
[36] Ibid.
[37] Adams.
[38] Ibid.
[39] Ibid.

4

Peacekeeping on the Ecuador-Peru Border: The Military Observer Mission - Ecuador/Peru

Stephen C. Fee

"Caminante no hay camino...se hace camino al andar."
(Traveler there is no path...the path is made by walking.)

-- Machado

Introduction

In January 1995 the western hemispheric sense of unity, fraternity and peace championed by the region's Heads of State just a month earlier at the Summit of the Americas in Miami was shattered by the outbreak of a violent and conventional border conflict between two South American neighbors - Ecuador and Perú. The existence of border disputes among Latin American countries is both well known and widespread--the examples abound: El Salvador-Honduras, Nicaragua - Colombia, Colombia - Venezuela, Venezuela - Guyana, Chile - Argentina, Guatemala - Belize. These border issues are also very long standing, dating principally from the Spanish colonial days and the 19th century era of independence.

The Ecuador-Perú border dispute is arguably the most long-standing and most bitterly contested in all Latin America. Both Perú and Ecuador cite references from as early as 1500 to the present in support of their respective positions. This dispute in modern times has been simmering since a very serious clash in late 1941 when Peruvian forces invaded and occupied parts of southern Ecuador. Given the preoccupation with World War II, the United States, in conjunction with Argentina, Brazil and Chile, helped negotiate a quick peace. These foregoing countries (the Guarantors), and Ecuador and Perú (the Parties) signed the 1942 Protocol of Rio de Janeiro (the "Rio Protocol") which (1) outlined a demarcation process by describing geographic features to guide the installation of border markers and (2) bound the Guarantors to continued support of Ecuador and Perú until the process was complete.

The border demarcation process duly began in 1943 in accordance with the 1942 Rio Protocol. Paragraph 8 of the Protocol defined part of the border in the southeastern disputed area as: "from the Quebrada de San Francisco, the watershed ("divortium aquarum") between the Zamora and Santiago Rivers to the confluence of the Santiago and Yaupi Rivers."[1] However, the emplacement of "Hitos" or border markers in this area resulted in the discovery of a watershed not specified within the Rio Protocol between the Zamora and Santiago: the headwaters of the Cenepa River. Insofar as this affected only a relatively small portion of the border area to be demarcated. Perú maintained that the Rio Protocol was still a valid document and that the Cenepa area could be demarcated through further negotiations. Indeed, Article 9 of the Rio Protocol clearly states that "the Parties [Ecuador and Perú] will be able to, nonetheless, on proceeding to trace the border on the ground, authorize reciprocal concessions that they consider mutually convenient, to the end of adjusting the border to geographic realities."[2] Ecuador, however, felt that this discovery of the Cenepa River clearly invalidated the Rio Protocol and consequently stopped all demarcation efforts in 1948 calling for a complete review of the border issue. The result: a 170 kilometer stretch of land has remained undemarcated since 1947 (see Figure #1).

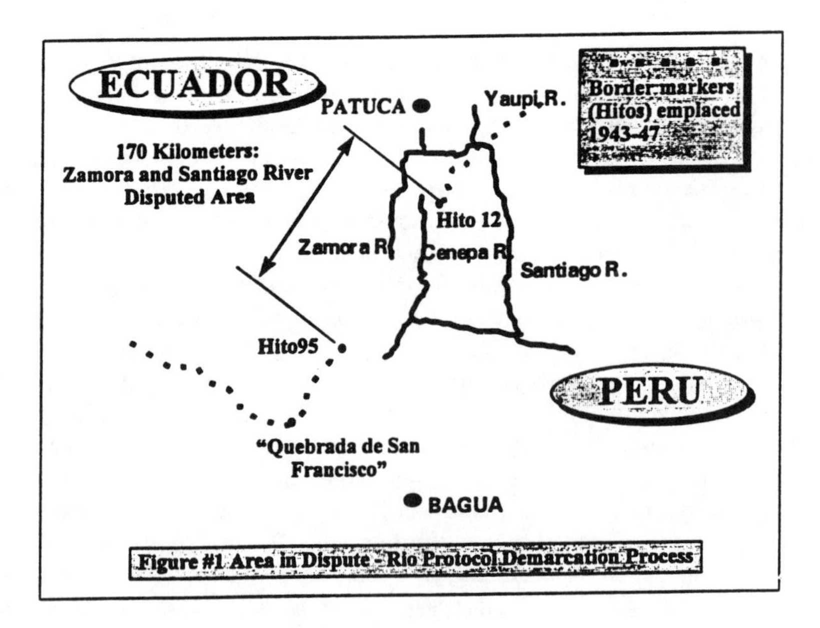

Figure #1 Area in Dispute - Rio Protocol Demarcation Process

Several flare ups (notably in 1981 in the Paquisha area and in 1991 near the Ecuadorian Border Outpost Teniente Hugo Ortiz) have kept continuous pressure in this inadequately demarcated area where an uneasy modus vivendi has existed between Peruvian and Ecuadorian military border outposts which dot this sparsely populated and undeveloped jungle area (Interestingly, this dotting of military outposts has indirectly defined a general conception of the border).[3]

In December 1994, Perú identified the establishment of a series of Ecuadorian base camps in the Upper Cenepa area. Perú denounced this as encroachment on what has historically been Peruvian territory and demanded the withdrawal of these military elements. Ecuador refused and by January 1995, these movements resulted in initial military contact. By late January, Ecuador and Perú had poured a total of over 5,000 troops into a 70 square kilometer area of the Upper Cenepa resulting in both ground and air combat operations (see Figure #2).

With national fervor exploding in press reports on both sides, politicians were incapable of controlling the wave of nationalist sentiment. Both militaries mobilized all along the frontier -- a total of about 100,000 in the border area; their respective navies put to sea -- the stage was set for an all out conventional conflict. During the ensuing 35 days of combat operations in the Upper Cenepa, about 300 lives were lost. The numbers are unconfirmed; both sides claiming victory.

Figure #2 - Perú-Ecuador Area of Operations 1995 Conflict

Through the intervention of the Guarantors of the Rio Protocol, the fighting remained limited to the Upper Cenepa area and was brought to an end with signing of the Declaration of Peace of Itamaraty in Brasilia on 17 February 1995 (although sporadic fighting/incidents continued for the next nine months). The Guarantors had acted swiftly and aggressively through their commitment declared in the 1942 Rio Protocol. With this as an initial point of departure, what followed has been perhaps the world's most unique and successful peacekeeping operation: the Military Observer Mission - Ecuador/Perú (MOMEP). Within twelve months after signing the Declaration of Peace, Peruvian and Ecuadorian troops in the Upper Cenepa were separated, forces along the border were demobilized, a Demilitarized Zone (DMZ) and a Security Zone (Zone Alfa) were established in formerly conflictive areas, the belligerents themselves were fully integrated into the Peace Force as Observers and, at this writing, are maintaining a 24 hour multinational presence at border points of greatest tension. The purpose of this Chapter is to analyze MOMEP operations using the seven factors of the Manwaring Paradigm. Does the paradigm highlight factors which have made MOMEP so successful? Does the paradigm highlight factors which may provide insights into the long term prospects for success in the demarcation of the Perú-Ecuador border? Will the end of the fighting signal positive steps towards a final resolution of the Perú-Ecuador border issue or is this just one more skirmish in a dispute destined to move into the 21st century unresolved?

Unity of Effort

The conditions for Unity of Effort were established well prior to the outbreak of hostilities on 24 January 1995: in the 1942 Rio Protocol, the Guarantors and the Parties agreed that "the participation of the United States, Argentina, Brazil and Chile, will continue until the border between Ecuador and Perú has been demarcated definitively with this Protocol (Rio Protocol) and the execution (of the border demarcation) under the guarantee of the four countries."[4] The February 1995 Peace Declaration of Itamaraty continued to focus the efforts of the Guarantors and the Parties by clearly establishing the military and political objectives of the six signatories:

> **Paragraph 2: Separation of Forces**. ...Immediately and simultaneously separate all the troops of the two nations committed in the conflict with the end of eliminating any risk of reopening hostilities...
>
> **Paragraph 3: Establishment of a demilitarized zone**. Request that the Observer Mission of the Guarantor Countries [MOMEP]...recommend to the governments of Ecuador and Perú an area to be totally demilitarized...

> **Paragraph 5: Demobilization of Forces along the border**. Initiate immediately, as a confidence building measure, in the frontier areas not directly committed in the conflict and with the supervision of the Guarantor Countries, a gradual and reciprocal demobilization...
>
> **Paragraph 6: Agreement to begin political discussions to demarcate the border**. Initiate conversations...to find solutions on the substantive points of disagreement as soon as the previous points are accomplished...[5]

To accomplish paragraphs 2, 3 and 5 (technical, military objectives) -- the Parties agreed to the deployment of a Peacekeeping Force to the Upper Cenepa: 10 Observers from each of the four guarantor nations and a 90-man administrative/logistical support package from the United States: The Mission of Military Observers - Ecuador-Perú (MOMEP) was born. Paragraph 6, the agreement to begin political discussions to demarcate the border, is a political objective dependent upon the success of MOMEP in executing the tasks laid out in paragraphs 2, 3 and 5. The resolution of Paragraph 6 has been left in the hands of an ad hoc committee of ambassadorial level representatives from the six nations, "the altos funcionarios" (High Functionaries) who have operated principally from Brasilia.

There has been a clear coincidence of Guarantor and Party interests. The Guarantor interests are quite straightforward: regional peace and stability and compliance with the Rio Protocol of 1942. Perú and Ecuador support these objectives, albeit for different reasons. Ecuador was in a good position tactically after the fighting and had once again successfully raised the border issue publicly -- Ecuador was militarily vindicated after its embarrassing defeat at the hands of Peruvian forces in 1941. However, it was in no position to continue a long term conventional struggle with Perú. Perú, on the other hand, was poorly prepared to conduct military operations in this distant and isolated part of its national territory -- its lines of communication were stretched thin and support infrastructure was inadequate. Additionally, Perú was in the apparent final stages of its struggle against Sendero Luminoso, still facing the daunting challenges of the counterdrug war and President Fujimori continued to battle to consolidate himself politically. While Perú was clearly in a position to win a long term conventional struggle with Ecuador, the aforementioned complicating and priority demands argued that it was in Perú's best interests as well to fully support the Itamaraty peace process and the consequent deployment of the MOMEP Peace Force.

Further reinforcing this Unity of Effort was the rapid deployment of the Peace Force. The Declaration was signed on 17 February 1995 -- by 12 March 1995, the Peace Force contingent of more than one hundred observers and support personnel was on the ground in its base in Patuca, Ecuador (some 90 km to the north of the Upper Cenepa) with an Observer element also based out of Bagua, Peru (250 km to the south of the Upper Cenepa). The deployment of MOMEP elements, as of December 1996, is shown in Figure #3.

It is also important to highlight the unity of effort within the US government in responding to this crisis -- specifically the teamwork between the Department of State (Ambassador Luigi Einaudi) as the lead agency and the Department of Defense (US Southern Command Commander, General Barry McCaffrey) as the force provider. This cooperation played a key role in establishing the US position of leadership in the organization, deployment and operational employment of MOMEP and served as a further reinforcement of Guarantor commitment to the Parties. The rapid assembly and deployment of the US Support element was the key which allowed the political will of the Guarantors to be quickly translated into a reality on the ground in Patuca, Ecuador. This US Joint Task Force (JTF) was designated JTF Safe Border and, as of December 1996, consisted of approximately 60 US Military, 4 UH-60 Black Hawk Helicopters and periodic USAF C-27 logistical support flights originating from Howard Air Force Base in the Republic of Panama).[6]

A final point should must be made regarding the unity of effort within the MOMEP Staff itself -- since the beginning of observer operations, Guarantor MOMEP officers had worked as a single team -- for the most part putting aside national identities -- even to the point of proudly referring to themselves as "Los Momepianos," -- the Momepians. There was also a clear effort to keep the MOMEP mission squarely focused on impartiality -- this too aided in reinforcing a sense of Unity of Effort. The integration of 18 MOMEP observers

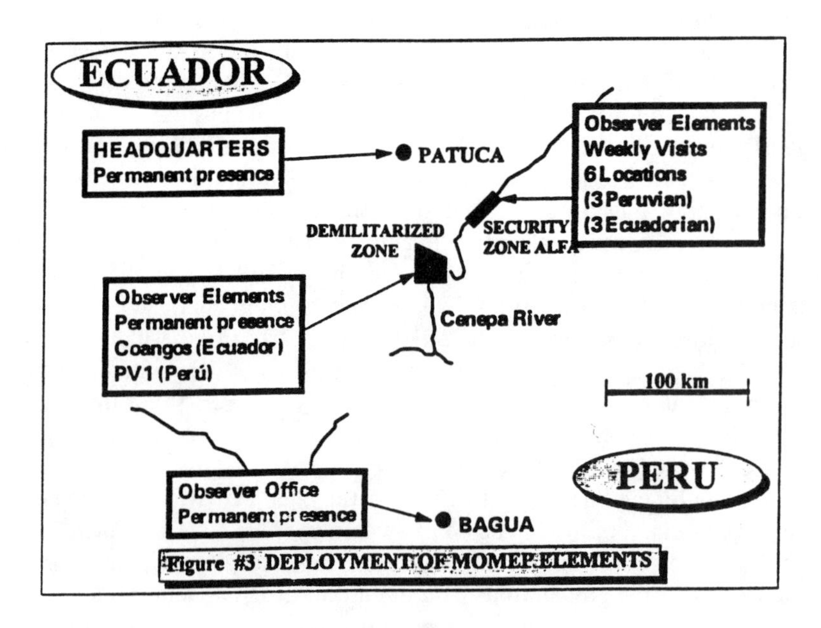

Figure #3 DEPLOYMENT OF MOMEP ELEMENTS

from Ecuador and Peru, from September 1995 through January 1996, far from upsetting this Unity of Effort, actually served to reinforce MOMEP's Unity of Effort. A humorous anecdote clearly highlights this unity: MOMEP verification missions into the DMZ and Zone Alfa were carefully balanced to insure appropriate participation by the Parties and the Guarantors. During one of the daily morning air mission briefs in the fall of 1995 an imbalance of Guarantors and Parties was noted on one of the UH-60 Blackhawk verification missions into the DMZ -- there were too many Peruvian Observers. As if to dispense with nationalism in favor of a smooth execution of the mission as planned, a Peruvian Major calmly announced that he was participating in the mission as the Assistant Personnel Officer of the MOMEP Staff, not as a Peruvian, and therefore there was no imbalance!

Legitimacy

MOMEP has enjoyed the full support of the Parties and the Guarantors since its deployment to the Upper Cenepa area in March 1995. Its mandate under paragraphs 2, 3 and 5 of the Declaration of Peace of Itamaraty was specific. Its success in separating the forces in combat by April 1995, verifying the demobilization of forces along the border by May 1995 and the establishment of a DMZ by August 1995 have contributed to its legitimacy as a mechanism to resolve future border incidents and as a foundation for the political talks on Paragraph 6 -- the demarcation of the border.

MOMEP's existence and activities are well known by the general public in both Perú and Ecuador and press reporting has been wholly positive thus contributing to MOMEP's overall legitimacy as a mechanism for maintaining peace. Regional coverage of MOMEP continued to be strong through the first 12 months of its operation: the numerous denunciations reported by one side or the other and border incidents both in the Upper Cenepa area and elsewhere almost without exception invoked MOMEP for clarification or action, in some cases beyond the scope of MOMEP's mission as defined in the Declaration of Peace and the related Terms of Reference (TOR) -- an indicator of press and public perception that MOMEP is the legitimate mechanism to clarify border incidents. A few quotes from a variety of Ecuadorian and Peruvian dailies make this point:

> ...Peru must confine itself...to the mechanisms established by MOMEP.[7]
>
> ...In response, the Armed Forces of Ecuador have exhorted MOMEP to clarify the Peruvian denunciations and Ecuadorian overflights of Peruvian territory[8]
>
> ...the Armed Forces (of Ecuador) must publicly accept in theory, not only the security norms established by MOMEP but also the direct dialogue between the Foreign Ministries in Lima and Quito.[9]

> ...In terms of complying with the Security Handbook (Cartilla de Seguridad)...this is an issue that must be addressed by the Guarantor Generals and MOMEP.[10]
> ...Nonetheless, the presence of Military Observers (MOMEP) in the area of the Upper Cenepa is still necessary.[11]
> ...MOMEP is an instrument of peace.[12]

There also appears to be a general sense of public support for MOMEP both in Perú and Ecuador -- man on the street reactions in downtown Lima to a MOMEP vehicle passing by: a thumbs up and the head nod of approval; or the little old lady in Cuenca, Ecuador who approached several MOMEP Observers on the street to wish them good luck and to comment on the importance of the mission. These anecdotal observations, while not scientific, were both strong and frequent enough to convince this author that the Legitimacy of MOMEP is real and is a foundation upon which political talks can proceed.

MOMEP's impartiality has been questioned from time to time, but overall the perception is that it has maintained a neutral position -- thus reinforcing its Legitimacy. Nonetheless, as in the case of Unity of Effort, Legitimacy is only an underlying condition which must exist for talks to occur. Unity of Effort and Legitimacy are preconditions for a political solution (Paragraph 6 of the Declaration of Peace of Itamaraty -- the demarcation of the border) -- however, they do not guarantee success.

Support to Belligerents

Ecuador and Perú began the conflict with force structures in place and developed over the previous decade -- Ecuador with a combination of US/European military equipment and Perú principally with Soviet equipment. The conflict was fully conventional in nature and while weapons procurements and deliveries were made by and to both sides, there was no massive external support to one side or the other during the fighting. The early 1996 scandal concerning the reported shipment of Argentine weapons/munitions to Ecuador (despite a guarantor nation agreement not to supply weapons to either side while the fighting continued), while of considerable press interest, was not a significant factor in the military balance during the period of active combat operations (January - February 1995) nor has it adversely affected Argentine Observers' ability to continue active participation in MOMEP operations.

There have been and will continue to be concerns voiced by both sides as each goes through the natural processes of military force modernization: the Ecuadorian purchase of four Israeli KFIRs in late 1995 to replace prewar KFIR training/accident losses is a good example. More recently, Peru announced the purchase of MIG-29 aircraft from Belarus. Both countries have legitimate defense requirements and the focus must remain on the military balance in the disputed border region and how modernization efforts relate to that balance. In summary, this was a "come as you are" conflict with little third country involvement. The overwhelming focus of outside involvement has been to bring the fighting to an end and work towards a peaceful settlement of the conflict -- There was no noticeable diplomatic or political support to one side or the other. Ecuador and Perú have historically had border issues with their neighbors: Colombia, Brazil and Chile. Yet in this conflict none of the aforementioned took sides -- in fact, third party involvement was conspicuous by its absence. This clearly was a positive factor which weighed heavily towards a rapid cessation of the fighting.

Support Actions of Peace Forces

There has been both constant and active support for the actions of MOMEP since its inception. The commitment on the part of the Guarantors has been strong. A clear problem, however, is Guarantor patience in sustaining a peace force operation while political talks continue to show little progress. The prospects of a decades long series of discussions while MOMEP remains deployed in the Amazon jungle is not appealing to a US administration already scrambling to find ways to make good on the pledge to the American people to pull 20,000 US military out of Bosnia after a one year stay -- the situation in Bosnia, like the Perú-Ecuador border conflict, has root causes going back centuries.

The initial Guarantor focus was on the separation of military forces and demobilization -- with that completed, the prospects of waiting years to see the border demarcation process bear fruit is problematic. While the Peruvian and Ecuadorian Foreign Ministers, and even the Presidents, have met, they have yet to agree even on the points of disagreement let alone the mechanisms to resolve them.

The integration of the former belligerents into the Peace Force has been perhaps the most unique and distinctive characteristic of MOMEP and, in this author's judgment, remains the operational cornerstone to long term success. (Figure Four shows the integration of the parties into MOMEP.) As discussed earlier, integration has also been a major factor in establishing and sustaining unity of effort. This integration of the Parties into the Peace Force has minimized "us" and "them" feelings in day to day MOMEP operations and has reinforced the commitment of the Parties to the peace process. It has also allowed for the development of a strong linkage between political and military activities through the creation of a 6 nation military Superior Consultative Committee (Comité Consultivo Superior, CCS) which serves to provide a compass for MOMEP activities and a communications link to the ad hoc High Functionaries in Brasilia and Guarantor Ambassadors in Lima and Quito.

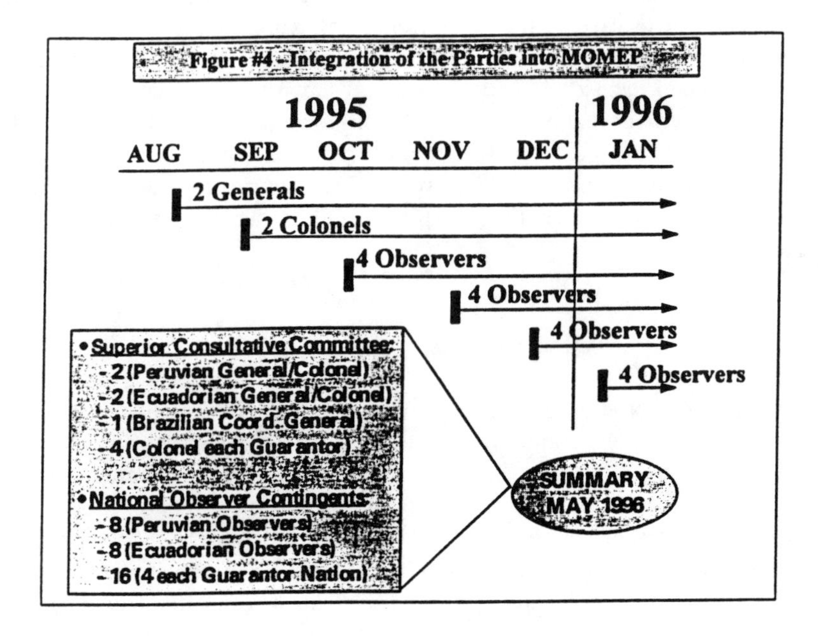

The participation of Peruvian and Ecuadorian military observers within the MOMEP structure was initiated in September 1996, less than six months after the fighting in Jan-Feb 1995.[13] Even if the political process drags on for years, MOMEP can serve as a mechanism for Peruvian and Ecuadorian Military Officers to interact on a one-on-one basis and develop common understandings of the border problem from a ground level perspective -- the Majors and Lieutenant Colonels who today serve as MOMEP Observers will be in positions of leadership in the Ecuadorian and Peruvian militaries in the next decade. From that perspective alone, MOMEP is clearly an investment in the future.

This dimension of support to the Peace Forces is also closely linked to legitimacy -- the participation of Ecuadorian and Peruvian Officers in the observing their peace accords provides a practical mechanism to communicate MOMEP's legitimacy back to the military and political leadership of the Parties. The first MOMEP contingent chiefs from the Parties, COL Wilbur Calle from Peru and COL Jorge Brito Albuja from Ecuador, were in constant daily contact with their respective military chains of command passing not only operational information on MOMEP activities but also perceptions and assessments of MOMEP's impartiality, MOMEP's legitimacy.

Military Actions of Peace Forces

The military actions of MOMEP have been a positive factor in establishing the environment for a political solution. The continuous verification presence in the DMZ and weekly visits to Security Zone Alfa have demonstrated MOMEP's ability to serve as a stabilizing mechanism. In addition to successfully addressing the "specified" missions in the Peace Declaration of Itamaraty (force separation, DMZ establishment and demobilization verification), MOMEP has also actively pursued its "implied" mission of promoting confidence building measures (CBMs) that will further strengthen the environment for political talks. Listed below are a few examples of MOMEP sponsored CBMs:

1. **"Cartilla de Seguridad**." This border security manual, approved by both militaries and distributed, was facilitated by MOMEP. The Parties wrote and jointly published this guide to "border behavior" intended for use at the lowest echelons (individual patrols and outposts) with the intention of minimizing border incidents and outlining actions to be taken in the event of contact. This Cartilla is now issued to all MOMEP Observers (October 1995).
2. **Recovery of war dead from the DMZ**. MOMEP sponsored a joint Peruvian-Ecuadorian operation in the DMZ to recover war dead remaining in Cueva de los Tayos (Ecuadorian remains) and Tiwintsa (Peruvian remains)(November 1995).
3. **Unit Contacts along border**. MOMEP has fomented a wide series of contacts between border outposts intended to increase personal contact at the tactical level and thereby reduce the chances of inadvertent military contact resulting in an incident. These initiatives have included a soccer game between the border outposts of Soldado Monge (Ecuador) and Cahuide (Perú), reciprocal visits between Battalion Commanders Ampama (Perú) and Santiago (Ecuador) (January 1996).
4. **Peace Ceremony at Hito 21**. General Officers from the Guarantor Nations and the Parties gathered at Hito 21 (Yaupi-Santiago) as a demonstration of commitment to the peace process. This Southern Command/MOMEP sponsored event included a historic meeting and embrace between Ecuadorian military chief, General Ortega and his Peruvian counterpart, General Hermosa (11 February 1996).

These are just a few examples which highlight the MOMEP focus on confidence building measures which keep the militaries of Perú and Ecuador engaged with one another in peaceful interaction. These are also activities which would probably not have occurred through bilateral initiatives by the Parties -- in that sense, MOMEP's contribution has been significant. These activities also served to bolster the legitimacy of MOMEP -- not only in the eyes of the Peruvian and Ecuadorian militaries but in the eyes of the public as well as these activities were publicized through MOMEP press releases.

Military Actions of the Belligerents and the Peace Forces

This action has been neutral at best. The occurrence of border incidents and evidence of renewed active patrolling are indicators of continuing distrust on both sides of the border at the military tactical and operational levels. The mere continuance of incidents is indicative of a command and control environment which permits activities which most innocently could be interpreted as "unfortunate mistakes" but which are more likely to indicate the intent at the tactical/operational level to avoid any military "surprises" should MOMEP be withdrawn and/or political discussions either fail or drag on. The danger in slow progress on the political front is that it wears down the patience of operational level military leaders on both sides (Division/Corps Commander equivalents) who take very seriously their respective constitutional charges to defend the national territory.

Perú was clearly embarrassed by its military performance in the Upper Cenepa and surely is determined that this not be repeated in the future -- some Peruvian problems at the tactical level can be traced to a sparse military presence in the region. Peru has already addressed this shortfall by the creation of Military Region 6 (with headquarters in Bagua, Peru) -- replacing the 5th Jungle Division Headquarters which had not served them well during the fighting. Ecuador, on the other hand, sensing this Peruvian reaction, is working to improve its infrastructure and ability to act/reinforce in the region if it becomes necessary. This has created problems: Ecuador interprets the Peace Declaration as a mandate for military forces to return to the ante bellum status of forces (i.e. with an Upper Cenepa balance clearly in favor of Ecuador); Peru, on the other hand, interprets the Declaration more literally as a mandate to demobilize forces but not as a prohibition of either Party to take sovereign actions to redistribute its forces as it sees appropriate. Thus the creation of the 6th Military Region (i.e. an increased deployment of forces in the Peruvian Province of Amazonas) was a sovereign act not related to demobilization of forces in frontier zones required by the Treaty of Itamaraty .

Both militaries are clearly supportive of the political process -- but have taken the most conservative position and are working to assure the presence of a military option. This position has unfortunately been reinforced by the snails pace at which the political talks are proceeding. The impact of this factor can be mitigated and perhaps turned around by continued and increased actions by MOMEP to stimulate and actively promote more confidence building activities, such as those outlined above in Military Actions of Peace Forces.

Actions Targeted on Ending Conflict

Actions targeted on ending the Jan-Feb 1995 conflict have been singularly successful. The isolated and sparsely populated character of the conflict zone and the quiet professional work of the MOMEP leadership were key. Once the declaration was signed -- MOMEP froze the forces in contact and proceeded to separate units one by one. This was accomplished over a period of about two months (March and April 1995). By May 1995 forces in the conflict zone had been reduced to 50 Ecuadorian soldiers in Coangos and 50 Peruvian soldiers in PV1 ("Puesto de Vigilancia #1) -- in accordance with the Declaration of Peace. This situation is maintained today and verified through a 24 hour a day presence of MOMEP observers in both PV1 and Coangos and through periodic overflights of the DMZ and Security Zone Alfa to insure no new forces have been reintroduced into the area.

Again, the success of MOMEP to date in accomplishing its original missions (force separation, DMZ establishment and mobilization) and its follow-on missions of confidence building, will have long term and lasting impact only if progress is made on the underlying issue of the border itself. MOMEP has proved it can reduce the prospects of renewed fighting. However, the resolution of the border issue itself remains a political issue in the hands of politicians.

Conclusion

The paradigm is clearly applicable to assess the performance of MOMEP operations. While quiet but clear military preparations on both sides remain of concern, the problem is now political in nature. Can Perú and Ecuador break the cycle of border clashes/combat operations followed by the failure of political initiatives to find a solution? MOMEP is a proven successful tool. The key factors which must remain if MOMEP is to continue to be successful are Unity of Effort (Factor #1) and the continued success of the Military Actions of the Peace Forces (Factor #4) -- with emphasis on the role of a fully integrated Observer force. We are left with one final question: Is there enough political will and patience on the part of the Guarantors and the Parties to leverage this MOMEP success while a political solution is hammered out?

Notes

1 Gustavo Pons Muzzo, Estudio Histórico Sobre el Protocólo de Rio de Janeiro: El Ecuador - País Amazónico, Lima, Perú, 1994, page 18.

[2] Gustavo Pons Muzzo, page 18.

[3] The maps shown in figures 1-3 are representations intended to show the relationships between place names, key geographic features and general distance factors. These are not intended as definitive maps. These figures have been modified from maps used in MOMEP/SOUTHCOM briefings.

[4] Gustavo Pons Muzzo, page 17.

[5] Declaration of Peace of Itamaraty, 17 February 1996. Translated from Spanish version of original document.

[6] Sources for events which occurred prior to the author's arrival in Patuca on 23 August 1996 are based on official SOUTHCOM reports and discussions with the first US Contingent Commander, COL Glenn Weidner, and COL Jorge Gomez Pola, Senior Argentine Representative to MOMEP, March - November 1995.

[7] Diario La República, Peru, Friday, 29 December 1995, pg. 3.

[8] El Comercio, Lima, Peru, 29 December 1995, pg. A4.

[9] El Comercio, Lima, Peru, 30 December 1995, pg. A2.

[10] El Telégrafo, Guayaquil, Ecuador, 12 February 1996, pg. 1.

[11] El Comercio, Quito, Ecuador, 17 November 1995, pg. A6.

[12] Article headline from El Comercio, Quito, Ecuador, 14 November 1995, pg. A9.

[13] Events described during the period August 1995 - February 1996 are based on the author's personal observations as a participant in those events.

Wider Peacekeeping

5

UN Peace Operations in the Congo: Decolonialism and Superpower Conflict in the Guise of UN Peacekeeping

J. Matthew Vaccaro

The history of the former Belgian Congo, formerly Zaire and now again Congo, its early independence and attempts at state building during the 1960s is a complex and interesting story. Intertwined with this story is the history of the controversial four year UN peacekeeping operation to the country, known as ONUC, from its French name, *Opération des Nations Unies au Congo*. The UN operation became the organization's first attempt at more than monitoring and reporting from the field. The immense cost of ONUC, relative to the UN's previous activities, and the violence inflicted and incurred by the robust operation stunned the organization and its member states. Twenty-eight years elapsed until another UN operation of similar scale was attempted. This chapter will not attempt to record the tangled history of these events for, as William Durch has written in his concise case study of the operation, "Its mission, and how it unfolded over many months, are not easily summarized."[1] Rather, this chapter will draw from a number of histories already completed to infer conclusions concerning each of the dimensions of analysis presented in this volume. A brief review of the key events of the Congo's history is useful.

The area of central Africa that became the Congo, the third largest country on the continent, was endowed generously with natural resources and located in the strategic center of Africa. These two factors attracted colonial interests and later, superpower interests. The area was under Belgian control from 1884 until independence in 1960. The Belgian colonial administration did not develop an indigenous elite or professional class, from whom a competent government could be formed. At the time of independence, not one Congolese had attained officer rank in the 25,000 person national army; only a few thousand had advanced beyond primary school education, and there was not a single qualified Congolese doctor. Further complicating independence was the fact that the country was not a nation-state. Colonial administrative boundaries, and indeed the international borders, had not been designed to create a stable state. The Congo was composed of numerous tribal groups that generally felt little allegiance to a unified state or each other.[2]

The Congolese were unprepared for independence which was suddenly granted on 30 June 1960 after only six months notice. The nascent government was led by Prime Minister Patrice Lumumba and Head of State Joseph Kasavubu, political rivals. Belgian nationals held almost all substantive positions within the government ministries. Less than a week after independence, elements of the *Armée Nationale Congolaise* (ANC) mutinied. They demanded the removal of their Belgian officers and greater pay. By 10 July, the mutiny had spread throughout the country and civil disorder was widespread. Some harassment of Europeans had occurred. Many of the approximate 100,000 Belgians in the country began to flee which contributed to the breakdown of effective government. In short, the embryonic state became a failed state. Belgium intervened without invitation to impose order and protect its nationals. By 19 July some 10,000 Belgian troops occupied several key areas of the Congo, including the national capital, Léopoldville, the port at Matadi, and Elisabethville, the capital of the southern province of Katanga. The day after the Belgians arrived in Katanga, the provincial president, Moise Tshombé, declared the province independent of the Congo. Tshombé appointed Belgian nationals to the civil administration and built an army around seconded Belgian officers and mercenaries. Many viewed the Belgian actions, especially those in Katanga, as an attempt to subvert Congolese independence and retain the economic benefits of empire.

On 14 July, in response to requests from the Congolese government, the Security Council established ONUC to provide military assistance to the Congolese government until the indigenous security forces were able to accomplish their tasks. The next day, UN peacekeepers were on the ground in the Congo without a strategy, command element, or logistics tail. Thus began the long and controversial UN operation. During the course of its tenure, ONUC would supervise the withdrawal of the Belgian Army, restore a Congolese central government after it split into leftist and centrist camps, and terminate the Katangan secession. For analytic purposes, the operation can be considered to have had four phases as indicated in table one. These phases are retrospective; they were not part of a UN strategy.

Table 1: Phases of the Operation

Phase	Primary Activity of ONUC	Period
Phase 1	Civil Order and Removal of Belgian Army	July 1960 - September 60
Phase 2	Restore Central Government	September 1960 - August 1961
Phase 3	Terminate Katangan Secession	August 1961 - February 1963
Phase 4	Maintain Stability and Withdraw	February 1963 - June 1964

During phase one the UN deployed 16,000 troops, built its communications and command structure, and began to develop a strategy to maintain the tenuous public order which the Belgian intervention had restored. Significantly, once the UN troops had established a presence, the Belgian troops largely withdrew to their bases and began to leave the country, partially ameliorating the major complaint of the central government and several stridently anti-colonial troop contributing states. However, they were not fully satisfied because the Belgian forces supporting the Katangan secession did not withdraw and the Katangan leadership refused to cooperate with ONUC. Meanwhile, the political rivalry between Kasavubu and Lumumba erupted and the central government split into two camps, causing phase two of the operation. ONUC was able to prevent full-scale civil war and eventually facilitate a political framework that allowed the Parliament to reconvene and elect a new government. Phase three followed in which the UN was able to finally turn its full attention toward ending the Katangan secession. ONUC, acting as an ally with the reunited central government, eventually conducted two police-like actions and two military actions in December 1961 and 1962 to disperse or disarm much of Tshombé's mercenary led army. Subsequently, Tshombé declared an end to the secession. Phase four saw meager attempts by ONUC to quell new political unrest in the Congo, but the UN, broken financially and unable to find the political will to sustain further involvement, beat a gradual withdrawal following the reintegration of Katanga. The last UN forces withdrew in June 1964.

Unity of Effort

Unity among the principle external actors to the Congo crisis was severely lacking. This is not surprising given the different, and often opposed, objectives of the principle actors. In macro terms, the US wanted to sustain the West's access to Congo's strategic resources and geography while denying de facto Belgian recolonization. The Soviet Union hoped to increase its influence in the Congo and saw opportunity to curry favor from emerging nationalist leaders in Africa. The European metropole states preferred to keep Africa firmly in their sphere in order to retain the benefits of empire, but tended to moderate this aspiration in order maintain American-European solidarity for the defense of Europe. Meanwhile, the rapidly expanding group of nonaligned, or newly independent, states wanted to end colonialism, prevent neocolonialism, and strengthen nationalist governments throughout the world.

The principle external actors papered over their differences and fielded the peacekeeping force with a vague mandate to help the Congolese government maintain civil order and ease Belgian forces out of the country. Security Council members hoped to influence implementation of the vague mandate to sway the activities of the peacekeepers toward national objectives. The resultant UN force represented states which had different goals for the operation. Throughout phase one and half of phase two (August 1960-February 1961), between 30 and 56 percent of the force came from nationalist, anti-West states (Ceylon, Ghana, Guinea, Mali, Morocco, the United Arab Republic, and Yugoslavia). During the same period, the other large portion of the force was Western leaning (between 23 and 43 percent). The remainder of the force (20 to 27 percent) was provided by states that were mutually suspicious of both the Western and Eastern blocs, but sided more with the US on issues relating to Congolese decolonization.[3] As it began to be evident that the US was, more or less, able to dominate the UN Security Council and the Secretariat, some of the anti-West states threatened various actions in an attempt to change the UN's orientation; Guinea threatened to transfer its UN contingent to the Congolese government if its contingent was not deployed to quell the Katangan secession.[4] The UAR contingent was singled out as a partisan of the leftist camp by Force Commander, General von Horn. He alleged they became overly involved in the local politics, maintained an unauthorized airlift, and dispersed funds to pay antigovernment Congolese troops, among other criticisms.[5] These actions in support of the leftists hindered unity of effort, since the UN strategy, under the influence of Secretary General Dag Hammarskjold was to behave impartially among the contending factions.

Over its duration, the ONUC military force was fielded from 35 different countries -- a group of countries with diverse military traditions and varying military professionalism. Furthermore, the coalition did not share a common language and was ill-equipped for the necessary communication between the national contingents. As the UN's bias toward the West's objectives became clear, the coalition self-sorted; all but a small number of the anti-West troops were withdrawn by their governments by April 1961. Troops from anti-West states comprised less than ten percent of the total force for the remaining three years of the operation. From August 1961 to December 1962, the majority of phase three in which ONUC undertook its greatest and most effective military actions, the composition of the coalition was relatively stable. The countries contributing the four largest contingents (Malaya, Nigeria, Ethiopia, and India) did not change, were similar to each other in their orientation and compatible with the orientation of the UN's political guidance, and provided an average of 70 percent of the force during the period. Greater homogeneity of the coalition improved unity of effort and effectiveness of the force.

Decisions made in the field also contributed to improved unity of effort as the operation progressed. Initially, the force was deployed in small units throughout the Congo, dispersing and dividing the efforts of the force. During phase two, a new deployment scheme was implemented that consolidated ONUC into company and battalion sized elements and located them in the areas of tension. This decision greatly facilitated logistical support and communications and enabled the forces to support one another. Furthermore, the decision, by happenstance or design, to concentrate the efforts of ONUC on reestablishing a central government before dealing decisively with the Katangan secession provided a concentration of effort to both activities which helped improve unity of effort.

To orchestrate a complex political-military operation with unity of effort throughout a theater of operations the size of the Congo would require a rather coherent coalition with competent leadership at every level from the SRSG down through the battalion commanders. The coalition would need to be able to develop common strategies and execute them with continual modification while maintaining the unity of a single organism. The right hand must know what the left hand is doing in order to achieve unity of effort. ONUC never achieved such a degree of unity. However, unity of effort improved over the duration of the operation, climaxing during the military actions of December 1962. The effectiveness of the force improved as unity of effort increased.

Legitimacy

The usefulness of "legitimacy" as a predictive dimension of analysis for peace operations will rely on determining among whom legitimacy might be important. This question seemingly could have many answers; among the general population within the area of operations, among the leadership of the belligerents, among the governments of the intervening states or even within their armed forces, or among the groups that affect government decisions within those states. This list could be longer, which would make this dimension more opaque and of lesser value.

The history of the Congo suggests that a peace operation must have enough legitimacy among external actors to preclude their subversion of the operation. The Congo operation teetered on the precipice of external subversion. In addition to the activities of the anti-West states discussed above, other states took actions which indicated they did not view the purposes of ONUC as legitimate. France and Portugal banned the use of their territory, or its overflight, by UN aircraft. Under French influence, Congo (Brazzaville) and the Central African Republic did the same. The United Kingdom was opposed to ending the Katangan secession by force and, together with the colonial government of Rhodesia, allowed the use of Rhodesia as temporary sanctuary for some Katangan elements and slowed the transit of UN supplies into Katanga. The UK and Portugal opposed the imposition of economic sanctions on Katanga from the UN. The Soviet Union provided mobility assistance (trucks and air lift) to Lumumba which he used to transport loyal ANC units to combat in Kasai (see below, Support to Belligerents).[6] However, France, England, and the Soviet Union did not choose to completely stymie ONUC, which they could have done through their veto power in the Security Council. The evidence from the Congo supports the finding: greater consensus among the external actors for the purpose and costs (financial and others) of a peace operation increases the likelihood that the purposes of the operation will be accomplished.

At the local actor level of analysis, the analysis of legitimacy is similar to the analysis of consent, the term used to describe local actors' orientation toward the peace operation. If the local actors view the peace operation as legitimate, they view its purposes as warranted and will likely consent to its activities. In the Congo, legitimacy, or consent, from the local actors proved to be of great import.

Security Council resolution 143 authorized the Secretary-General to take actions to support the Congolese government, as requested by that government. Upon arrival, UN forces had cordial relations with their host. The central government viewed the UN presence as legitimate. The leadership of the Katangan secession did not view ONUC's activities as legitimate and resisted the deployment of UN troops into Katanga. The situation worsened, however, when the Security Council adopted resolution 161 seven months later, after the central government had split into two camps. The resolution gave the Secretary General authority to reorganize the ANC (Congolese army) and ordered foreign advisors and fighters out of the country, except those under the auspices of the UN. The Kasavubu faction of the central government opposed these steps; they were seen as violations of Congolese sovereignty and as a veiled effort to disarm elements of the ANC loyal to Kasavubu. The ANC (Kasavubu) initiated a campaign of deliberate harassment of UN personnel including denial of freedom of movement, detention, theft, beatings, and one instance of rape. The campaign escalated into an attack of the UN-held port facilities at Matadi and a small naval facility at Banana, both at the mouth of the Congo River. Outnumbered and outgunned, the UN troops were forced to accept a cease-fire, were disarmed, and transferred control of the port facilities to the Congolese. Eventually, the UN conceded to the armed opposition and agreed not to implement aspects of the mandate viewed by the Kasavubu camp as illegitimate.[7]

ONUC which had been initiated to support the central government was unprepared, militarily or politically, to oppose the wishes of the Kasavubu faction of the central government. However, ONUC did persist in opposing the Katangan secession, despite being viewed as illegitimate by the leadership of the secession. A review of ONUC actions in relation to the various local actors shows that the UN worked to develop and maintain a level of consent or legitimacy for their actions from among the various local actors commensurate with ONUC's ability to impose solutions, i.e. to act without consent. This indicates that obtaining legitimacy among the local actors may not be a clear-cut indication of the probable success or failure of a particular peace operation, but rather, a barometer of the level of effort required to reach the desired objectives. The evidence from the Congo suggests an important planning consideration; if one's objectives are not seen as legitimate by the local actors, the level of effort required to accomplish them can be expected to be higher.

Support to Belligerents

In the case of the Congo, it is important to assess support to various local actors. ONUC was initiated to support the central government of the Congo. At its initiation, two challenges confronted the central government; the Belgian violation of the country's sovereignty and the secessionist movements. The Belgian intervention had already halted, more or less, the threat caused by the ANC mutiny and the resultant civil disorder.

The Belgian presence made them an actor in the local calculus. Presumably, the deployed elements had the full backing and support of the Government of Belgium. Yet, despite this political and military strength, Belgium chose to grudgingly comply with demands that it withdraw its forces from the Congo. The objectives of the Belgians seem to have been limited since their forces behaved cooperatively despite having the full backing of an external state and military superiority, at least initially.

During phase one of the operation, ONUC focused on replacing the Belgian forces and getting itself established. Its stance toward the central government was a bit reserved and measured because Secretary General Hammarskjold intended ONUC to be impartial. In the eyes of President Kasavubu and Prime Minister Lumumba, the UN was to be in direct support of the central government. As such, ending the Katangan secession should have been a high priority. Dissatisfied with the type of support from ONUC, Lumumba requested direct military aid from the Soviet Union on July 14, 1960 and again on August 15. In response to the first request, Moscow sent 100 trucks and support technicians by ship. The second appeal was answered more strongly. On August 25, 1960, Soviet planes began airlifting ANC troops to Kasai province to launch an assault first on a new secessionist movement in southern Kasai and then against the Katanga secessionists. The Soviet trucks arrived by sea on September 3rd and were diverted to the ANC effort in Kasai province. The UN Force Commander had expected the equipment would be placed at his disposal. This provision of mobility support gave a large advantage to the central government's forces compared to the relatively stationary nature of the secessionist forces. The UN intervened to stop the fighting. On September 5th, Andrew W. Cordier, the SRSG, ended most of the advantage gained by ANC forces from the Soviet Union by closing the major airports to non-UN aircraft. Mediation achieved a brokered agreement whereby ONUC would establish a neutral zone in southern Kasai and northern Katanga -- the areas that had been largely cleared of secessionists by the ANC.[8]

Although the provision of Soviet aid helped the central government deal a blow to both secessionist movements, it also served to fuel the rivalry between Kasavubu and Lumumba. Lumumba had conducted the military campaign without consultation with Kasavubu. In early September Kasavubu and Lumumba dismissed each other from office, effectively splitting the central government and the ANC into two factions. On September 14, 1960, Colonel Joseph D. Mobutu, Chief of Staff of the ANC, seized control over the Kasavubu faction based in the national capital, Leopoldville. Mobutu, not a leftist, ejected all Soviet bloc missions from Leopoldville, ending overt support to the Congo from the Soviet Union. The rival regime was eventually established in Stanleyville, the capital of Orientale province.

Support provided by some national contingents of ONUC to the Lumumba faction (discussed above under Unity of Effort) proved to be more political encouragement than tangible material. Nonetheless, until it ended with the withdrawal of those national contingents, the endorsement must be counted as support to one of the local actors coming from the peace force itself during a period in which the force's strategy was to behave impartially toward the factions. Eventually, in August 1961, the central government was reunited through the dedicated efforts of the UN. It was no small deed; much credit is due. Thereafter, ONUC acted as an ally of the government, and by so doing, purposefully provided support to that actor. Indeed, from August 1962 until February 1964 a contingent of the ANC of about 700 soldiers served as part of the UN force.[9]

The poorly organized secession in southern Kasai province had little indigenous support and no records of external support were found. Perhaps largely due to the lack of support, the secession was short lived (12 months).

The Katangan secession on the other hand survived for thirty-one months. This was due in part to the split in the central government which divided the main opponent of an independent Katanga and diverted ONUC's attention. The other main factors of the secession's longevity was the support given to the movement from external actors and the economic strength of the province. Katanga benefited being adjacent to Northern Rhodesia (UK) and Angola (Portugal). Both states, under strong influence from their European colonizers, were sympathetic to the Katangan secession. Their territory provided sanctuary and easy access to lines of supply, both inbound and outbound, which allowed the Katangan economy to continue to function and bankrolled the secession. Belgium and France provided at least tacit support of the secession. Belgian military officers served with the secessionist forces with Brussels' approval and later as mercenaries. French and South African mercenaries eventually replaced most of them. About eight tons of Belgian weapons and munitions were provided to Katanga on September 7, 1960, via a Sabena flight from

Brussels.[10] (Other actions of European states indirectly supporting the Katangan secession are above in the Legitimacy section.) One area that deserves greater inquiry is the role of transnational actors, especially the large natural resource conglomerates at work in the region at the time. It is unclear if these companies behaved as organs of the states in which they were they were headquartered or acted in their own interests, as a state would, or were motivated by a combination of these factors.

Support Actions of Peace Forces

This dimension is intended to gauge the perceptions of the local actors concerning the commitment or determination of the peace force to accomplish the mandate. If the local actors perceive a strong, large peace force with ample reserves or replacements and unwavering political support from the international community, are they likely to see the writing on the wall and cooperate with the peace force? It seems logical that greater perceived strength or determination by the local actors of the intervenors would enable the intervenors to deter or coerce the local actors more effectively. However, the Western concept of logic does not always prevail; the Eastern concept of "saving face," or other notions may be stronger. Further, the motives of nationalism or revolution may actually cause anti-interventionist fervor to rally on the perception of greater strength of the intervenors.

Peace operations are all about changing the behavior of local actors with actions short of warfare. Understanding and successfully shaping the perceptions, and consequently, the actions, of the local actors is critical. The "science" of reading the minds of local actors should be further advanced. We should not rely solely on attempting to deduce perceptions from the actions of local actors. This method may underestimate their cunning and finesse.

The UN operation in the Congo was perhaps the most controversial peace operation ever conducted. As already discussed, the lack of real consensus over what the operation should accomplish -- indeed, the opposed objectives of the various involved states -- plagued the operation throughout its four year duration. The international debate, often centered at UN headquarters in New York or emanating from Washington, Moscow, or various European capitals, projected massive uncertainty over the future of the operation and its course of action. It is difficult to determine the extent to which this sense that the operation teetered on political failure, premature closure, and financial bankruptcy permeated the perceptions of the local actors. We do not know their thoughts. In the midst of the information revolution of the late 20th Century, it is easy to forget the remoteness of the Congo in the 1960s. The country and the indigenous population had little ability to access the international debate. However, events in the theater were witnessed by the local actors and undoubtedly affected their perceptions of the peace force's determination and continued viability. The quick replacement of the six contingents withdrawn in early 1961 with a complete regular infantry brigade from India numbering over 3,000 men surely demonstrated resolve and increased competency and military strength of the force. The effective use of the peace forces to aid diplomacy and provide the security environment needed to restore the Parliament demonstrated a constructive and determined role for ONUC, at least to all those who chose to participate in the reformulated national government. The consolidation of the peace forces into Katanga, the arrival of UN combat aircraft, and the attachment of a Congolese unit to the UN peace force (albeit, not in Katanga) indicated the UN was finally serious about ending the Katangan secession. Over time, the local actors should have perceived that the UN peace force was credible and determined to implement its mandate.

One measure of a peace force's determination is its response to incurring casualties. The local actors will form perceptions based on this response. Actually, since a coalition peace force is a conglomerate of national views, it would be better to assess the willingness of significant troop contributing countries to accept casualties and the commensurate views developed by the local actors in response to this willingness. In the Congo, the casualties incurred by the peace force were not insignificant -- 235 deaths of which 126 were classified as battle deaths.[11] They were spread over the duration of the operation and among several troop contingents.[12] It seems that the troop contributing countries were willing to accept these casualties. ONUC was not withdrawn because of unacceptable casualty levels. The strategies employed by the local actors against the peace force do not indicate the local actors believed ONUC could be sent running through attrition or a mass casualty terrorist-like event.

Military Actions of Peace Forces

The initial deployment of ONUC was designed to achieve presence throughout the country. In August 1960, one month after the operation was initiated, 14,295 troops were under UN command in the Congo. They were spread across an area about the same size as western Europe in 77 separate locations.[13] This dispersed type of deployment pattern was familiar to the UN at that time because previous peacekeeping operations had relied mostly on monitoring international borders and showing the UN flag. The UN had not previously needed to use force and, initially, did not intend to do so in the Congo. Nonetheless, the deployment pattern proved to be a logistical nightmare. The forces were gradually concentrated in areas of tension as new units rotated into the theater.

The size and composition of a peace force relative to the capabilities of the local belligerents becomes a much more critical factor to success of the mission when the peace force is required to conduct activities that do not have at least the tacit consent of the local actors. This point became obvious to the UN command in the Congo as it attempted to end the secession in Katanga. ONUC had four major confrontations over the course of sixteen months with the Katangan forces before they achieved that result. Thus, the UN force was incrementally built up until it was able to dominate the Katangan forces militarily.

During the first two confrontations (August and September 1961) the UN Security Council had not yet authorized the use of force in the Congo. Hence, the UN did not intend to employ its combat power in a militarily significant manner. Rather, their strategy relied on police-type tactics to round up Katanga's mercenaries. ONUC had about 4,920 troops throughout Katanga, 1,700 in Elisabethville, 1,200 in Albertville, 1,000 in Kamina, and 1020 in three other locations. Tshombé had a much larger force; eight to ten thousand indigenous troops in the gendarmarie led by a cadre of about 100 Belgian, French, South African, and Rhodesian mercenaries. An additional 200 mercenaries were formed into an elite, "International Company" under command of a British national.[14]

The UN force was strengthened a bit before the next police-type action, later termed Round One. The garrison in Elisabethville was raised to about 2,600 troops, composed of an Indian brigade headquarters, two Indian infantry battalions, one Swedish and two Irish infantry companies, two small armored car units, an Indian heavy machine gun unit, and an Indian heavy mortar detachment. The total UN force throughout Katanga was about 6,800.[15] Approximately ten thousand UN troops were deployed in other provinces of the Congo. Katanga attained a huge technological leap by deploying a French jet fighter aircraft against UN troops, who were unprepared to conduct air defense. The introduction of the aircraft combined with the complete encirclement of the Irish contingent compelled the UN to seek a cease-fire. The eight to ten thousand Katangan ground forces, with their new air threat, bested the UN force.

In November 1961 the Security Council authorized the use of force to expel mercenaries from the Congo. The next confrontation, Round Two, occurred a month later. Subsequent to the new authority to use force, ONUC's planning took on a more traditional military tenor. Total UN strength in Katanga was about 8,450. Over 5,000 troops were in Elisabethville, including; the two Indian infantry battalions and the full Swedish and Irish infantry battalions, plus two Ethiopian infantry battalions which were deployed once the engagement began.[16] Of great importance, the UN fielded its own combat air force to counter the Katangan threat. The UN flew four Ethiopian F84 fighters, six Indian Canberra bombers, and four Swedish Saab S29 fighter aircraft.[17]

Round Three, the final confrontation between UN troops and the Katangan forces took place a year later at the end of December 1962. By this time the UN had concentrated the majority of its combat power (about 13,500 troops) in Katanga. Only about 5,400 troops covered the remainder of the country. Eight infantry battalions under the control of two brigade headquarters operated in Elisabethville, three infantry battalions were at Kamina, a Malayan regiment was located in Albertville.[18] By the time of Round Three, Tshombé had reassembled a mercenary cadre of between 300-500 serving as leaders, trainers, and shooters in a much expanded gendarmarie force. The Katangan air force was reported to consist of two jet Vampires, six or seven Harvards with machine guns, and some "other small planes and transport craft." The UN air force at about the same time (January 1963) provided a distinct advantage to ONUC (8-10 Swedish J29 jet fighters, two Swedish S29 photo reconnaissance jets, and four Iranian and four Italian F86 jet fighters).[19]

The UN force was not able to accomplish its purpose by force until it was strong enough to dominate the forces of the local actor concerned. In any peace operation where consent is lacking or marginal, the correlation of force must be considered as one of the primary consideration of analysis -- the stronger force is apt to have its way in the end. Since peace operations may have numerous local actors with which to contend, the UN force, if it is intended to coerce, should be able to dominate militarily all the local actors combined.

Military Actions of the Belligerents and the Peace Forces

This dimension measures the military professionalism of the forces involved in order to determine the peace force's potential to accomplish the mission successfully. The four bouts of military confrontation between ONUC's military arm and the Katangan gendarmarie are useful to evaluate ONUC's military professionalism. Although all the external actors expected ONUC to end the Katangan secession, the force was never given the explicit mandate to do so. Rather, ONUC, under sanction of the newly centralized government, was authorized to expel foreign nationals from the Congo. It was anticipated that removing Tshombé's mercenaries would cause the secession to buckle.

The first two bouts of confrontation were intended to be police-type actions to round up and expel the mercenaries: the first Operation Rumpunch was largely successful for the UN, the second turned into an embarrassing tactical failure. Operation Rumpunch was launched early in the morning August 28, 1961. UN military forces in Katanga successfully occupied the Elisabethville post office and radio station and cordoned the Katangan Interior Minister's home. Aided by the element of surprise, other ONUC elements in the city and in northern Katanga surrounded and arrested some 338 mercenaries. Shocked by the sudden and effective aggressiveness of ONUC and facing the rancor of the

Europeans living in Katanga, the Belgian Consul in Elisabethville intervened with the UN command. Conor Cruise O'Brien, Deputy SRSG for Katanga, (the top UN civilian representative in the province) halted the police action that evening when the Belgian Consul agreed to expel all mercenaries from Katanga including the 104 on ONUC's list that had not been captured. A significant portion of the mercenaries were expelled, but European diplomats refused to expel all of their nationals serving as mercenaries. In all, about half of Tshombé's supply of mercenaries was removed. ONUC's forces performed well during Operation Rumpunch.[20]

The effectiveness of Rumpunch caused Tshombé to temporarily replace the mercenaries with less well qualified leaders and trainers. The action also raised the ire of the Katangan forces. On September 11 a 150 man Irish contingent in Jodotville was surrounded by Katangan gendarmarie and the following day were attacked by Katangan aircraft twice. As this standoff continued, on September 13, ONUC launched Operation Smash which is more widely known by its post facto name Round One. This action was hurriedly planned in collusion with the central government and included more ambitious goals that exceeded the legal authority of ONUC. O'Brien intended to compel Tshombé to end the secession by placing the five Katangan ministers, including Tshombé, under house arrest; securing and holding the post office, radio studios and transmitters, and the Information Ministry; and arresting as many mercenaries as possible. The operation started at four in the morning. Before daybreak the operation had taken a bad turn when the Katangan forces resisted. UN Indian troops became fully engaged taking the post office and radio facilities. Hand-to-hand combat resulted. The Katangan troops mounted a counteroffensive using armored cars. In the heat of battle, Indians troops were reported to commit some atrocities -- killing captured Katangan troops, shooting nonmilitary vehicles, etc.[21]

The unanticipated stiff resistance delayed ONUC's coordinated actions in Elisabethville and allowed four of the Ministers to avoid capture. Tshombé escaped to Northern Rhodesia with the assistance of the British Consul. ONUC held the post office and radio facilities. ONUC's attempt to establish elements of the central government in Elisabethville failed. In northern Katanga, where its goals were mostly military in nature, ONUC was more successful; they captured a number of gendarmarie posts. Set back by these inconclusive results and held hostage by the tremendous international debate over the apparent disregard for their limited mandate, the UN signed a cease-fire with Tshombé which basically returned the situation to the *status antebellum*. Round One was a planning failure not an execution failure. The plan had not anticipated the resistance and made little provision for flexibility. Ultimately, ONUC accomplished its military tasks, but too late in the day to achieve their political purposes.

From the signing of the cease-fire until early December, a tense stalemate existed between the UN force and the Katangan forces who were operating in close proximity. In November the UN force for the first time was given authority to use force to expel mercenaries. The combat strength of the peace force in Katanga was strengthened considerably as discussed above. On December 2, the gendarmarie fired on ONUC forces at the Elisabethville airport and established road blocks to constrain the UN forces. On December 3, UN medical personnel were detained and more road blocks set up. On December 5, the UN launched Round Two ostensibly to restore its freedom of movement, a provision of the cease-fire agreement. ONUC moved to dismantle the road blocks and was attacked with heavy mortars, machine guns, and small arms fire. ONUC responded with offensive tactics using its air force and mobile ground forces to engage the immediate threat and to expand its area of control throughout Katanga. Fierce fighting resulted in and around Elisabethville. Relative to previous UN actions in the Congo and elsewhere, casualties from Round Two were significant. UN troops reportedly killed 206 Katangan troops, and 50 civilians. ONUC suffered 21 killed. Nonetheless, ONUC was successful in its military objectives. Freedom of movement was restored and the Katangan secession suffered a significant political and military blow. Shortly thereafter, on December 21, Tshombé signed an agreement with the central government which, *inter alia*, acknowledged Katanga could not secede from the Congo and placed Katangan troops under the control of the central government. However, once military pressure was eased a bit, Tshombé reneged on this agreement.[22]

For the next year another military standoff occurred as the UN and central government attempted through diplomatic means to get Tshombé to live up to his agreement to end the secession. During the period both the UN force and the Katangan gendarmarie were built up, although ONUC made relative gains. The overall professionalism of the UN force in Katanga increased. Military planning and command and control became more effective due to the familiarity of habitual relationship among the staffs and leadership. The Indian Force Commander in Katanga at this point was also regarded as a highly effective leader. While waiting for the diplomatic efforts to take hold, ONUC developed and continually refined a military plan to exert control throughout Katanga under the guise of protecting freedom of movement.[23]

Round Three was launched on December 28, 1962, in response to four days of intermittent harassing fire on UN troops. The UN troops faced ineffective resistance in Elisabethville and easily secured the city by nightfall the next day. Tshombé was reported to have little control over his forces. The other major success of the first few days of the operation was elimination of the Katangan air force. UN aircraft attacked Katangan air bases and destroyed seven planes on the ground, as well as fuel and hanger facilities. The few remaining planes were stolen by their mercenary pilots as they fled the country. Subsequently, the UN aircraft were able to conduct extensive aerial reconnaissance in support of

ONUC's ground movement to seize Kaminaville on December 30 and Jodotville on January 4, 1963. The final phase of the operation involved seizing the city of Kolwezi, where Tshombé was holding out, and moving UN troops to the border areas with Northern Rhodesia and Angola. During Round Three the majority of the mercenaries escaped to Angola and the gendarmarie melted away from engagements. Consequently, casualties were limited; ONUC suffered ten killed and 77 wounded; Katangan casualties were reported as light. Following the dispersal of Tshombé's forces, the central government was able to exert control over the province.[24]

Throughout these four engagements which eventually caused the secession to fail, the UN's military actions were significantly constrained by their restrictive mandate that, at its strongest, only allowed the use of requisite force to expel mercenaries. The mandate's origin can be traced to the different objectives of the various external actors as previously discussed. Additionally, the novelty of a UN peace force needing to employ force caused a significant debate and division in the international community which, in turn, caused the UN Secretariat and its field operation commanders to be quite tentative in the use of force. Another constraint on the military actions was the preference within the UN command to obtain political settlements rather than decisive military victories. The first police action and Round Two were halted before they reached their full potential. These political constraints on the peace force seem to have been a greater detractor from its effectiveness than the force's professionalism. For Round Three, most of the political constraint had been removed and the force was at its maximum in terms of strength and professionalism. Not surprisingly, Round Three was ONUC's best demonstration of the effective employment of military means to end the secession.

Actions Targeted on Ending Conflict

The instability in the Congo - the splits in the central government and the secession attempts - was largely the result of power-hungry men attempting to control as much of the emerging state as possible. (There is ample blame to be shared by internal and external actors for this situation.) Hence, ending the conflict or the instability from very weak governmental institutions required state building. Intertribal tension and warfare were part of the Congo crisis, but these were manifested by the manipulation of the actors contending for power; tribal tensions did not cause the conflict.

ONUC effectively employed diplomatic and military means to help rebuild a unified and broadly accepted central government in the Congo following the Government's split into rival factions. This was accomplished by tireless mediation efforts and by using military means to provide a secure setting and safe political space for an indigenous agreement to emerge.

Under pressure from the UN and international community the rival factions agreed to reconvene Parliament to attempt to develop a unified government. ONUC forces made the Parliament session possible by securing the meeting area, Lovanium University near Leopoldville. The University was cleared of all personnel and replaced with a UN security detail. The entire campus was sealed off with an electric fence illuminated by lamps and covered by guard dogs. One battalion of troops patrolled the grounds and controlled entry and exit. All persons entering the compound were searched. The factions agreed that armed ANC soldiers and police would not be allowed to roam in Leopoldville or near the University during the Parliamentary session. ONUC forces patrolled to verify ANC and police compliance. No violence marred the Parliamentary session. After two weeks of meeting a new Prime Minister was unanimously endorsed by the Parliament. The unprecedented security functions carried out by ONUC were essential to getting the opposed factions together to work out an arrangement.[25]

In addition to the military component and the diplomatic elements of ONUC, the operation employed over one thousand civilians in civic action-type duties. These persons were heavily involved in state building efforts. In large part the UN civilian component filled the gaps, which were manifold, in the country's administrative structure caused by the exodus of many Europeans during the initial mutiny. UN civilians reactivated the ports and railway system; provided most of the technical staff to operate the airports and telecommunications system; controlled the Congolese Monetary Council which influenced strongly the country's economy; and attempted to coordinate bilateral aid to the country. To ease human suffering from the conflict, ONUC distributed food and medical supplies; organized resettlement of displaced persons; and organized public works projects to provide relief from unemployment. To help the country develop its human capital, the UN provided extensive technical training assistance. Approximately 800 secondary-school teachers, 200 medical personnel, and 50 legal experts were involved in direct training of the Congolese people. Furthermore, the UN provided fellowships for Congolese students to pursue advanced study abroad and established institutions of higher learning in the Congo. All of these activities helped to end the conflict by preventing the further deterioration of state structures and by enhancing the capabilities of self governance.[26] In the long run, however, the UN intervention was unable to develop a lasting state. Thirty years later the Congo is under the control of foreign troops supporting the revolutionary leader, Laurent Kabila, who overthrew the dictator, Mobutu.

Conclusion

The Max Factors present a useful mechanism to evaluate the UN operation in the Congo. One important area to be determined is the relative weight to place behind each dimension. Which dimensions are more important? This can be determined by evaluating a number of cases. In the case of the Congo, "Unity of Effort," "Legitimacy," and the two interconnected dimensions of military power seem to have been most determinate.

Here, the analysis of unity of effort and legitimacy produced similar conclusions; external consensus is a prerequisite of unity of effort, and greater consensus among the external actors for the purpose and costs of a peace operation increases the likelihood that the purposes of the operation will be accomplished.

A detailed correlation of forces analysis is less important for a peace operation than it is for a combat operation. However, if a peace force is required to coerce local actors -- due to the absence of legitimacy or consent as was the case in ending the Katangan secession -- the capability to effectively employ military force is necessary. In a peace enforcement operation the two dimensions dealing specifically with military capabilities are quite important to one's conclusions. ONUC's ability to adapt militarily to the changing situation in the Congo aided its ability to prevail, eventually. Effective peace forces must be responsive to dynamic situations.

In sum, the paradigm generally provides a useful analytical tool to describe the various aspects of a peace operation and the operation's strengths and weaknesses. The operation in the Congo when viewed through this lens was an operation that gradually improved its capabilities and probability of success. As the operation proceeded, unity of effort of the peace force improved, the purposes of the operation (ending the secession) eventually were viewed by the majority of the local actors as legitimate, and the military strength and professionalism gained until ONUC was able to dominate the one local actor who viewed the operation as illegitimate.

While ONUC accomplished its narrow goals, it did not succeed in building state structures in the Congo that would enable the country's nascent Parliamentary system to withstand the pressures of further secessionist or revolutionary movements nor the corrosive effect of Mobutu's consolidation of autocratic rule with the assistance of the west shortly after UN troops had departed. Today the country continues to struggle with the absence of adequate state structures.

Notes

[1] William J. Durch, *The Evolution of UN Peacekeeping*, (New York: St. Martin's Press, 1993), 315.

[2] David W. Wainhouse, *International Peacekeeping at the Crossroads*, (Baltimore: Johns Hopkins University Press, year), 267-268.

[3] All analyses of force levels are dependent on the gross numbers from Lefever, Volume 3, Appendix H, Chart E.

[4] Wainhouse, 316.

[5] Karl von Horn, Soldiering for Peace, pp. 203, 213, 228, and 237.

[6] Wainhouse, 310, 314, 325, and 328-329.

[7] Ernest W. Lefever and Wynfred Joshua, *United Nations Peacekeeping in the Congo: 1960-1964 An analysis of political, executive and military control.* (Washington: The Brookings Institution, 1966) Volume 3, Appendix P-9 and P-17.

[8] Wainhouse, 325-326. Lefever, Volume 3, Appendix P-3 and P-5.

[9] Wainhouse, 310.

[10] Lefever, Volume 4, 13. And Wainhouse, 307.

[11] Wainhouse, 301.

[12] Lefever, Volume 3, Appendix P includes brief sketches of the military incident and related information about casualties.

[13] Lefever, Volume 3, Appendix O-4.

[14] Lefever, Volume 2, 360.

[15] Lefever, Volume 2, 361.

[16] Lefever, Volume 2, 363.

[17] Wainhouse, 297.

[18] Lefever, Volume 2, 365.

[19] Lefever, Volume 2, 123 and footnote 56, page 367.

[20] Lefever, Volume 2, 107-108.

[21] Lefever, Volume 2, 109-117.

[22] Lefever, Volume 2, 117-122 and 363-364.

[23] Lefever, Volume 2, 365-367.

[24] Lefever, Volume 2, 117-122 and 363-364 and Volume 3, Appendix P-25.

[25] Lefever, Volume 2, 92-93 and 346-347.

[26] Harold Karan Jacobson, "ONUC's Civilian Operations: State-Preserving and State-Building," World Politics, Volume XVII October 1964-July 1965, pp. 75-107.

6

UN Operations in Cambodia: (A Second "Decent Interval")

Joseph G.D. Babb and George W. Steuber

From the 1991 deployment of the United Nations Advance Mission In Cambodia (UNAMIC), to the establishment of the United Nations Transitional Authority in Cambodia (UNTAC) in 1992, through the 1995 presence of UN military advisors, the UN has played a critical role in the emerging political and military environment in that troubled nation. The debate over the success or failure of this action in the international community continues. Whatever the outcome of the discussion, the UN effort in Cambodia provides numerous lessons learned for serious students of peace operations.

> The United Nations' involvement in seeking a resolution to Cambodia's long-standing political conflict represents an unparalleled international diplomatic effort. Massive in size, comprehensive in scope and precise in its mandate, the United Nations Transitional Authority in Cambodia (UNTAC) set a new standard for peacekeeping operations undertaken by the international community. As with any unprecedented endeavor, UNTAC, and the Paris Peace Agreements which articulated its mandate, contained certain risks and experiments within its framework and implementation. It is for this reason that the outcomes of such an operation deserve careful scrutiny.[1]

The Political and Military Context

In the summer of 1989, the Paris Conference on Cambodia was convened with the contending four factions and nineteen countries in attendance. France and Indonesia co-hosted the meeting with the Secretary General of the United Nations participating in his official capacity. In September 1989, Vietnam, which had occupied Cambodia since 1978, announced its intention to withdraw all military forces which created an immediate opportunity for a political settlement on the part of the factions. In addition, a series of events and actions involving outside powers related to the end of the Cold War and the regional economic boom added impetus to the talks and played a role in bringing the relevant parties to the table and forging an accord among the factions.

> Vietnam withdrew its troops in September 1989, leading to an improvement of relations with China. The dissolving Soviet Union and Warsaw Pact ended aid to both their long-standing ally Vietnam and the PRK [Democratic Party of Kampuchea], while Thailand and other members of ASEAN [Association of Southeast Asian Nations] concluded that Indo-China was more lucrative as a market-place than as a battlefield. China, the Khmer Rouge's principal foreign supporter, and the Soviet Union began a slow rapprochement, hastened by the Soviet withdrawal from Afghanistan. The USA and other Western countries began to fear a return to power of the KR [Khmer Rouge].[2]

In 1990, the Cambodia political-military factions agreed to establish the Supreme National Council (SNC) as a framework body to work out a peace settlement. By the fall of 1991, after a difficult series of sessions over various proposals for power sharing and methods of verification, a peace plan consisting of a Final Act and three separate instruments was signed by all the participants including representatives of all four Cambodian factions. While the United Nations and interested outside powers were needed to provide security, economic and political assistance, and humanitarian aid, the critical element for the success of the agreement was the opposing factions' willingness to abide by the accords.

These factions were very diverse and included a broad political and military spectrum that reflected the turbulent history of Cambodia traditionally a buffer between Vietnam and Thailand. French colonization of Vietnam, Laos, and Cambodia, in the 19th Century sowed the seeds of nationalism that began to emerge after the First World War, but which blossomed in the period immediately following the Second World War. Cambodia had been only one of the Southeast Asian battlegrounds in the decades long conflict in Indochina involving the, Japanese, the French, the Americans, the Russians and the Chinese during the Second World War and the overarching big power confrontation of the Cold War that followed.

All four of the factions solidified their identities in the period from the first Indochina War to the exit of the Americans in 1975. Cambodia's role as a US "sideshow" changed dramatically with America's abrupt withdrawal from Southeast Asia. Cambodia soon became a centerpiece of the emerging Sino-Vietnamese contention for regional power and influence, that once again thrust the Cambodia factions into another round of internal turbulence. None of the Cambodia factions, alone or in coalition, had shown the political or military strength to prevail over time. All four factions were able to persevere and influence the conduct of UNTAC's mission, to a greater or lesser degree.

The largest faction represented at the talks was the People's Revolutionary Party of Kampuchea (PRK) which was established as the government in exile by the Vietnamese. This element, which was called the State of Cambodia (SOC) at the time the accords were signed, was placed in power by the Vietnamese after the 1978 invasion. This faction was led by Hun Sen, the Cambodian Prime Minister. Its political wing was called the Cambodian People's Party (CPP). The faction, originally led by Heng Samrin who was installed by the Soviet supported Vietnamese invaders, controlled and occupied all major population centers in the country. At the time of the accords, the SOC controlled the largest regular military in the country, the Cambodian People's Armed Forces (CPAF), which was reported to have approximately 130,000 troops with a militia of over 200,000.

There were two smaller factions that did not have large military forces and did not control significant amounts of territory, but did occupy small enclaves along the Thai border and maintained operational bases in many areas of the interior. These two factions constituted the noncommunist resistance forces which received limited support from the West and several Asian nations and both played key roles in the settlement. The United Front for an Independent, Neutral, Peaceful and Cooperative Cambodia (FUNCINPEC--from the French name for the organization) was led by Prince Ranariddh who had replaced his father, Prince Sihanouk, as the leader of this organization. This faction won the May 1993 election and Ranariddh became the first president of Cambodia's constitutional monarchy under the new power-sharing constitution, however the government bureaucracy remained firmly controlled by the SOC faction.

Prince Sihanouk, who from the early 1980s had led a Cambodian coalition government that occupied that nation's seat at the UN, was backed by China, Thailand, and the other states of the Association of Southeast Asian Nations (ASEAN), and the West. He remained a very powerful and influential player in Cambodian politics. Sihanouk was made the king of the country, a position that he had renounced over 20 years before. The military arm of this faction, the National Army for an Independent Kampuchea (ANKI) was the smallest with from 12,000 to 15,000 personnel.

The other faction, the Khmer People's National Liberation Front (KPNLF) was led by Son Sann, the former Prime Minister of the US supported Lon Nol government. A split developed between the KPNLF and its armed element the KPNLAF. The result was formation of a new KPNLF political arm, the Buddhist Liberal Democratic Party (BLDP). The military arm, the Khmer People's National Liberation Armed Forces (KPNLAF) had about 25,000 troops. This unstable faction also occupied small enclaves along the Thai border with smaller elements throughout the country and was determined to play a role in the emerging Cambodian political arena.

The most notorious and most difficult faction was led by the infamous Pol Pot. From 1975 until the Vietnamese invasion of December 1978 the Party of Democratic Kampuchea (PDK or DK), more commonly known as the Khmer Rouge, had autocratically ruled Cambodia and had conducted offensive, revanchist military actions against Vietnam. The Khmer Rouge were also responsible for the deaths of perhaps a million people in its brutal campaign of "autogenocide" against its own people, and particularly against those of Vietnamese descent. The political arm of this organization was called the National Unity Party of Cambodia (NUPC). The military arm of the Khmer Rouge, nominally headed by Khieu Samphan, with about 30,000 guerrillas, was officially called the National Army of Democratic Kampuchea (NADK). This element had been opposed militarily by the Vietnamese and the SOC forces and was primarily located in sanctuaries in the mountainous areas along the Thai border with elements scattered throughout the country.

This faction had surprisingly widespread support, based predominantly on their anti-Vietnamese stance, and enjoyed significant freedom of movement and operation throughout the country. The Khmer Rouge had continued to fight the Vietnamese and the Cambodia government forces of the SOC in an on-again-off-again loose coalition with the noncommunist resistance factions. The most visible indications of success or failure of the UN effort in Cambodia were directly tied to the handling of the Khmer Rouge, during the periods of both the United Nations Advance Mission In Cambodia (UNAMIC) and UNTAC. Despite the fact that all the factions signed the accords voluntarily, understanding overt and covert factional opposition to the implementation is critical in assessing the overall effectiveness of United Nation's role in Cambodia.

The Paris Peace Plan called for the United Nations to virtually run Cambodia for a transitional period until formal democratic governmental structures could be created and begin to function. The United Nations was to supervise, control and expand the existing administrative structures in the country, manage the economic effort for rehabilitation and reconstruction, and organize and conduct elections. The UN was to coordinate for the repatriation of refugees, supervise, monitor and verify the cease-fire and withdrawal of foreign forces, and monitor and oversee the cessation of outside military assistance to all of the factions. In addition, the UN was to regroup, canton and disarm one hundred per cent of all four factions' military elements, excepting militias. Once the factional military elements were disarmed the UN was to assist in the demobilization of seventy per cent of the military forces of all four factions, work with the Red Cross for the release of all prisoners of war and civilian internees, and, last but certainly not least, foster a peaceful and stable environment. A critical element of this was task was the demining program. Literally millions of mines had been placed throughout the country and continued to exact a tremendous human toll on the people of Cambodia.

In October and November 1991 with resolutions 718 and 46/18, respectively, the Security Council and the General Assembly expressed support for the agreement and the UN's role in its implementation. However, there was little in the way of detailed instructions for the military and civilian implementors. There were some detailed engineering studies conducted on Cambodian infrastructure prior to the signing of the treaties, however, copies of the various agreements and mandates were not initially available to the UN military personnel on the ground.[3] In addition, the UN was woefully unprepared, militarily, organizationally, administratively and logistically, to move quickly into Cambodia and begin the tasks outlined in the mandate and the accords. A critical deficiency in the UN mandate was that this operation was to be conducted as a Chapter VI, "Peacekeeping" mission and no provision were made for either UNAMIC or UNTAC to enforce the peace accords.

In November of 1991, pursuant to UNSCR 717, a small group of military officers, under the title UNAMIC arrived in Phnom Penh, the Cambodian capital, to supervise the cease-fire, begin liaison work among the four factions, start the formidable task of mine awareness, and set the stage for the arrival of UNTAC. Problems immediately arose for this element in that UNAMIC was not specifically mentioned in the accords and, therefore, the legitimacy and operational mandate of this group was contentious and problematic.[4] Nevertheless, UNAMIC deployed liaison teams to all four faction headquarters before Christmas Day 1991 to demonstrate UN resolve to accomplish its mandate. Through January of 1992, UNAMIC continued to deploy, organize, and begin to implement its initial missions. In short order, UNAMIC received additional and expanded missions from the UN. These tasks included major engineering tasks such as road building and repair, and the instituting of a major mine clearance training program.

UNAMIC's "mission creep" continued when it was expanded in early 1992 under the terms of UNSCR 728 with the addition of 1800 people, predominately Thai and Malaysian engineer battalions. In February 1992, with UNSCR 745, UNTAC was officially approved and a Japanese diplomat, Mr. Yasushi Akashi, was appointed as the Special Representative of the Secretary-General (SRSG) for Cambodia. The period of November through February saw conditions in Cambodia deteriorate. Political jockeying for position and infighting among the factions, especially between the SNC and the Khmer Rouge, numerous ceasefire violations, and a Khmer Rouge attack on a UNAMIC helicopter during which an Australian officer was wounded, are indicative of the state of affairs in the country, before UNTAC was even officially on the ground.

On 15 March 1992, Mr. Akashi and the designated Force Commander, Australian Lieutenant General John M. Sanderson, arrived in Cambodia to begin the UNTAC phase of the operation which was not to exceed 18 months.[5] The UN personnel that had been in country from November until March working as part of UNAMIC now became part of UNTAC and the mandated clock began to run. While selected arbitrary start and end dates for missions may make sense for domestic political reasons in those countries participating in potentially dangerous peacekeeping missions and for the administrative and logistics bureaucracies that must plan to fund and support operations, they also provide the "losing" factions at fixed date to restart the conflict.

Unity of Effort

> The situation "on the ground" shaped the outcome of UNTAC as significantly as did the architecture of the Paris Agreements. UNTAC faced immense practical challenges from the very moment of its creation. The first was simply to establish a presence. By the time UNTAC was created, four months had elapsed since the signing of the Paris Agreements, during which time numerous cease-fire violations had taken place, including an attack on a UNAMIC helicopter. In addition, public demonstrations had been mounted against the return to Phnom Penh of PDK officials as well as against the Phnom Penh authorities, prompting an appeal for calm from the five permanent members of the Security Council.[6]

All of the factions had signed the accord and the involved outside powers had agreed to work through the UN to implement the agreement, at the strategic level there was an outward appearance of unity of purpose, if not unity of effort. However, by the time the SRSG, Mr. Akashi, and the Force Commander, Lieutenant General Sanderson, finally got into Cambodia opportunities had been lost despite the difficult, and often dangerous work conducted by the UNAMIC personnel over the past several months. While immediate unity of effort certainly could not be expected of the Cambodia factions and their followers who had violently opposed each other over the last decade or more, the military and civilian implementors working under the aegis of the UN mandate were expected to conduct a unified operation to bring peace and stability to Cambodia. However, the various UN contingents and contracted personnel arrived in a piecemeal manner from dozens of countries and detailed instructions and standard operating procedures were still being formulated months into the effort.

Table 1, from the official UN report on Cambodia,[7] provides the numbers of uniformed personnel from the UN member states that were on the ground at the peak period in June of 1993. Coincidentally, the UN was also fully involved with mounting the United Nations Protection Force (UNPROFOR) in Bosnia which further delayed deployments and support and competed for resources and planning time with UNTAC.[8] The scale of the effort needed in Cambodia to bring this disparate grouping of military and police units, humanitarian relief organizations, and contracted individuals together is self-evident.

Table 1: UN Personnel On The Ground, June 1993

Military Component	
Algeria	16
Argentina	2
Australia	685
Austria	17
Bangladesh	942
Belgium	5
Brunei Darussalam	3
Bulgaria	748
Cameroon	14
Canada	218
Chile	52
China	444
France	1,350
Germany	137
Ghana	912
India	1,336
Indonesia	1,779
Ireland	11
Japan	605
Malaysia	1,090
Namibia	43
Netherland	809
New Zealand	67
Pakistan	1,106
Philippines	127
Poland	666
Russian Federation	52
Senegal	2
Singapore	35
Thailand	716
Tunisia	883
United Kingdom	130
United States	49
Uruguay	940

Civilian Police Component	
Algeria	157
Australia	11
Austria	19
Bangladesh	220
Brunei Darussalam	12
Bulgaria	74
Cameroon	73
Colombia	144
Egypt	100
Fiji	50
France	141
Germany	74
Ghana	218
Hungary	97
India	421
Indonesia	224
Ireland	40
Italy	75
Japan	66
Jordan	83
Kenya	100
Malaysia	224
Morocco	98
Nepal	85
Netherlands	2
Nigeria	150
Norway	20
Pakistan	197
Philippines	224
Singapore	75
Sweden	36
Tunisia	29

Moreover, this does not include the other UN agencies, such as the United Nations High Commissioner for Refugees (UNHCR) which was responsible for the relocation and care of more that 360,000 Cambodia people in the refugee camps, or the 1500 international personnel from 44 countries who would assist in the organization of elections.[9] Achieving unity of effort under these circumstances was a monumental task for both the civilian and military leadership of UNTAC.

In Cambodia, the absence of clear and unambiguous chains of command internal to UNTAC, as well as proper coordination between the Secretariat in New York and the field, resulted in a loss of operational efficiency. Within UNTAC, a major challenge confronting Akashi and, especially, the Force

Commander, Lieutenant General Sanderson, from the outset, was how to ensure the loyalty of the individual battalion commanders while making them accept the chain of command within the mission.[10]

Under most strict military doctrinal definitions, Unity of Command or even Unity of Effort did not exist in Cambodia. National contingents, in the main, refused to grant the commander operational control or even tactical control of the units on the ground. All the national contingents maintained direct links back to their home governments which gave them the ability to avoid, evade, or delay implementation of orders and tasks from the Force Commander. Even if the languages spoken within the headquarters staff elements could be narrowed to English and French, which they were not, there was very little common ground, operationally or doctrinally, for the communication of orders and tasks, at least initially.

The headquarters staffs, the military officers assigned to the Mixed Military Working Groups that were charged with setting up liaison missions to the four factions, the operational military units that were to be assigned sectors through the country, and the support personnel had no opportunity to train together or conduct preparatory work ups before arriving in country and beginning their missions. What was accomplished was done by force of personality (Akashi Sanderson, and individual lower level commanders and staff officers), locally agreed upon standard operating agreements, and the demands of the specific situations on the ground. The official organization chart is depicted:[11]

There was a clear mandate and an official organizational structure designed to unite the efforts of the military and civilian agencies and contingents in Cambodia at the strategic level. However, since the military had no mandate to compel compliance, the individual national contingent commanders had a ready fallback position whenever the Force Commander attempted to use force or the threat of force to bring the factions into compliance with the accords that they had signed. At the operational and tactical levels, the major factor that contributed to the situational unity of effort that evolved was the legitimacy of the accords and the desire of most of the Cambodians to see an end to the fighting, an improvement in the climate of human rights, free and fair elections, and the repatriation of the long-suffering people from the refugee camps.

Legitimacy

> By their very nature, United Nations peacekeeping and peacemaking operations tend to be Utopian. Driven by the higher ideals of the UN Charter and the good intentions of the states not directly involved in the conflict at hand and, some would say, by the unworldliness of the UN bureaucracy in New York, such operations tend to assume goodwill where little exists, to take written agreements at face value and to side count the corrosive effects of self-interest and power politics after peace accords have been concluded.[12]

UNTAC ORGANIZATIONAL CHART

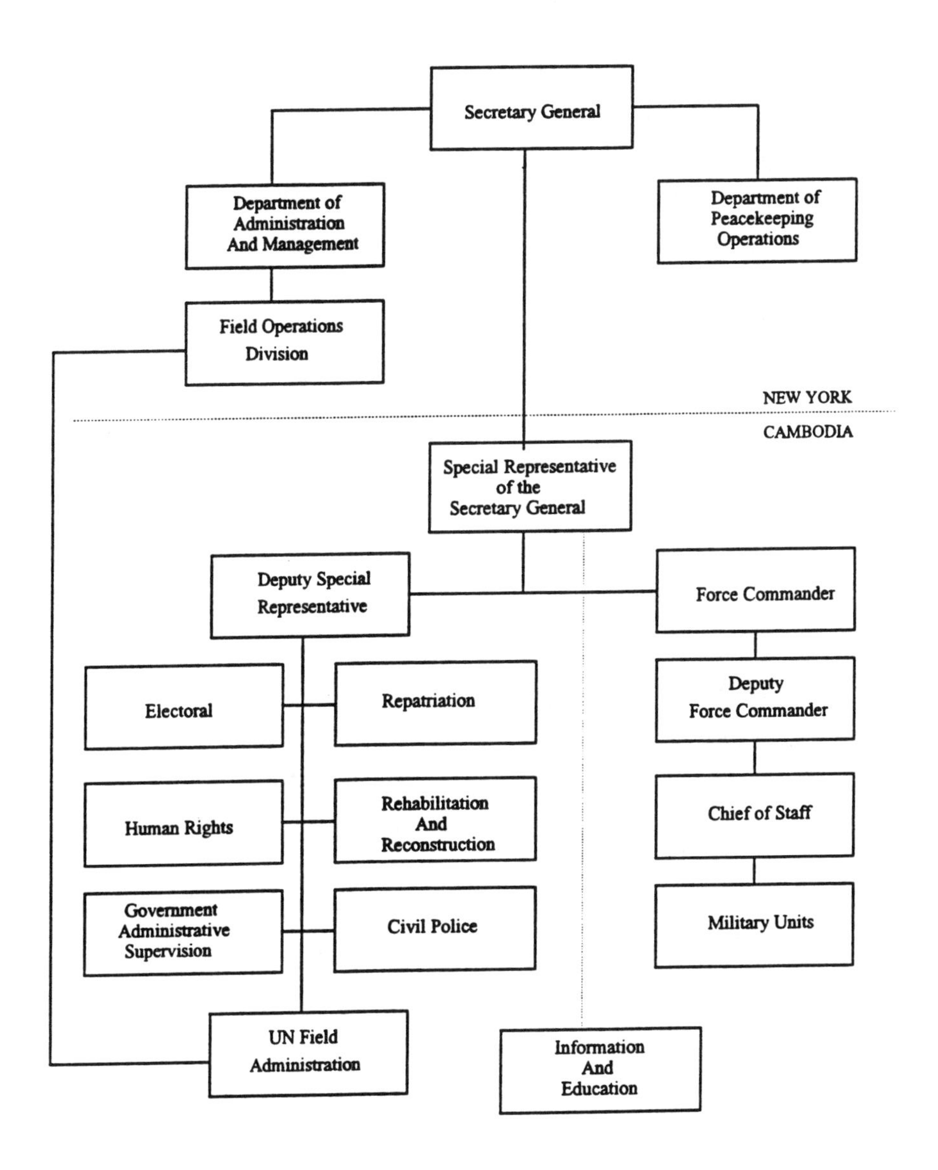

At the strategic level UNTAC was outwardly viewed as a legitimate exercise of international diplomacy. There was substantive agreement among the five permanent members of the UN Security Council who were willing and able to support the Paris accords which had been brokered primarily by the Indonesians and the French. The regional players and governmental and nongovernmental contributors to the peacekeeping and humanitarian efforts in Cambodia, broadly accepted the overall concept of the mission and supported the implementation process. There was a sense of legitimacy among the nineteen nations that signed the accords with the factions that the agreement had been properly and fairly negotiated. However, there is little doubt that external pressure from outside powers had played a significant role in bringing the factions, especially the Khmer Rouge and the State of Cambodia into line. When outside pressure subsided, the factions slowly returned to the status quo ante.

This external legitimacy and the UN "good offices" provided an overarching mechanism with the potential to gain and maintain support among the factions who had signed the accords, but it was critical that the major powers and the regional neighboring states continue to support the peace process outlined in the accords. Probably the most significant legitimizing factor was the desire for peace and stability among the people of Cambodia. Although UNTAC was unable to completely execute the entire range of tasks called for in the mandate, its efforts were generally seen as fair and impartial, and in the best interests of the Cambodian people. Where this impartial approach wavered (especially with in the eyes of the Khmer Rouge faction) the seeds of mission failure were planted.

General Sanderson is quoted as believing that the: "key to success in Cambodia lay in UNTAC's ability to 'forge an alliance' with the Cambodian people, to 'overcome the intrigues of their factional leaders and deliver an opportunity to them to break free from the prolonged cycle of fear and coercion.'"[13] It can certainly be argued, that in spite of the failures and partial successes in implementing the mandate to the letter of the agreement, UNTAC was seen by the people of Cambodia as more legitimate than any of the factions and offered a very real hope for the end of decades of violence and dislocation. Another critical element of UNTAC's success in implementing the mandate within the borders of Cambodia was a significant change in outside support and assistance, overt and covert, to the belligerent factions.

Support to Belligerents

By 1989 Russia and the United States, as the Cold War receded into history, had ended any significant direct or indirect aid to the factions or their supporters in Cambodia and were strongly behind the peace process as members of the UN Security Council. Indonesia, which saw itself as a regional leader, and France, the former colonial power, had a major stake in the success of the diplomatic accords they had engendered. Nevertheless, the three nations that were the primary supporters of the belligerent factions, China, Vietnam, and Thailand, were the key regional actors over the long term.

1. ***China.*** China played a critical role in the negotiations and in the implementation of the accords both as a member of the UN Security Council and as a key player in the regional calculus. China's past support to the Khmer Rouge and Prince Sihanouk in opposition to the Vietnamese backed government was part of a larger contest with Hanoi over regional hegemony. When Vietnam agreed to withdraw, China seized the opportunity to support the peace process and began to exert pressure on the Khmer Rouge to sign and abide by the accords. An independent Cambodia was seen by China as in its long term interest and in the interest of stability and economic growth in Southeast Asia. China's movement to a more neutral position in regard to the factions and the ending of support to the Khmer Rouge was a major contributing factor in the success of UNTAC. In addition, China contributed over 400 troops to UNTAC.
2. ***Vietnam.*** The removal of all Vietnamese forces from Cambodian territory and a de-linking of Vietnam from the State of Cambodia government were necessary prerequisites for progress, not only during the period leading up to the accords, but in their implementation on the ground. External pressure, diplomatic and economic, from its primary supporter, Russia, and from the United States, that held out the carrot of official recognition and increased trade, and a rapprochement with China, made Vietnam's withdrawal, which had been part of discussions since the mid 1980s, more palatable to the leadership in Hanoi. The evidence indicates Vietnam did in fact withdraw its forces as promised. Nevertheless, the Khmer Rouge continued to use the fact and fiction of the illegal presence of Vietnamese troops as a reason for its non-compliance with specific areas of the mandate. In addition, since the SOC government, which had been set up by the Vietnamese during its occupation, retained significant administrative and political control after the accords, (UNTAC did not take over several ministries of the government from the SOC as required by the accords) the Khmer Rouge rightly perceived that the political playing field was not level and that they were at a significant disadvantage. With a significant ethnic Vietnamese minority in Cambodia, historical animosities, and a long, common border Hanoi has significant interests in the final outcome and remains a factor in Cambodia's future.

3. ***Thailand.*** Thailand was another long term supporter of the Khmer Rouge and of the noncommunist resistance in Cambodia. In addition, Thailand also served as a relative safe haven for literally hundreds of thousands of refugees settled in numerous camps along the border. Despite the fact that many humanitarian relief organizations were present to assist the refugees, the Thai government claimed they were a drain on Thailand's economy. However, this was more than offset by Thailand's large economic stake in cross border trade in lumber, drugs, gems and other goods. This trade provided funds that were critical to the Khmer Rouge leadership and to the financing of their continued resistance efforts. UN attempts to get the Thai government to close off the border and to end trade with the factions was a very touchy issue and compliance was uneven. Nevertheless, the Thai government and military provided some assistance in the refugee relocation effort and provided engineer units to rebuild and repair lines of communication in Cambodia as part of UNTAC. However, it is fair to say that Thai assistance and compliance remained problematic, and overall was counterproductive to the UNTAC mission.[14]

Military Actions of the Peace Forces

The following maps outline the initial UNTAC military sector assignments and the deployment and order of battle supporting the election effort.[15] The more than 15,000 troops in 12 infantry battalions with supporting formations (including the controversial deployment of Japanese military forces, an engineer battalion) in this peacekeeping mission were given more tasks than they could reasonably be expected to carry out in the best of circumstances. The majority of the force did not begin to arrive until five months after the accords had been signed. The problems of the command was exacerbated by the uneven state of training of many of the units, the ad hoc nature of the headquarters and sector staffs (which reflected back to the lack of Unity of Effort at the operational and tactical levels), the lack of sufficient logistics and transportation assets for many of the national contingents, and the problems of command and control mentioned earlier. The many tactical accomplishments of UNTAC have to be attributed to the leadership and perseverance of Lieutenant General Sanderson and many of the individual members of his multinational staff and of the national contingents participating in the mission.

While arguably a bit simplistic, perhaps the best method to assess the military actions component of UNTAC is to evaluate the effort in each of the specific military tasks and sub-tasks assigned in Annex 1, UNTAC Mandate, Section C, Military functions of the agreement signed in Paris on 23 October 1991.[16] In

UNTAC Sectors of Cantonment and Demobilization

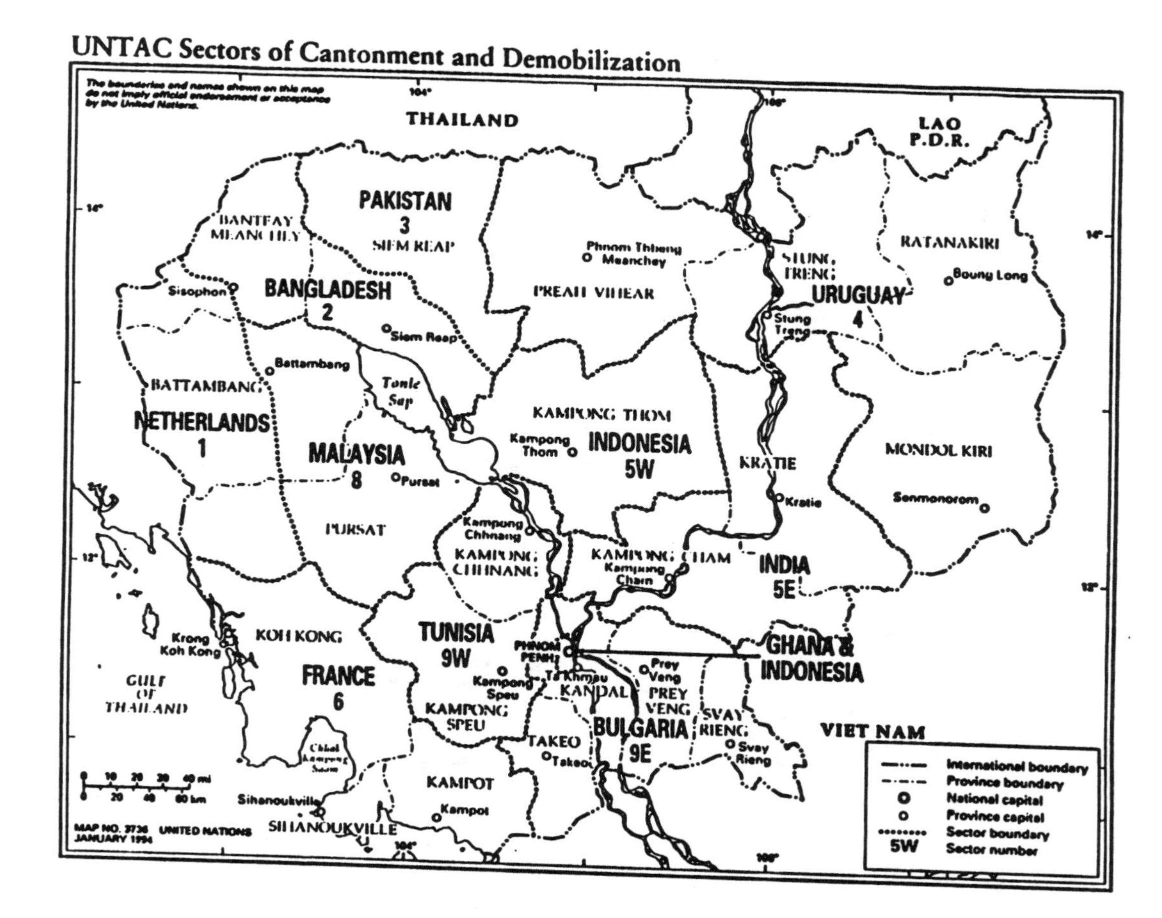

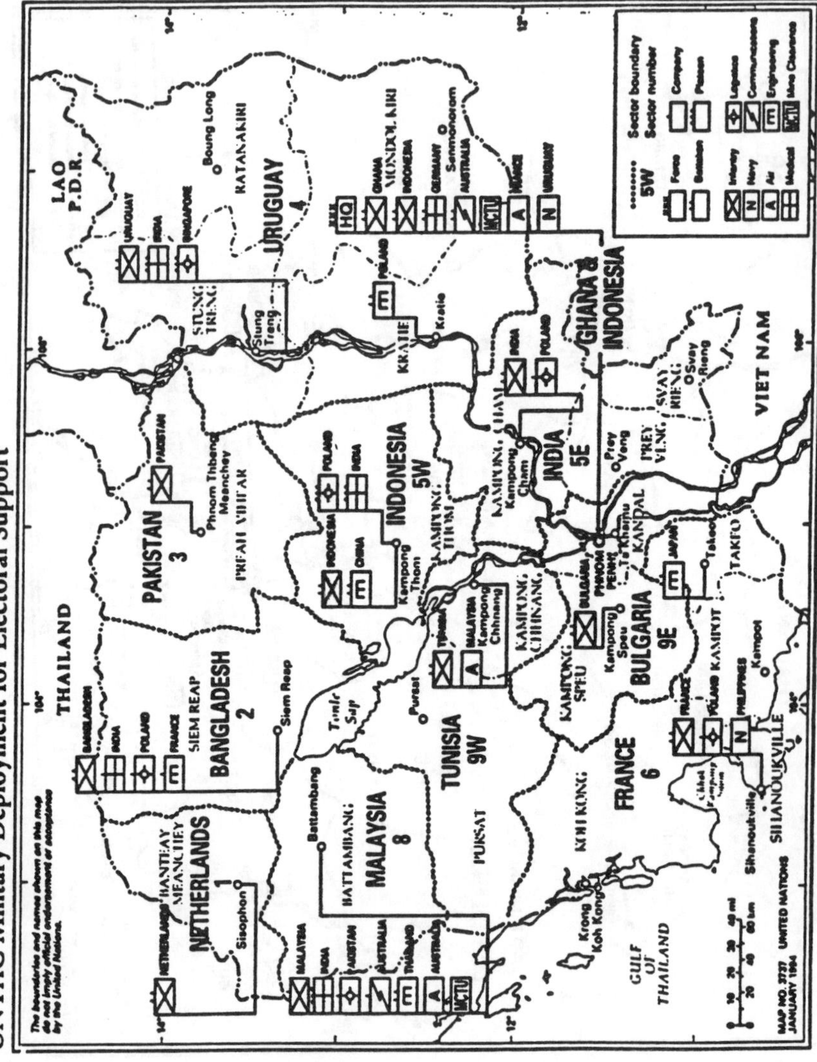
UNTAC Military Deployment for Electoral Support
THAILAND
LAO P.D.R.
VIET NAM
GULF OF THAILAND
NETHERLANDS 1
BANGLADESH 2
PAKISTAN 3
URUGUAY 4
INDONESIA 5W
INDIA 5E
GHANA & INDONESIA
FRANCE 6
MALAYSIA 8
TUNISIA 9W
BULGARIA 9E
Sisophon
Battambang
Siem Reap
Pursat
Tonle Sap
Phnom Thbeng Meanchey
Kampong Thom
Kampong Cham
Kampong Chhnang
Kampong Speu
Kampot
Takeo
Prey Veng
Svay Rieng
Kratie
Stung Treng
Boung Long
Senmonorom
Sihanoukville
Krong Koh Kong
PHNOM PENH
KANDAL
SIEM REAP
PREAH VIHEAR
BATTAMBANG
PURSAT
KOH KONG
KAMPONG SPEU
KAMPONG CHHNANG
KAMPONG THOM
KAMPONG CHAM
PREY VENG
SVAY RIENG
KRATIE
STUNG TRENG
RATANAKIRI
MONDOL KIRI
KAMPOT
TAKEO
SIHANOUKVILLE
Sector boundary
Sector number
MAP NO. 3727 UNITED NATIONS
JANUARY 1994

addition to these five specific tasks there are two other significant areas of military support to the mission: support to UNHCR efforts to repatriate the refugees; and secondly, providing a stable environment for and assisting the conduct of free and fair elections. Critically, this all was to be done under artificially constructed time limits that allowed the factions to delay and stonewall controversial issues.

> 1. UNTAC will supervise, monitor and verify the withdrawal of foreign forces, the cease-fire and related measures in accordance with Annex 2, including :
>
> (a) Verification of the withdrawal from Cambodia of all categories of foreign forces, advisors and military personnel and their weapons, ammunition and equipment and their non-return to Cambodia:
>
> (b) Liaison with neighboring Governments over any developments in or near their territory that could endanger the implementation of this agreement;
>
> (c) Monitoring the cessation of outside military assistance to all Cambodian parties;
>
> (d) Locating and confiscating caches of weapons and military supplies throughout the country;
>
> (e) Assisting with clearing mines and undertaking training programs in mine clearance and a mine awareness program among the Cambodian people.
>
> 2. UNTAC will supervise the regrouping and relocating of all forces to specifically designated cantonment areas on the basis of an operational timetable to be agreed upon, in accordance with Annex 2.
>
> 3. As the forces enter the cantonments, UNTAC will initiate the process of arms control and reduction specified in Annex 2.
>
> 4. UNTAC will take necessary steps regarding the phased process of demobilization of the military forces of the parties in accordance with Annex 2.
>
> 5. UNTAC will assist, as necessary, the International Committee of the Red Cross in the release of all prisoner of war and civilian returnees.

The overall assessment of the first major task can only be judged as marginally successful at best. It took several months to put in place the liaison elements and man the Vietnamese, Lao and Thai border monitoring sites with impartial UN observers. Isolating Cambodia from external support was a critical task necessary to reassure the four factions of neighboring states' compliance with the peace accords, and that no faction would benefit unfairly from the UN presence. Since the Thai never allowed full UN control of their border, cross-border trade remained crucial to Khmer Rouge survival. Thai compliance remained a key issue throughout the UN deployment.

The mission of locating and confiscating weapons and military supplies is nearly impossible to assess. All of the factions provided numbers of forces that were suspect and locations of caches of military supplies had to be volunteered. Even when intelligence was collected and sites identified, if the areas in which the caches were located were defended by military elements of the factions, UNTAC had no authority to seize the caches by force of arms. All of the factions remained armed and this task was not accomplished.[17]

The tasks of demining and refugee repatriation deserve special mention. A major effort was undertaken to accomplish these related tasks. Some of the units assigned to the demining effort were not adequately prepared for this difficult task. Initially, there was no mechanism in place to ensure standardization of training for the designated demining teams. Perhaps even more critical given the numbers of mines in the country and the difficulty in finding them, was the inadequate numbers of personnel assigned to the demining task at the outset. The terrain, the haphazard implantation and marking of minefields and the ingenuity of guerrilla fighters who had learned their trade over decades of war all contributed to the complexity of this task.

Directly affected by the problems in the demining effort, were the refugee repatriation operations. The UNHCR's movement of refugees commenced before UNTAC had the forces available to carry out its fundamental mission of regrouping, cantoning, disarming, and demobilizing the armed factions. More importantly, the enormous task of training mine clearing teams was just starting. The influx of people into areas that had not even been adequately marked, let alone cleared, further complicated UNTAC's mission.

Poor planning, coordination, and execution of UNHCR repatriation operations also limited the amount of help UNTAC could provide to the civilian returnees. The returnees were supposed to be given a plot of land, building materials for a house, seed grain for the first year's crop and food to last until the first harvest. Returnees were polled as to where they wanted to live, and mine-free land was supposed to be identified and allocated according to the results of the poll. Unfortunately, since the repatriation operations was not tied to UNTAC progress in identifying mined areas and demining prospective relocation sites, there was not enough land available to meet repatriation requirements.

In addition, UNHCR did not have sufficient building materials, seed grains or food to meet the project requirements. The fact that UNTAC was still deploying into Cambodia when the relocation effort began and there simply were not enough forces on the ground to provide protection along the convoy routes or at the relocation sites was critical. Although the UN declared the repatriation a success because it emptied the refugee camps in Thailand, no one attempted to ascertain the human costs of this uncoordinated and ill-timed operation.

Civilian casualties caused by mine incidents, banditry, and continued inter-factional fighting could probably have been reduced if the UNTAC mandate to control all UN activities in Cambodia had been exercised. In the end more than 360,000 refugees were resettled, but additional civilian casualties resulted because this operation began before UNTAC had been given the time to properly implement key precursor aspects of the accords and prepare safe lines of communication and resettlement areas.

Military Actions of the Belligerents and the Peace Forces

The regroupment, cantonment, disarming, and demobilization of the four fighting factions' regular armed elements was the primary mission of UNTAC. The UN conducted a preliminary survey of the factions prior to deploying UNAMIC. This survey was designed to inform the factions of their responsibilities under the peace accords and gather information on the numbers of combatants, weapons, and ordnance controlled by each faction. In addition, the factions were asked to designate areas to be used as cantonment sites. ANKI, KPNLAF, and SOC forces were reasonably forthcoming with the required information, but there were misunderstandings as to what infrastructure building and site preparation activities UNAMIC/UNTAC would undertake. Eventually, through negotiations, the number and location of cantonment sites was resolved with these three factions and UN forces occupied many of these sites. The Khmer Rouge was the least forthcoming of the factions. After intense negotiations, the number and location of sites was agreed upon, but unlike the other factions, the Khmer Rouge never allowed UNTAC full access to these sites. This action by the Khmer Rouge derailed the regroupment and cantonment process.

Since the regroupment and cantonment of the regular armed elements of the factions never occurred, large-scale disarmament of the contending factions could not take place. While the UN was able to take control of some weapons, this was only a small fraction of the total armaments available to the factions. When external assistance to the ANKI and KPNLAF ceased, these forces lacked the resources to keep paying their soldiers. Some soldiers sold their weapons; many turned to banditry to support their families. Failure to disarm the Khmer Rouge meant that the UN could also not control weapons in the hands of the SOC forces. This is one of the primary reasons FUNCIPEC was not able to capitalize on its election victory and displace the SOC bureaucracy. Cambodia's high level of violence still evident in the summer of 1997, is largely attributable to UNTAC's failure to carry out the disarming of the factions as specified in the accords.

Related to the failure to disarm, was the failure to demobilize and retrain former fighters. Demobilized soldiers were to receive vocational training in a variety of technical skills to assist in their transition into civilian life. The UN sent survey teams to all of the factions to poll the commanders and soldiers on what technical training would be most helpful. Again, the Khmer Rouge refused to cooperate with the UN. This program had the potential to assist in the overall economic development as well as reduce the future potential for violence. The failure to regroup and disarm the factions' military elements, two of the primary tasks of the accords, had significant second and third order effects on the stability of the country.

As noted previously, the regrouping process had not begun before UNHCR repatriation operations started. The soldiers of the KPNLAF and ANKI factions were faced with the choice of staying with their leaders, who could no longer pay and support them, or repatriating with their families currently in the refugee camps. This caused a serious erosion, if not disintegration of command and control in most of these factions' armed elements along the northwestern border. The Khmer Rouge saw themselves as the biggest losers in this shift in power which in effect rapidly decreased the strength of the coalition forces opposing the SOC.

By late April 1992, it was obvious that neither ANKI or the KPNLAF could account for their declared numbers of combatants or weapons, nor could UNTAC verify the regroupment, cantonment, disarmament, or demobilization of these factions. This provided both the Khmer Rouge and the SOC with a convenient excuse for not complying with the accords. The Khmer Rouge so distrusted the UN and the SOC, which seemed to be the primary beneficiary of the UN intervention, that the KR refused to cooperate further with the UN. Thus, the core element of the UNTAC mission died without ever having a legitimate chance at success.

In simplest terms since the Khmer Rouge refused to comply fully with the accords, and the other factions reacted to protect themselves and their areas of influence, the ceasefire could never be fully implemented. The following quote from the official UN report summarizes the problem and response. Again, because of Chapter VI guidelines UNTAC did not have the mandate to enforce the ceasefire and avoided offensive action to the greatest extent possible.

> The PDK [Khmer Rouge] refused to allow UNTAC troops to proceed with their deployments in the areas under the PDK's control, failed to provide information on the numbers of its soldiers and material, did not mark minefields and was responsible, UNTAC believed, for many cease-fire violations. In addition on one occasion the armed forces of the PDK prevented senior UNTAC personnel, including my special representative and the Force Commander, from proceeding through PDK-controlled territory to the Thai border. A personal appeal from me to Mr. Khieu Samphan, President of the PDK and a member of the SNC, seeking the compliance with the Paris Agreements, went unheeded.... The PDK's lack of cooperation challenged the very foundations of the Paris accords and gravely compromised UNTAC's ability to adhere to its timetable.[18]

Actions Targeted on Ending Conflict

Both UNAMIC and UNTAC undertook numerous actions to end the conflict in Cambodia. UNAMIC's early formation and deployment in and of itself (UNAMIC was not mentioned in the accords) was a UN action designed to foster and improve direct communications between the UN and the factions. Military Liaison Teams were sent to the headquarters of all four of the factions to provide direct communications between the factions' headquarters (HQ) and the UN. (ANKI HQ at Phum Ku, KPNLAF HQ at Banteay Meanrith, supposedly the NADK HQ at Pailin, and the CRAF regional HQ at Battambang.) Inserting unarmed liaison teams in all faction areas before December 1991 was designed to show that the UN was impartial; security and support depended on mutual trust and cooperation; and that UN members were willing to make personal sacrifices to help Cambodia keep the peace.

The next significant action in stopping the conflict was the formation of the Mixed Military Working Groups (MMWGs). These groups were composed of two officers from each faction and a UN officer(s) as the facilitator. The UNAMIC Force Commander, Brigadier General Loridon chaired the first MMWG meeting in Phnom Penh with general officer level participation from all four factions. MMWGs at all levels provided the primary forum for negotiating military issues involved in disengaging the combatants, deploying UN forces into contested areas, and investigating alleged violations of the peace accords.

Since all of the factions were represented on the MMWGs, all factions had to cooperate to ensure the security of the group. An example of this principle and of the effectiveness of these organizations is the actions of the Kampong Thom MMWG. This group stopped the fighting in Kampong Thom Province (started by a Khmer Rouge attack on 27 Feb 92) by physically interposing themselves between the factions guaranteeing that no faction could fire without hitting their own senior officers. MMWGs were invaluable as a confidence building measure and communications channel for both the UN and the factions.

As noted previously, UNTAC was required to ensure that outside aid and interference in Cambodia stopped. Accomplishing this would have placed pressure on all factions to cooperate more fully with the UN. Border checkpoints were one method of doing this, and UNTAC increased the number along the Vietnamese border specifically in response to Khmer Rouge demands. UNTAC leaders hoped this effort would increase Khmer Rouge cooperation, but this did not happen. Sealing the border between Cambodia and its neighbors was an impossible task given the assets available and the lack of international political will to take the steps necessary to cut off Thai-Khmer Rouge activity. UNTAC and the international community's failure to successfully isolate the factions, especially the Khmer Rouge, from outside assistance, meant that they could continue to rely on resources to support their operational agenda.

Although UNTAC also failed to achieve its key mission of regrouping, cantoning, disarming and demobilizing the majority of Cambodia's armed combatants, UNAMIC and UNTAC did take other actions to stop the conflict. A weapons buy-back program was established by UNAMIC and continued by UNTAC. This should have been an adjunct to the disarmament program, however, it quickly became the primary method of identifying and collecting arms and munitions from the faction areas as the factional command and control diminished.

In addition, UNTAC carried out an extensive multimedia information campaign to inform Cambodians of the provisions of the accords and UN actions designed to support the peace plan. This information campaign was crucial to providing rural Cambodians with information on the progress of the peace process. This program also was instrumental in support of the election process and in the transition of UNTAC at the end of the mission.

Conclusion

Several years and thousands of lives after UNAMIC/UNTACs departure, Cambodia appears to be more peaceful that it has been for decades. The Khmer Rouge have fallen under the weight of their own faulty ideology, international opinion, and a push from their erstwhile Thai supporters. The standoff over power sharing between the Sihanouk faction and the Hun Sen backers closely resembles the situation when UNTAC left Cambodia -- which speaks volumes about the success of the UN in that troubled country.

First and foremost, this illustrates that there is no quick fix or easy solution to problems that have multiple causes and historic roots going back generations. The problems in Cambodia stem from hundreds of years of ethnic conflict between the Khmer, Vietnamese and the Thai. In addition, urban-rural class differences and pressures to modernize as part of one of the most dynamic economic regions in the world exacerbate Cambodia's developmental problems. A UN mandate to solve all these problems in eighteen months was unworkable even if UNAMIC/UNTAC had been provided massive military, political and economic sanctioning powers. However, the problems could begin to be addressed by the Cambodia people in a more stable and secure environment.

Second, Unity of Effort is absolutely essential to the successful accomplishment of any peacekeeping mission. The peace plan signatories and UNAMIC/UNTAC participant elements all had hidden agendas and individual reasons for becoming involved in the process. Individual nations and UN and nongovernmental organizations were involved in costly refugee support operations and had direct and indirect economic interests in Cambodia. As previously noted, UNAMIC/UNTAC participant units did not accept UN command and control in every instance, and were not necessarily equipped or trained for assigned missions. All of these factors had an impact on how successful UNTAC could be in accomplishing this prodigious mission.

Finally, the ad hoc nature of UN operations and the lack of true centralized control within the UN were key factors that degraded the ability of UNTAC to carry out its mission. Officers could not communicate with one another or with Cambodians because of language problems. No standard operating procedures existed for the mission and there were no training requirements for participating units. In addition, the military-civilian working relationships were often strained and too often uncoordinated, although this relationship improved over time. Even though Mr. Akashi was given full authority over all UN elements working in Cambodia, perhaps the most critical factor in UNTAC not achieving its core military mission was the early and uncoordinated UNHCR refugee repatriation operation.

The political process begun with the elections in 1993, continues into the summer of 1997, not with ballots but with bullets. UNTAC provided a decent interval and a promise of real change, but Cambodia appears to be returning to government by military coup and dictatorship. Nevertheless, the precedents for good governance, democratic processes and elections are there, the brutal Khmer Rouge faction and its leadership has been virtually eliminated as a factor, and regional states are attempting to bring Cambodia into the family of nations in Southeast Asia. Progress had been made and the UN played a significant and positive role in that transition.

Notes

1 Boutros-Ghali, Boutros, The United Nations and Cambodia: 1991-1995 (UN Blue Book Series Vol. II.) New York: Department of Public Information, United Nations, 1995, p.3.

2 Findlay, Trevor. Cambodia: The Legacy and Lessons of UNTAC. Oxford, UK: Oxford University Press, 1995, p 3-4.

3 Brown, Jerold E. UN Peacekeeper in Cambodia, 1991-1992: An Interview with Major George Steuber. Fort Leavenworth, KS: Combat Studies Institute Report 14, 1992, p. 16.

4 Ibid., p. 1.

5 Boutros-Ghali, p. 15.

6 Ibid.

7 Ibid., 23.

8 Mayall, James. The New Interventionism, 1991-1994: United Nations experience in Cambodia, former Yugoslavia and Somalia. Cambridge, UK: Cambridge University Press, 1996, p. 66.

9 Boutros-Ghali, p. 33-38.

[10] Mayall, p. 50.

[11] Heininger, Janet E., *Peacekeeping Transition: The United Nations in Cambodia*. New York: Twentieth Century Fund Press, 1994.

[12] Findlay, p. 101.

[13] Ibid., p. 112.

[14] Findlay, pp. 43-45.

[15] Boutros-Ghali, pp. 18, 36.

[16] Ibid., p. 139.

[17] Thompson, Eugene L. Interview conducted at Fort Leavenworth, Kansas 7 August 1997. LTC Thompson served as UNTAC Military Observer Team Leader in Cambodia from January through July of 1993.

[18] Boutros-Ghali, p. 17.

7

Piecemeal Peacekeeping The United Nations Protection Force in the Former Yugoslavia

John A. MacInnis

The lightning strike by the Croatian army in October 1995 which overran the Krajina, effectively ended the rebellion by the Croatian Serbs and along with it, the mission of the United Nations Protection Force (UNPROFOR) in Croatia. In Bosnia, NATO intervention followed by the signing of the Dayton Peace Accord) 25 November 1995 ended the conflict, and along with it, the mission of UNPROFOR in Bosnia. Both missions were clouded in controversy: the Bosnian mission in particular came under severe and repeated criticism, particular from those who believed that UNPROFOR was too hesitant in the use of force to exercise what they assumed to be its mandate. In Croatia, UNPROFOR was taken to task repeatedly for either failing to protect the Serbs in the sectors or for failing to have them comply with UN Security Council Resolutions.

This chapter examines both components of the UNPROFOR operation in relation to the applicable dimensions. In so doing, an attempt is also made to understand the reasons behind the controversy, and in particular why the UN effort in the former Yugoslavia left much to be desired and why the mission evolved as it did.

UNPROFOR1 and the War in Croatia

The collapse of the Yugoslav Communist Party in February 1990, the country's major unifying force since 1940, signaled the beginning of the end of the Yugoslav Federation. The Serbs, who had the most to lose from a breakup pushed hard for both unification and centralization. Slovenia and Croatia, however, had other ideas and in 1991 their moves towards independence prompted action by the only Federal institution with power remaining, the Yugoslav National Army (JNA) which quickly became an instrument of Serb nationalism. Indeed, as it became apparent that the prospect of a unified state was becoming unlikely, the Serbian objective changed to that of achieving unification of the Serbs, in other words, the formation of a Greater Serbia. To achieve its purpose, the JNA launched assaults against Croatia beginning in May 1991. On 25 June, Slovenia and Croatia declared independence. The JNA, in coordination with hyper nationalistic "irregulars" such as the Arkanovci,[1] followers of the notorious criminal-turned-patriot, moved to crush the secessions.[2] Thus began a war of extreme violence with an ugly twist: ethnic cleansing.

The war in the gulf and the collapse of the Berlin Wall, symbols of both the end of the cold war and the emergence of a so-called new world order, held the attention of the West to the extent that it was caught off guard by the outbreak of war in the former Yugoslavia. In fact it was not only the outbreak which was surprising, but also its hyper-nationalistic nature. The international response, therefore, was slow, tentative and disjointed. In fact early actions concentrated on holding the Federation together and seemed to encourage military action by the JNA.[3] Efforts by the European Union, which had assumed leadership in trying to resolve the conflict, proved inadequate prompting the UN Security Council to call upon the Secretary General to offer his assistance. Former US Secretary of State Cyrus Vance was sent as his envoy. UNPROFOR began its deployment in early 1992, mandated to implement the "Vance Plan".[4] The operation was mandated to "create the conditions of peace and security required for the negotiation of an overall settlement of the Yugoslav crisis".[5] The specific tasks set out for UNPROFOR were to verify the withdrawal of the JNA, to ensure the UN Protected Areas (UNPAs) were demilitarized through the withdrawal of all armed forces and that all persons in them were protected from fear of armed attack, to monitor the function of local police to ensure nondiscrimination and full respect for human rights, and to facilitate the return of displaced persons.

Unity of Effort

If unity of effort is to be achieved within a mission area, the politico-strategic guidance given to the mission must itself be focused - in UNPROFOR it was not. To be fair, no one anticipated the intensity of communal strife which blanketed Croatia, nor knew how to deal with the consequences of a conflict the basic aim of which was population dislocation by any means. Nor was the UN ready to move from its traditional position on Peacekeeping, that is, one based upon the consent of the parties, impartiality, and the use of force only in self defense. Battalions were to be lightly armed, and after much discussions, were authorized to possess no more than 15 Armored Personnel Carriers, (APCs) to be used essentially for self-protection while on patrol. Following a reconnaissance however, both the Canadians and French insisted that their battalions were to be fully mechanized.[6]

The Vance Plan showed its fragility while UNPROFOR was still deploying: Croatia demanded return of the "Pink Zones", those areas around the UNPAs into which the Serbs had extended their presence while the agreement was still being negotiated. The first addition to the mandate was contained in resolution 762 of 30 June 92 which tasked the Force to monitor the reintroduction of Croatian authority into the Pink Zones, to verify the withdrawal of all forces from the Zones, and to maintain custody of the heavy equipment of the JNA forces.

At the operational level, few of the components of the basic mandate were definable in military terms with sufficient precision to ensure unity of effort. This was exacerbated by the machinations of the headquarters which found itself in Sarajevo, next in Belgrade and finally in Zagreb. Meanwhile, four sectors were established in the Serb-held areas of Croatia, each containing three or four infantry battalions and commanded by a brigadier-general. The detailed command structure of UNPROFOR however did little to promote unity of effort as several parallel chains of command existed at once: logistics and finance under the Chief Administration Officer (CAO), civil affairs and police reported to the Deputy Chief of Mission (DCM) and unarmed military observers (UNMOs) reported to the Chief Military Observer. While several attempts were made to correct this, the fluctuating quality of leadership and command at the sector level meant that parallel chains could never truly be eliminated.

Note that UNPROFOR's mandate was a composite which meant that with its three disparate imperatives - military, political, and humanitarian - "mission creep" was front-end loaded, in other words, responsibility was so diffused that success in one area was immediately offset by lack of progress elsewhere. For the military, this presented challenges and problems which the force alone was unable to resolve and which detracted from the relative success which it was able to achieve.

The greatest impediment to Unity of Effort by far, however, was the diverging and in many cases contradictory aims of the peace forces and the parties to the conflict, a condition made worse as the mandate evolved. Security Council Resolution 815 of 30 March 1993 stated that the UNPAs were "an integral part of the territory of the Republic of Croatia" whereas the basic mandate had been, as stated earlier, to maintain peace while political negotiations proceeded to resolve the Yugoslav question. This resolution, in the view of the Serbs, prejudged the outcome of the political dialogue and resistance intensified.

Similarly, the lack of success in negotiating a return of the Pink Zones convinced the Croatians to take matters into their own hands which they did by launching four attacks into the Zones in 1992-1993.

Unity of effort required a degree of consent and cooperation from both the Croatian Government and the Serbs. This UNPROFOR did not enjoy and could do little to obtain.

As of March 1994, therefore, the only major success achieved in the basic mandate was the withdrawal of JNA forces. The same month, however, produced a breakthrough which permitted UNPROFOR to keep the peace in a more traditional fashion. On 29 March,[7] Zagreb and Knin signed a cease-fire agreement, as part of a wider accord, which reduced military tensions throughout the UNPAs. The agreement was to be part of a three-step program, a cease-fire to stabilize the situation, a package of economic measures to further cooperation, and discussions leading to a political solution. Unity of Effort, following from a precise and workable mandate on the cease-fire, was finally at hand and remained in place for a year. However, while the first two steps were completed successfully, the third and most important step was never taken. The Croatians who had previously coined the phrase "Cyprusization" to refer to a state of affairs in which the result attained is peace in its narrowest sense - the absence of armed conflict - went on to prove that this "Cyprusization" or state of stalemate was not seen as an acceptable solution to the problem at hand.

Legitimacy

Some of the same factors which prevented Unity of Effort were also instrumental in undermining the legitimacy of the mission. Political groups in Yugoslavia were still expressing objections to the UN plan as of 15 February 1992; nevertheless, the UN Secretary General pushed for the establishment of UNPROFOR based upon the lesser of two evils: that the risk of mission failure was less grievous than that of renewed conflagration.[8] With this dubious underpinning, the legitimacy of the Vance Plan was repeatedly eroded to the extent that "each side, for its own reason, blames UNPROFOR for failing to fulfill its expectations - of the restoration of normal conditions and the return of refugees, in the case of Croatia, or of protection, in the case of the local Serbs."[9]

Jurisdictional disputes over the "Pink Zones" led to the set up of a joint commission of the parties essentially to oversee the return of these zones to Croatian authority.[10] The joint commission process ended in failure: this challenge to the legitimacy of the mission so early in the mandate led to other problems which began to impede the demilitarization process such as the handing over of weapons from the JNA to the local armed elements or police/militia as well as making it difficult to reestablish local law enforcement.[11]

The lack of legitimacy was reflected in the actions of the Croatian government and people. In Zagreb, a so-called "wall of shame", built of bricks each containing the name of a missing, dead or displaced person, was erected around UNPROFOR headquarters. Furthermore, access to sectors and units were repeatedly blocked, and each extension of the mandate was more and more difficult to achieve, until, with the overrunning of the Krajina by the Croatian army in 1995, UNPROFOR's presence became irrelevant.

As the crisis loomed, the lack of agreement on the question of political legitimacy in Yugoslavia prompted an international response which proved to be a substitute rather than a recipe for effective action. Repeated attempts were made to hold Yugoslavia together long after the federal structure, less the JNA, had ceased to function. Similarly, the Vance Plan, the basis for UNPROFOR's mandate in Croatia, preceded Croatia's recognition as an independent state within borders which included Serb-held territory. This recognition placed the legitimacy of the Plan in serious doubt especially as it resolved the legal, but not the practical, question of territorial ownership. The real tragedy, however, was the failure to recognize that the Belgrade government, by using military force against civilians in the siege and destruction of Vukovar in the fall of 1991, had morally and ethically shattered its own legitimacy.

Support to Belligerents

On its departure from Croatia, the JNA left behind weapons, vehicles and "demobilized" personnel for the local armed elements, the so-called border police. Demilitarization therefore was far from complete and more than 16,000 well armed "militia" remained. The war in Bosnia, and a change in strategy in Belgrade kept military support for the Knin Serbs to a minimum. Nevertheless, Croatia was insistent that UNPROFOR should halt the flow of goods across the UNPA boundaries into and out of Serbia and Bosnia. As the Vance Plan preceded Croatia's recognition, and therefore did not address the question of borders, it offered little help. Despite possessing neither the experience nor the resources to engage in customs and immigration duties, UNPROFOR was mandated to carry out these tasks,[12] an undertaking which proved impossible to carry out without the consent of the Serbs, which of course was never obtained.

But, in a twist to this dimension, it was the Croatians who benefited from UNPROFOR's continued presence. It gave them the necessary breathing space to strengthen themselves both economically and militarily to the point that their 1995 campaign in the Krajina was a quick success.

Support Actions of the Peace Forces

While UNPROFOR in Croatia had little difficulty in obtaining and retaining troop presence, the capability, credibility and conduct of some of the troops provided tended to degrade UNPROFOR's performance. Frequent rotations, lack of experience with peacekeeping, and diverging concepts of operational capability meant that common standards and practices were almost impossible to achieve. As an example, the initial success of UNPROFOR in placing Serb heavy weapons under a double lock system was quickly reversed following the Croatian attack into Sector South in January 1993. While it is true that commanders had no direct orders to stop the Serbs from forcing their way in and removing the weapons, few contingents possessed either the will or the capability to stop them. Only the Canadians in Sector West challenged the Serbs by setting up a strong defensive position and showing their will to defend the sites for which they were responsible. Following the move of the Canadian battalion in late 1993 to the more volatile Sector South, Sector West became essentially a "third world" sector, a fact which was not lost on the Croatians who began the recovery of their territory in that Sector, Western Slavonia. Although the Sector Commander had received orders to implement a contingency plan to resist, the Croatians entered the area unopposed.[13]

UNPROFOR in Croatia consisted of thirteen battalions from twelve countries, four of which were NATO. The reality was, however that only four, Canada, Russia, France and Belgium possessed the doctrine, logistics, training and experience commonly associated with complex, out-of-country operations. This proved to be a definite drawback, especially in situations calling for sophistication, restraint and above all credibility, all vital characteristics especially when the underlying mandate is imprecise.

Military Actions of the Belligerents and the Peace Forces

In the Croatian conflict, based as it was on ethnic nationalism, separation of the underlying issues into their political and military components proved an impossible undertaking. Military commanders of both warring factions were indistinguishable from the politicians in power and most of them were hard-line in their pursuit of nationalist goals: in many cases, they were the politicians. Bringing the military components of the warring factions together in any sort of common undertaking, therefore, proved temporary at best. Combining that with yet another set of goals as set out in the mandate of the peace forces proved all but impossible. Only infrequently were all three in agreement that conflict was not in their best interests, although the Krajina Serbs, being on the defensive and partially isolated within the UNPAs, had more to lose in continuing the conflict. The Croatians, on the other hand, deemed it unacceptable that the Serbs should consolidate their position, and as the international community had nothing to offer in the way of a political solution, conflict to end the impasse proved inevitable.

The question of military professionalism among the warring factions and its potential to abate conflict quickly became moot. The perception of professionalism and credibility of UNPROFOR military and civilian police UNCIVPOL did, initially, have a deterrent effect. Police were able to gain respect within the UNPAs and together with the military at first were able to impose their will by presence alone. By January 1993, however, after it became apparent that to the Croatians that the word "protection" in the label of UNPROFOR did not mean "defense", Croatian forces attacked into and through the Pink Zones in Sector South, simply avoiding the widely dispersed French troops. The Serbs, convinced that UNPROFOR had provided assistance to the Croatians, inflicted several casualties upon the French and no longer tolerated police presence in certain areas. It was not until late in 1993, following the Canadian action at Medak[14] against the Croatians and General Cot's "step by step" strategy, (see next dimension), was professional credibility reestablished sufficiently to allow a cease-fire to go ahead.

Actions Targeted on Ending Conflict

The Vance Plan, and its associated negotiations, was successful in bringing the conflict under control. The issue of the Pink Zones however kept the war smoldering, especially in Sector South where artillery duels occurred constantly. The International Conference on the Former Yugoslavia (ICFY) appointed two ambassadors to deal with the situation.

Within the UNPAs, expulsions on an ethnic basis were a daily occurrence especially in Eastern Slavonia, despite the constant presence of UNCIVPOL who had integrated themselves in to the communities. In July 1993 an agreement on the Pink Zones had been reached at ERDUT calling for the withdrawal of Croatian forces from sensitive areas and their replacement by UNPROFOR troops. Despite considerable effort by the UN including redeployment of several battalions to carry out the mission, the Croatians pulled out of the agreement on 15 July, the date on which it was to go into effect. UNPROFOR itself had gone about as far as it could in pursuit of its mandate but, following this failure, its activities had been reduced to that of presence and patrolling within the UNPAs.

By December 1993, cease-fire negotiations in the UNPAs in Croatia had come to a complete standstill. Meanwhile, the new Commander of Sector South, Colonel George Oehring of Canada began to achieve a series of low key, short term cease-fires by striking up personal and professional contacts with the military leaders on both sides of the line. Exploiting this phenomenon, the Force Commander at the time, General Jean Cot, embarked on a "small steps approach" in which he encouraged small low level local agreements that were less likely to be politicized. He built on each one of these in order to achieve increasingly larger successes. When completed, he had created a de facto cease-fire, albeit one based on a series of "gentleman's agreements." The conditions conducive to a formal agreement had been created and as a consequence a cease-fire agreement was signed on 29 March 1994. By changing the situation on the ground, General Cot had also altered the political environment. As indicated earlier, however, even this well-maintained cease-fire foundered because of the inability to address the underlying political issue of who ruled the UNPAs and the people in them. Until this fundamental issue was finally resolved, (through Croatian military action) military, humanitarian or other political actions by the peace forces provided only temporary respite at best.

UNPROFOR2 Bosnia-Hezegovina Command

On any had scale of measurement, the UN operation on Bosnia evolved to become many times more complicated than the parent operation in Croatia. Following international recognition of Croatia and Slovenia, Bosnia had little wish to remain part of a Serb-dominated rump Yugoslavia. Many of the Bosnian Serbs, however, had other ideas, and the resort to rabid nationalism by all parties and the spillover of conflict from Croatia, began one of the most vicious inter-ethnic conflicts witnessed in Europe for many decades. The response of the international community as represented by the UN Security Council was to avoid the fact of the conflict directly and to concentrate on its consequences by giving UNPROFOR a humanitarian role[15] "to create the necessary conditions for unimpeded delivery of humanitarian supplies to Sarajevo and other locations in Bosnia and Herzegovina". This mandate was later expanded to include, *inter alia*, the following tasks:

- to provide support to the UN High Commission for Refugees (UNHCR) in the delivery of humanitarian relief, particularly through the provision of convoy protection when so requested, and
- to provide protection for convoys of released detainees on request of the International Committee of the Red Cross (ICRC).

The UN Protection Force therefore, although deployed under Peacekeeping rules, had nothing to do with peace and little to do with protection. Meanwhile, four conflicts waxed and waned: the Serb-Croatian conflict in Croatia, the

Serbs against Muslims and (on occasion) Croats in Bosnia, the Croat-Muslim war in central Bosnia and the Muslim - Muslim war in the Bihac.[16]

The evolution of the Bosnian conflict and the role of UNPROFOR played out in four phases:[17]

1. Phase one, from about April 1992 until May 1993, was the period of the Bosnian Serb revolt and military offensive against the Muslims, with the Croats mainly sitting on the sidelines. The same brutal paramilitary groups which had refined their grisly methods in Croatia, moved into Bosnia on a campaign of ethnic cleansing. The international response was the dispatch of UNPROFOR as mentioned including the operation of a relief air bridge into Sarajevo.
2. Phase two, from roughly May 1993 until February 1994, saw the Croats launch their attacks on the Muslims, while the Serbs began consolidating their position and intensified their pressure on the enclaves. The Muslims, meanwhile began to recoup some of their losses while fighting on two fronts. The international community tried to put in place a safe area regime essentially as an extension of the humanitarian based mandate, thereby requiring UNPROFOR to adopt a partisan stance on the one hand while operating as an impartial third party for humanitarian purposes on the other. How this was to be reconciled was never fully addressed. As time went by and expectations remained unfulfiiled, UNPROFOR's credibility deteriorated.
3. Phase three began with the mortar attack on the Markale Market on 5 February in which 68 people were killed and 197 wounded. Weapon exclusion zones were put in place and a decrease in fighting occurred on all fronts as the Serbs stopped their bombardment under threat of NATO air attacks. More importantly, the Croat-Muslim war came to an end by means of a UN brokered cease-fire and a US sponsored peace plan. The Bosnians were gaining strength and became less and less willing to accept cessation of hostilities. In the spring of 1994 the five nation Contact Group issued a "take it or leave it offer" to the Bosnian Serbs, which was rejected. The Contact Group found itself in disarray and unable to react; contact with the Bosnian Serbs was broken and remained that way for several months. UNPROFOR picked up more and more tasks, including peacekeeping along traditional lines between the Muslim and Croat communities.
4. Phase four, from spring 1995 until the Dayton peace, began with the collapse of the truce brokered by former President Jimmy Carter. The Bosnian army went on the offensive and the Serbs reacted in characteristic fashion by attacking safe areas thereby prompting NATO bombing, which in turn resulted in widespread hostage taking.

A rapid reaction force was introduced into UNPROFOR, but while this force was deploying the Serbs overran the safe areas of Srebrenica and Zepa, massacring thousands. This was followed by the Croatian attack in the Krajina, more NATO bombing and finally the Croat-Muslim thrust towards Banja Luka.

Unity of Effort

A degree of constancy is needed in order to maintain clarity of purpose and unity of effort: constancy was not one of the characteristics displayed by the UN Security Council as the war progressed through its four phases.. Between the period 25 September 1991 and 15 March 1994, the Council issued 50 Presidential statements and adopted 55 Resolutions relating to the former Yugoslavia, most of them relating in some way to UNPROFOR's mandate.[18] The effect was one of creeping incrementalism, a process in which many "lines in the sand" were drawn; lines which were either too late in coming or which were blatantly unenforceable.

As time went on, the pattern of unity, or rather disunity, could be seen in the makeup of UNPROFOR, one which seemed to mirror the international bias: one element comprised the original troop contributors, mainly NATO countries, who had subscribed to the original humanitarian mandate, another element, mainly Russians and Ukrainians which tended to side with the Serb cause, and in the middle a large number of Muslim states, some of whom were openly advocating joining the fray on the side of the Bosnians.

Successful campaigns are characterized by a unity of purpose throughout the strategic, operational and tactical levels of war. In order to operate effectively, commanders at all levels must understand both the intentions of their superiors and what role they themselves are to play in the achievement of the desired end state. In a large and complex mission trying to manage someone else's conflict such as UNPROFOR, where the end state remained undefined, and where commanders were often called upon to make decisions whose effects could be far reaching, it was most important that each level and element to be following a common path. Among the operating levels of the mission (UN New York, ICFY, and UNPROFOR civilian and military), the requisite unity was lacking. By way of illustration, two examples of the failure to achieve coordination at the strategic and operational levels are cited: following the Sarajevo market place shelling on 5 February 1994, at the strategic level, the UN Secretary-General dispatched a letter to the Secretary-General of NATO asking that body to delegate air strike authority to CINCSOUTH. At the same time, at the operational level, the Special Representative of the Secretary-General (SRSG) Mr. Akashi and the Force Commander General Cot attempted to achieve a local ceasefire. Meanwhile, ICFY, again at the strategic level, was diffusing the pressure by trying to convince the Bosnian Serbs to pursue the concept of UN administration for Sarajevo, and secondly, in the winter of 1994, after much planning, the Force Commander announced his intention to refocus UNPROFOR's efforts on the Operation LIFELINE route along the Neverta River into central Bosnia and the reconstruction of bridges destroyed by the Croats south of Mostar in order to speed up the delivery of humanitarian aid. ICFY, on the other hand, was pursuing a solution to the Mostar problem itself, these two initiatives ran the risk of undercutting each other.

At the operational level, a change in the command and control structure did little to improve matters. In July 1993, the first civilian head of mission, Thorvald Stoltenberg of Norway, was appointed SRSG, while Genera Jean Cot of France became Force Commander. Stoltenberg, however, was one of the co-chairman of ICFY, a position which demanded most of his attention. Despite the appointment of a Zagreb-based deputy, the negative effect was twofold: first of all, the parallel chains of command for logistics and civil affairs described earlier effectively bypassed the erstwhile head of mission, the Force Commander, and secondly UNPROFOR, although ostensibly guided by Security Council resolutions and, for Bosnia, mandated to assist UNHCR in the conduct of humanitarian operations, became to a large degree an instrument of ICFY negotiations. As an example, in early August 1993, President Itzetbegovic threatened to walk out of negotiations on the Stoltenberg-Owen peace plan unless the Serbs were removed from Mount Igman, overlooking the Sarajevo airport. After receiving the order to "do something, General. Now!",[19] General Francis Briquemont negotiated the deployment of French troops between the Serbs and Muslims. The Geneva talks subsequently failed but the French troops remained easy targets in no-man's land, effectively blocking the use of NATO air power in that area for some time. (See also the discussion on safe areas under a following dimension.)

In his desire for clarity of purpose, General Cot pressed for clear political oversight and guidance so that he in turn could develop a unified operational strategy. The best advice he could receive from the SRSG's staff was - read the Resolutions. The arrival of a permanent SRSG in January 1994 was an improvement but by then the complexity of the situation was such that coherent political oversight was no longer achievable.

Changes within BH Command did much to improve the quality and unity of effort at the tactical level. As the war proceeded into its second phase and with the increased number of troops called for as a result of the declaration of safe areas, in early 1994 Lieutenant General Sir Michael Rose reorganized the Command by adding two brigade level (sector) headquarters and greatly reducing the size of his own. This had the advantage of eliminating the practice of battalion commanders reporting directly to a division level headquarters thereby relieving them of levels of responsibilities for which they were rarely qualified, as well as introducing higher level commanders and a broader range of staff functions outside the Sarajevo area. Commander British Forces (COMBRITFOR) became Commander Sector Southwest in Gornji Vakuf, and the commander of the Nordic battalion (made up of Swedes Danes and Norwegians) became Commander Sector Northeast, in the newly occupied Tuzla area. This move increased flexibility considerably and allowed UNPROFOR to move quickly into a standard peacekeeping mode between the Muslims and Croats during phase three of the war.

During phases 2 and 3, the UN-NATO planning effort was a unified endeavor while the conduct of tactical operations tended not to be. The plan for peace in Bosnia developed in 1993-1994 saw UNPROFOR remaining in place as long as there was no peace; NATO was to enter the scene once a formal peace had been negotiated. Several iterations of transition planning and handover were worked out. UNPROFOR, however, because of the equivocal position of the United States at the time on the issue of US troops in Bosnia, was required to keep a contingency plan up its sleeve whereby it would carry out the post-peace operation on its own.

As the war evolved through its four phases, however, the UN-NATO relationship became more fragile as the effort tended to split along institutional lines. Tensions began in summer 1993 with the emerging US "lift and strike" proposal, one which caused serious difficulties within the North Atlantic Council (NAC), especially among UNPROFOR's troop contributors. A crisis was averted through the set up of the so-called "dual key" approval process for air strikes;[20] this same process, however, later strained NATO - UNPROFOR relations as the mandates of the two began to, or at least appeared to, separate. Unity of effort was maintained somewhat precariously until August 1994 when CINCSOUTH, US Admiral Leighton Smith, while acknowledging the gravity of what he was suggesting and the concern for the safety of UN forces, nevertheless recommended the conduct of air strikes.

The UNPROFOR commander, French General Bertrand de LaPresle clearly points out the opposing view of the mandate:

> ... just as the United States is understandably concerned about the threat to their soldiers prior to any decision to commit ground troops, I am similarly concerned, as well as responsible to the troop contributing nations, for the safety of the soldiers who have been provided for a mission of peace keeping and not peace enforcement. Before engaging in a totally new mission I would have to seek the approval of these nations whose concurrence cannot be assumed.[21]

The UN-NATO relationship was sometimes characterized as one of competing credibilities. Although UN resolutions describe the relationship as one in which NATO was to act in support of UNPROFOR in the execution of its mandate, NATO made it clear that it was not a UN subcontractor, and in fact it twice declared heavy weapon exclusion zones around Bosnian towns, which UNPROFOR helped to maintain on the ground, without specific Security Council authorization.[22]

The two finally achieved unity of effort in August 1995 when UNPROFOR's rapid reaction force and NATO took military action against the Bosnian Serb Army (BSA). Impartiality had been left behind, and the humanitarian mandate which brought UNPROFOR into the theater in the first place, had become transformed.

In summary, it had taken more than three years to achieve a semblance of a unified effort in relation to the conflict in Bosnia, albeit one which bore no relation to the original mandate. The Security Council's lack of unified direction from 1992 until 1995 was a reflection of the disparate policies of the major powers and players involved. The initial humanitarian-based strategy, however, for which unity of action was achieved, did sustain over 2.2 million civilians and probably prevented a swift Serb victory. Unity of purpose in ending the conflict achieved earlier however, especially within the Contact Group at phase three, might have had ended the war sooner. By failing to impose a solution on the basis of the map that they had presented to the Bosnian parties a year before, the Contact Group had lost authority (and indeed legitimacy) in the region. As a result, the Croatians and the Bosnian Serbs moved in to fill the vacuum by a series of military actions - in Western Slavonia, Zepa, Srebrenica, Bihac, and in the Krajina.

Legitimacy

The warm welcome which greeted UN troops when they arrived in Sarajevo in July 1992 quickly turned to hostility when the locals realized that the troops had come to feed and cloth them while the siege and war continued. While the UN Security Council may have good reason to conclude that a military solution to the conflict was unlikely, there had to be less legitimacy to the conclusion that there could be a humanitarian one. Granted, the extremes of military intervention on the one hand and doing nothing on the other were less acceptable at the time so that helping the victims, containing the war and, by presence alone, reducing the conflict seemed reasonable, and was undoubtedly the only mandate to which many troop contributors were willing to subscribe. Nevertheless, each passing resolution which added yet another expectation and task to the mandate decreased the credibility of UNPROFOR and legitimacy along with it. A reason, not readily apparent, is that each additional resolution and each additional mandate element represented an add on, none of the previous components was dropped which meant that impartiality was necessary in order to ensure that humanitarian action was not politicized, yet partisanship was needed in order to effect certain mandate requirements such as protection of the so-called safe areas.

As with the effort in Croatia, the international community could not agree on the nature of the conflict, whether it was intra-or international in nature. This failure to gain international consensus on the issue of political legitimacy with respect to the responsibilities of Serbia, the newly recognized Bosnia, or its constituent ethnic groups lead once again to the adoption of a mandate which proved to be weak and inappropriate to the task.

Support to Belligerents

The Security Council imposed an embargo on the import of weapons against the republics of the former Yugoslavia in September 1991[23] in an effort to curb the emerging conflict. Although the embargo may have helped to contain the conflict, it did little to prevent the destruction of over sixty percent of dwellings in Bosnia nor to restrict the employment of the many heavy weapons available to the Bosnian Serbs. As in Croatia, the JNA left much in place for use by the Bosnian Serbs. Bosnia itself, however, had been an arsenal in which much of Yugoslavia's reserve of arms were stored: its manufacturing capacity for small arms and ammunition was retained throughout the war. This, coupled with the porosity of the embargo permitted the conflict to continue unabated. The Bosnian government, which maintained that the embargo denied its right to self defense, was nevertheless able to make gains while facing two foes at once, essentially through the employment of its superior infantry on terrain which muted the employment of heavy weapons. This however did not apply to Sarajevo and locations where Bosnian Serb heavy weapons were used with devastating consequences.

The intermingling of Croatian soldiers with Bosnian Croats and Serbs with Bosnian Serbs across adjoining borders allowed uninterrupted support for these two factions. The Bosnian Muslims on the other hand received support in spite of the embargo, in the form of small arms from, *inter alia*, Iran and manpower reinforcements from a source not always welcome
Mujahadeen ready to pursue an Islamic Jihad.

Lacking the mandate, access, and capacity to counter these developments, the peace force made significant efforts to observe and publicize this activity. As a result, Mujahadeen involvement began to decline from the spring of 1994 especially after the deployment of the Turks to the Mujahadeen stronghold of Zenica where the Turkish battalion systematically wrenched control of the area from them. As for the Croatians, their involvement was reduced well prior to the Washington Accord of April 1994 through the threat of sanctions and political pressure placed upon Croatia's President Tudjman. The scope and extent of support from Serbia however remained unquantifiable.

Support Actions of the Peace Forces

While troop contributors were ready to support the humanitarian based mandate, most shied away from efforts to pursue a more robust approach against one or more of the parties. As the war evolved, it became more and more difficult to obtain troops for the mission. The demand reached a high pitch in 1993-1994 when the safe areas, the Muslim Croat cease-fire, and weapon exclusion zones all combined to raise the need. In an attempt to meet demands, the UN Military Advisor sent letters of request to over 100 countries asking for units. Only two responded, both of whose militaries required substantial resources and training before deployment.

As UNPROFOR increased in size, it not only began to mirror international bias as previously discussed, but became unwieldy and unbalanced as no sophisticated resources, such as engineers and logistics accompanied the newly arrived infantry units. As the war unfolded, nations increasingly placed more and more restrictions on the employment of their contingents no matter what command arrangements they had agreed to with the UN. The Nordic battalion insisted on being deployed to Tuzla only and refused an order from the UN commander in Bosnia, Lieutenant General Briquemont to deploy a company to Srebrenica. Governments of troop contributing countries intervened at the highest level in April 1994 to prevent its troops from being deployed to Gorazde. British forces although provided under tactical control (TACON) (later operational control) of the UN commander only, nevertheless remained flexible throughout.

Military Actions of Peace Forces

Even without a mandate to intervene, successive UN commanders in Bosnia found they could not ignore the reality of the conflict. General Morillon, after he had found a solution to the flow of humanitarian aid which worked most of the time, attempted to influence the conflict by personally entering the besieged town of Srebrenica with a handful of escorts. Although the result of his action was to reduce the pressure on that town for up to two years, the strategic response by the international community was the ill-fated safe area concept (see Action Targeted On Ending Conflict). General Briquemont took a different tack and concentrated more fully on the desperate humanitarian situation which existed during late 1993 by keeping open the routes from Split to Central Bosnia and initiating Operation LIFELINE through the Croat-Muslim conflict around Mostar. Moreover through persistent efforts, he was able to achieve a consensus among the commanders of the warring factions, Mladic (Bosnia Serb), Petcovic (Croat), and Delic (Muslim) on the modalities of a ceasefire.

Unfortunately the political efforts did not keep pace; however the groundwork for the eventual ceasefire which did occur in 1995 was laid out.

Actions Targeted on Ending Conflict

The demand for action to end the conflict increased as the war evolved through its phases. Only during the final phase, after unity of effort was established, was combined, systematic military and political action taken The aim of this action was to exert sufficient military pressure upon the Bosnian Serbs, and sufficient political pressure upon the Bosnian Federation, to accept both a cease-fire and negotiations leading towards a political settlement. This aim was achieved, but it was long in the making

Actions prior to this phase were, in the main, ineffective if not counterproductive, primarily because of failure to follow-up, or because of an incrementalist approach, or failure to foresee the consequences of initiatives taken. For example, the Vance-Owen peace plan for Bosnia the first in a series of options based upon territorial division, did not receive sufficient international support to force the Bosnian Serbs to comply thereby leading to its rejection. Following its failure however, the Bosnian Croats, in a apparent effort to increase their potential land holdings, attacked the Muslims and began ethnic cleansing on their own, an activity not unconnected with the content and failure of the Vance-Owen initiative itself

Additionally, some actions reflected an incremental approach which made it difficult to convince the belligerents that the international community was ready to follow up on its threats. For example, Resolution 781 banning aircraft from Bosnian airspace, was passed on 9 October 1992 but enforcement of the No-Fly Zone did not begin until six months later (Resolution 816, 31 March 1993).

The initiative which caused the most confusion and which raised unfulfillable expectations, was that of the so-called safe areas. Here again, a series of incremental measures took place in the form of what appeared to be increasingly robust Resolutions. The first, Resolution 819 (16 April 1993) declared Srebrenica and its (unspecified) surroundings to be a UN-protected safe area Although it demanded Serb withdrawal, it did not give UNPROFOR the responsibility for defending Srebrenica. The second, Resolution 824 (6 May 1993) extended the concept to include Bihac, Sarajevo, Tuzla, Zepa and Gorazde and the withdrawal of all Serb (but not Bosnian) forces to a safe distance. The third, Resolution 836 (4 June 1993) passed under Chapter VII of the UN charter authorized, *inter alia*, UNPROFOR, in carrying out its mission in the safe areas, "acting in self-defense, to take the necessary measures, including the use of force. . . "

From the beginning, the sponsors of Security Council resolution 836 foresaw difficulties and wanted to ensure that the deliberately chosen words of the Resolution - "to deter" rather than "to defend" and to "promote withdrawal" rather than to "ensure or enforce" were clearly pointed out to the Force Commander. In other words, UNPROFOR's main purpose was deterrence which would flow from its presence in the safe areas. In the same vein, Serb withdrawal would be accomplished by persuasion rather than coercion. Demilitarization would be accomplished through UNPROFOR negotiating certain voluntary arrangements with the Government and at the very least, assurances were to be sought that the safe areas would not be used for military activity. A token presence of 7000 troops was approved although the force commander's stated requirement was for over 30, 000. (In fact only 3000 were ever deployed.) As for the use of air power, it was foreseen that its use would result in serious threats to the personnel of UNPROFOR and therefore should be used in self-defense.

This initiative to limit if not prepare for the end of the conflict had several characteristics and effects:

1. The choice of towns left much to be desired. Tuzla and Sarajevo for example housed large - and active- Bosnian military forces;
2. The areas were never defined geographically. This allowed Bosnian officials to allege attacks against the safe areas when in fact military action was far off;.
3. "Safe Area" implied the existence, and acceptability, of unsafe areas elsewhere,
4. The Security Council authorized (quasi-) military action while possessing neither the resources nor the will (including that of several of the Resolution's sponsors) to carry it out.

The resulting inaction, the dichotomy between UNPROFOR's humanitarian mission with the blatantly anti-Serb mission outlined in the resolution, was the beginning of the end for UNPROFOR. A slow but inexorable move towards gridlock ensued wherein UNPROFOR, the agent of the UN Security Council became increasingly defiled and marginalized. The end result was the massacre at Srebrenica in 1995.

Conclusion

Note that several dimensions were not analyzed in detail. There are several reasons for this. The first is the overwhelming importance of the key principles of unity - of purpose, of effort, of command - as well as that of legitimacy. In the case of UNPROFOR, and indeed the overall international response to the crisis during UNPROFOR's lifetime, the complete failure to operate within either of these dimensions renders, in my view, discussion on some of the remaining dimensions somewhat meaningless. The real tragedy however was the dichotomy between public expectations and the reality: as far as UNPROFOR troops were concerned, their job was humanitarian in nature and they tried to do it well; but delivering food from armored vehicles bristling with heavy weapons while not being able to use those weapons to save lives became more and more impossible to accept. By engaging in displacement activity rather resolving to end the crisis politicians degraded their own military forces and undermined UN peacekeeping in all respects. Recovery will take a long time.

Notes

1 Arkan is the nom de guerre of Zeljko Raznatovic, a Belgrade playboy who has yet to be indicted for war crimes. *TIME*, May 13, 1996.

2 Samantha Power, *Breakdown in the Balkans, a Chronology of Events: January 1989 to May 1993*, Washington DC:The Carnegie Endowment for International Peace, 1993.

3 In late June 1991, less than a week before the forecast independence of Slovenia and Croatia, US Secretary of State James Baker visited Belgrade and reportedly stated that, although opposed to the use of force, there would be no penalties if it were used.

4 *Report of the Secretary-General Pursuant to Security Council Resolution 721* (1991), S/23280, December 11, 1991, Annex III.

5 Ibid.

6 The Author went to New York to argue the case with the Direct of Political Affairs, Marrack Goulding who relented, but only after I agreed to lend 15 APCs to the Nepalese.

7 The signing actually took place at 0400 hours, March 30 in the Russian Embassy but the documents were already dated March 29.

8 UN reference paper on the situation in former Yugoslavia, March 15, 1994.

9 Further Report of the Secretary General Pursuant to Security Council Resolution (1992), September 20, 1993.

10 UN Security Council Resolution 762 (1992), June 30, 1992.

11 Report of the Secretary General Pursuant to Security Council Resolution 749 (1992).

12 UN Security Council Resolution 769 (1992), August 7, 1992.

13 From a conversation with the Deputy Force Commander, Major General Ray Crabbe, August 8, 1995.

14 In September 1994, following a Croatian attack in the Gospic area of Sector South, the Canadian battalion, augmented with two French companies, blocked the Croatian advance and pushed them out of the pocket, but not before systematic ethnic cleansing had taken place.

15 UN Security Council Resolution 757 (1992) of May 30 and 776 (1992) of September 14.

[16] David Owen, *The Toronto Star*, September 26, 1994.

[17] *The War In Bosnia: A Turning Point*, Statement by Dr. Games A Schear, Carnegie Endowment for International Peace to the committee on National Security, US House of Representatives, November 2, 1995.

[18] *The United Nations and the Situation in the Former Yugoslavia*, Reference Paper dated March 15, 1994.

[19] Heard in the company of Brigadier Vere Hayes, COS BH Command, August 1993.

[20] It was in fact, a twin ladder process by which non-agreement at lower levels triggered a referral for decision at the next higher level. It was not a UNPROFOR construct but was designed by four NATO officers - Admiral Boorda as CINCSOUTH, Lt Gen (Canadian) Jack Dangerfield, Director of NATO's international military staff, Brigadier (UK) Phil Sturley, NATO LO to UNPROFOR and me.

[21] Ibid.

[22] "United Nations Peacekeeping in Europe," Shashi Tharoor, *SURVIVAL*, Summer 1995.

[23] UN Security Council Resolution 713 (1991) dated September 25, 1991.

Peace Enforcement

8

Intervention in the Dominican Republic 1965-1966

Lawrence A. Yates

The assassination in May 1961 of Rafael Leonidas Trujillo Molina, the dictator of the Dominican Republic for over thirty years, ushered a period of uncertainty and instability into that country's politics.[1] In the tumultuous year and a half that followed Trujillo's death, US pressure foiled attempts by the strongman's relatives to retain power, eight major political parties emerged to fill the vacuum created by the demise of the dictatorship, and in December 1962, national elections elevated Juan Bosch to the presidency. A poet, idealist, and leftist reformer, Bosch did not remain in office long enough to celebrate the anniversary of his triumph. In September 1963, he was deposed by conservative elements within the Dominican military, who created a civilian "Triumvirate" in his stead.

Headed by businessman Donald Reid Cabral, the new government tried to tackle the country's deep-seated economic woes, but Reid's austerity programs and political machinations succeeded mainly in alienating large segments of the Dominican middle class, business community, and labor movement. Reid fared no better with his promises to curb corruption and other abuses in the military, as his reforms upset the conservative officers who had placed him in power and left disaffected younger officers complaining that the changes were inadequate. By early 1965, Reid's political and military detractors across the political spectrum were actively planning his removal from power.

On Saturday, 24 April 1965, Reid, who two days before had dismissed seven junior officers accused of plotting against him, ordered the arrest of another group of conspirators located near the capital city of Santo Domingo. The move served only to trigger the uprising he was hoping to forestall. With weapons provided by sympathetic military units, a few thousand demonstrators took to the streets of the capital and, the next day, succeeded in toppling Reid's regime. The civilian and military leaders of the coup quickly proclaimed a provisional government--which later adopted the label "Constitutionalist"--and called for the return of Juan Bosch, then in exile. This move alarmed arch-conservative elements within the military, as well as anti-Bosch factions within the rebel movement itself. On Sunday afternoon, self-proclaimed "Loyalist" officers, having set up headquarters at the San Isidro military base northeast of the city, launched air and naval attacks on the provisional government. With this act, what had begun as a coup d'état was transformed into a civil conflict, albeit one confined largely to the capital.

Earlier on Sunday, officials at the American embassy in Santo Domingo had voiced strong concerns about "extremist participation in [the] coup." The revolt against Reid, they believed, represented not just an internal Dominican power struggle, but part of a Soviet and Cuban blueprint to promote instability and revolution in the Western Hemisphere. Concerned about the regional, even global, ramifications of the local crisis, the deputy chief of mission, in the ambassador's absence, had the embassy's military attachés inform key Loyalist military leaders of "our strong feeling that everything possible should be done to prevent a Communist takeover in this country and to maintain public order." Apprised well in advance of Loyalist plans to move militarily against the provisional government, the embassy gave its "reluctant support" to the attack.[2] In the next day or two, as fighting raged in the capital, US officials talked to both sides regarding a possible cease-fire, but given the animosities between the warring groups and the embassy's clear preference for the Loyalist faction, these efforts proved ineffectual.

On Monday, 26 April, a US naval task group of six vessels carrying a Marine Expeditionary Unit (MEU) composed of 1,700 officers and men arrived off the Dominican coast, prepared for any contingency. The next day, unarmed Marines came ashore and, in an operation agreed to in advance by both rebels and Loyalists, began evacuating American and other foreign citizens from the capital.[3] At this point, armed intervention by the United States seemed unlikely. To all concerned, it appeared that the Loyalists were on the verge of defeating the rebels, an impression confirmed when key Constitutionalist leaders asked the US ambassador, who had returned to the country on Tuesday, to mediate an end to the fighting. Ambassador W. Tapley Bennett, convinced that the communists were "taking full advantage of [the] situation," even calling the shots, rejected the request and urged the rebel leaders to capitulate. Instead, with a few exceptions, the suppliants sought political asylum at various embassies around the city.[4] One exception, a Colonel Francisco Caamaño Deño, refused to stop fighting, and by Wednesday morning, he had rallied the Constitutionalist forces sufficiently to halt the troops advancing on the capital from San Isidro. Alarmed by this unexpected development, Ambassador Bennett urged Washington to provide communications equipment to the

Loyalists, who only hours before had formally established a military junta as a counterpoise to the rebels' provisional government. Later in the day, as Loyalist fortunes continued to deteriorate, Bennett cabled Washington with an urgent appeal to land US troops. In response, President Lyndon Johnson ordered 536 Marines ashore to protect American lives and property. As fighting continued, the ambassador requested more troops and Johnson agreed. By week's end, the president had committed the rest of the MEU and a brigade of the 82d Airborne Division to armed intervention in the Dominican Republic.[5]

In the wee hours of Friday, 30 April, the first units of the 82d Airborne Division landed at San Isidro, the Loyalist base, and set up their headquarters nearby. At daybreak, the paratroopers began operations, clearing the east bank of the Ozama River, crossing the Duarte Bridge, and establishing a bridgehead in eastern Santo Domingo. Meanwhile, on the other side of the capital, the Marines maneuvered to establish a neutral International Security Zone (ISZ) around an area of the city that contained the US and other foreign embassies. Throughout the day, the Leathernecks and paratroopers both received small-arms fire and took their first casualties, but by Friday evening, they occupied secure positions. Separating them, however, was the bulk of the rebel force, which was firmly lodged in Ciudad Nueva in the southeastern corner of the capital.

A fragile cease-fire had been negotiated that afternoon, but virtually all involved regarded it as nothing more than a temporary respite from the bloodshed. Given the likelihood of renewed fighting, the new US commander on the ground, Army Lieutenant General Bruce Palmer, concluded that the wide gap separating US paratroopers manning the Ozama bridgehead from Marines in the ISZ was militarily unacceptable. Thus, while Loyalists and Constitutionalists regrouped, and as additional US forces, including two more brigades from the 82d Airborne, flowed into the country, Palmer requested and finally received permission from Washington to close the gap. At one minute after midnight on 3 May, a brigade from the 82d moved out of the bridgehead and began "leapfrogging" across a predetermined route that ran slightly north of the main rebel positions in Ciudad Nueva. A little over an hour later, a linkup with the Marines took place. The result of the operation was to create a corridor, or Line of Communication (LOC), that, once inundated with US troops, isolated most of the rebels in Ciudad Nueva.[6]

Realizing that the rebels could no longer achieve their goals through the use of force, the Johnson administration concluded that a military solution to the crisis was no longer necessary or wise. US interests in the area, the president and his advisers believed, would be best served by a stable, noncommunist Dominican Republic. A military victory over the rebels would certainly neutralize the communist elements who, US officials continued to argue, had seized control of the revolt,[7] but such a course of action would not redress the legitimate grievances held by large numbers of noncommunist Dominicans who supported the rebel movement. A military solution thus contained the seeds of future conflict, not the basis for long-term stability. The alternative was a political settlement that would appeal to as broad a range of Dominicans as possible, save for extremist elements on both sides.

Initial attempts at peacemaking by various emissaries from LBJ and representatives from the Organization of American States (OAS) produced few positive results. More successful were efforts by the Johnson administration to affix a fig leaf of regional legitimacy to what, in the beginning, had clearly been a naked case of unilateral intervention. Virtually ignoring the United Nations, where a Soviet veto in the Security Council could readily scuttle any US demarche in Santo Domingo, Washington concentrated on obtaining OAS support for the intervention. With prodding from US diplomats, OAS foreign ministers voted 15-5 on May 6 to create a multinational force, ultimately called the Inter-American Peace Force (IAPF), for the purpose of "cooperating in the restoration of normal conditions in the Dominican Republic, maintaining the security of its inhabitants and the inviolability of human rights, and the establishment of an atmosphere of peace and conciliation that will permit the functioning of democratic institutions."[8] To the thousands of US troops in Santo Domingo who would be integrated into the IAPF, the OAS action added nearly 2,000 soldiers, *guardia nacional*, military police, and staff officers from six Latin American countries (Brazil, Honduras, Nicaragua, Paraguay, Costa Rica, and El Salvador). Brazilian General Hugo Panasco Alvim arrived in the Dominican capital in late May to assume command of this multilateral, hemispheric force.[9]

In mid-May, before the IAPF became fully operational, Loyalist troops controlled by the Government of National Reconciliation (GNR), a US-backed entity that had been hastily cobbled together after the Constitutionalist "congress" had elected Caamaño "president" on 4 May, maneuvered around US positions in the capital to clear out pockets of rebel resistance north of the LOC. The "president" of the GNR, General Antonio Imbert, then demanded that his forces be allowed to pass through the US-held corridor to finish off the main body of rebels in Ciudad Nueva. To his surprise and dismay, Washington not only refused the demand but issued General Palmer orders to prevent the GNR from mounting any kind of attack against the rebel stronghold. These instructions marked the point in the crisis at which the Johnson administration, despite the president's previous professions of US impartiality, actually adopted a neutral posture, in deed as well as in print. In Santo Domingo, American troops began training their guns on both rebel *and GNR* positios. Having come so close to achieving a military victory, Imbert and other conservative Dominican officers, most of whom had come to take US encouragement and support for granted, fumed over their setback, but Washington had made its point: following the "cleanup" operations in northern Santo Domingo, the Johnson administration's desire for a political settlement would override most entreaties to cut the Loyalists more slack militarily. As GNR leaders came to realize that the military option was no longer any more open to them than it was to rebel forces, the prospects for a political solution improved.

In early June, the arrival of a three-man OAS Ad Hoc Committee, led by the US ambassador to the OAS, Ellsworth Bunker, signaled the beginning of serious diplomatic negotiations. The talks were grueling and took place amid almost daily sniping incidents and cease-fire violations. But Bunker was persistent, and after drawing moderate Dominican leaders into the peacemaking process, his committee was able to forge a tenuous agreement in August, followed by the establishment of a new provisional government in September and promises to hold national elections within a year. To maintain order until then, the OAS put its peace force at the disposal of the provisional president. Consequently, the IAPF took on the tasks of disarming rebel forces, escorting extremist leaders out of the country, and protecting the temporary head of state from left-wing and right-wing challenges to his authority. When elections were held in June 1966, Joaquín Balaguer defeated Juan Bosch to become the new Dominican president, an office he had occupied during the last days of the Trujillo regime. After Balaguer was sworn in, remaining US and IAPF troops made arrangements to leave the country, the last units departing in late September.

Unity of Effort

The Dominican crisis had arisen literally overnight, but before it was one week old, Santo Domingo had been inundated with foreign troops and diplomats. The haste with which the intervention had been mounted precluded any one group or government from forging a consensus on what course of action, either military or political, was best suited to end the revolt. There was a good deal of communication and coordination in which concerned officials discussed various approaches, but so long as the situation remained highly unstable, these exchanges produced no general agreement on how to proceed. Indeed, confusion would dominate the first weeks of the crisis, as different groups often found themselves working at cross-purposes.

One of the first steps toward creating the unity of effort needed to manage the situation effectively was to ensure that existing command arrangements worked as they should and that modifications to any chain of command serve to enhance the prospects for resolving the crisis. For US participants, military and civilian, the formal lines of authority were fairly well drawn from the outset. On the military side, orders from the president and secretary of defense were conveyed by the Chairman of the Joint Chiefs of Staff (JCS) to the Commander-in-Chief of the US Atlantic Command (CINCLANT), a Navy admiral. Headquartered in Norfolk, Virginia, the Atlantic Command

(LANTCOM) had responsibility for US military operations in the Atlantic Ocean and the Caribbean Sea. For the first two weeks of the crisis, CINCLANT, in turn, issued orders down the chain to the next link, a Joint Task Force (JTF) commanded by a US Navy vice-admiral who exercised operational control over separate task forces of US Marine and US Army units in the Dominican Republic. After General Palmer arrived on 1 May, a series of interim command relations were implemented until 7 May, when the JTF was deactivated, and Palmer assumed a position under CINCLANT as Commander, U.S. Land Forces, Dominican Republic.

This military chain of command worked well enough, although not without a few snags. One stemmed from early attempts by the Chairman of the JCS, Army General Earle Wheeler, to cut CINCLANT out of the military chain, or at least to diminish his influence in it. Wheeler was irritated by what he perceived as the slowness and inaccuracy of reports on the crisis he was receiving from the JTF on the scene through LANTCOM. To streamline the command structure and to encourage more timely reporting, Wheeler told Palmer just prior to the latter's departure from Washington for Santo Domingo to report to him directly via "backchannel" messages. When the new CINCLANT, Admiral Thomas Moorer, got wind of the arrangement, he threatened to have Palmer relieved of command unless the general reported directly to Norfolk, thus allowing CINCLANT to frame how the reports would be passed up the chain. Palmer complied, although he continued to keep Wheeler informed by sending routine "info copies" of his messages directly to the JCS.[10]

Once Palmer arrived in Santo Domingo, he discovered the impact modern communications could have on the formal command structure. In short, if the president of the United States wished to by-pass officers in the military chain and talk directly to people on the scene of a crisis, he could and would do so. Thus, soon after Palmer set foot on Dominican soil, he found himself talking directly to President Johnson on a variety of issues of concern to the White House. This disruption of the formal chain of command could work to Palmer's benefit when he needed approval from higher authorities to execute what he considered to be an urgent undertaking, but it could also sow confusion if key officers in the chain remained ignorant of the information exchanged or agreements reached in this manner.

The activation of the IAPF in late May further complicated military command arrangements. As officials discussed how the peace force would be organized, Palmer strongly asserted his conviction that it should be commanded by a US officer, lest the United States lose much of its freedom of action in the crisis. The Johnson administration was sympathetic to Palmer's position, but overruled the general when the OAS insisted that the commander be a Latin American. Palmer thus became the IAPF's deputy commander, a position infused with potential conflicts of interest. When asked by newsmen what he would do if he received conflicting instructions from the IAPF commander and from the US president, the general allowed that he was bound by oath to obey the latter. The remark evoked protests from the OAS, and Palmer received strict instructions not to comment further on the issue. As things worked out, he had little reason to do so. Although General Alvim became the IAPF commander, Palmer, as deputy commander, retained virtual control over all US forces in the Dominican Republic. Also, by the time Alvim arrived in Santo Domingo, he inherited along with the IAPF standard a staff organization set up by Palmer with the intention of ensuring US leverage in any IAPF initiative.[11]

As with the military command structure, the chain of command under which US civilian officials operated during the crisis was well defined on paper but abridged sometimes in practice. The State Department generally served as the conduit for passing information between the US embassy and the White House, but the president and his advisers also relied on their own direct communications, reports from Pentagon and CIA crisis groups, and special emissaries outside the formal chain to keep themselves informed or to undertake various initiatives. During the first month or so of the crisis, Ambassador Bennett, as the senior US diplomat in Santo Domingo, generally orchestrated US policy on the scene, although his authority in this area was occasionally diluted by the presence of presidential envoys or special delegations. Furthermore, once the OAS Ad Hoc Committee arrived on 4 June, Bennett, in Palmer's words, found himself "definitely playing second fiddle" to Ambassador Bunker.[12]

That Palmer was in a position to render this observation indicates the extent to which he was involved in a politico-military operation. From the outset of the intervention, coordination between US military and civilian officials in Santo Domingo was exemplary. US commanders received their orders through the military chain of command, but on certain critical issues, including the timing and extent of the troop deployments, they were made to understand that they would take their directions from Ambassador Bennett. One of Palmer's first moves after arriving in the country was to meet with the ambassador, after which the general ordered that his headquarters be moved from San Isidro to a location next door to the embassy. During the move, Bennett offered Palmer the use of his living quarters and his communications facilities. Thereafter, the two conferred daily to exchange information and discuss the situation. They did not always agree on the wisdom of a given course of action, both recounted several heated arguments carried on behind closed doors, and each knew that the other was not always forthcoming with information received through his chain of command. Yet, circumstances, compatible personalities, and the conservative leanings of both men made for an amicable and professional working relationship that would be sustained throughout the crisis and establish the basis for a life-long friendship.

The establishment of effective chains of command and methods of coordination did not necessarily translate into unity of effort when it came to determining what courses of action to take in resolving the crisis. To begin with, there was the military question: Should US troops remove the rebel threat by armed force? Bennett, Palmer, and Major General Robert York, commander of the 82d Airborne Division, initially entertained few doubts that President Johnson would approve the combat option. When, instead, LBJ decided in favor of a political settlement, Palmer and York continued to plan for military operations against rebel locations both north of the LOC and in Ciudad Nueva. While prudence alone would have dictated such contingency planning, both generals, with the ambassador in agreement, continued to believe that military operations posed the most effective way of preventing a communist takeover of the country. As late as mid-May, just prior to the GNR offensive north of the LOC, Palmer and York were still lobbying for a US attack on key rebel positions in that part of the capital.[13]

Gradually, Palmer came to see the wisdom of a negotiated settlement over a military solution to the crisis, although the president's decision to seek a long-term political agreement acceptable to the vast majority of Dominicans was not accompanied by a blueprint on how that objective might be achieved. Within the administration, opinions on the course negotiations should follow were divided, generally with liberals and conservatives lining up against one another. The subsequent bureaucratic infighting undermined early efforts to arrange a diplomatic settlement, as presidential emissary McGeorge Bundy would have occasion to testify. Johnson's national security adviser and his entourage arrived in Santo Domingo in mid-May with the assignment of finding some prominent Dominican, not closely identified with either of the warring factions, around whom a coalition government could be created. Bundy settled on Sylvestre Antonio Guzmán, a political moderate, as deserving of this honor, but progress toward this end was thwarted by conservative US officials who, along with Imbert, were convinced that a government headed by Guzmán, a member of Juan Bosch's political party, would be susceptible to communist domination. When Guzmán's own behavior seemed to give weight to these allegations, criticism of the proposed appointment reached such intensity that Bundy had to concede the futility of his mission.[14] Ironically, the failure of the "Guzmán gambit" enhanced prospects for a political solution to the crisis. Soon after Bundy's return to Washington on 26 May, the Johnson administration decided to work through the OAS to obtain a peace settlement. Unity of effort, so elusive thus far in the Dominican intervention, was about to be realized.

On 4 June, the OAS Ad Hoc Committee led by Ellsworth Bunker arrived in Santo Domingo. From the outset, Bunker made it clear that he was his "own man," not an agent of the State Department, and that his dual status as the committee's principal delegate and as the US ambassador to the OAS meant that he spoke officially for both the OAS *and* the US government. He met daily with Bennett and Palmer to exchange information and to discuss developments, but it was clear that considered himself in charge. He intended, according to Palmer, "to tell Washington what should be done rather than the other way around." If any US official in Santo Domingo or Washington questioned his negotiating strategy or proposals, he would patiently employ his ample powers of persuasion to win over the critic. Failing that, he would simply refer the matter to the White House, where LBJ would invariably decide in his favor. Once Bunker's compatriots realized that he had the complete backing of the president, the political infighting characteristic of the early phases of the crisis dropped off markedly.[15]

The breakthrough in the peace process came on 30 August when both sides to the conflict accepted the OAS sponsored Act of Reconciliation. Under the terms of the agreement, a new provisional government would be set up under Héctor García-Godoy, a Dominican businessman and diplomat, the rebels would disarm in return for amnesty, the regular military would return to its bases, and general elections would be held the following year. On 3 September, García-Godoy took the oath of office. Over the course of the next several months, however, he faced one challenge after another to his fragile government, prompting the OAS to place the IAPF at his disposal for the purposes of peace enforcement. In taking this step, Bunker and other OAS representatives assumed that the IAPF commander, General Alvim, and his deputy, General Palmer, would carry out the orders they received from García-Godoy.

The assumption was open to question. Alvim and Palmer did not always see eye-to-eye, but on one point, they were in complete agreement: García-Godoy was a poor choice for the provisional presidency. Both generals regarded the new Dominican leader as a weak man, ever too eager to make disastrous concessions to rebel factions on the extreme left. Despite this conviction, Alvim and Palmer generally did what they were ordered to do on behalf of the provisional government. In those instances when they questioned the wisdom of a course of action, they might appeal over García-Godoy's head to Bunker, hoping that the ambassador would either dissuade the Dominican president or approve what they considered to be a more sensible course of action. On one occasion, the two generals took more extreme action. When the Dominican leader ordered the IAPF to move against his conservative military chiefs, Alvim refused to comply and Palmer wanted a decision from Washington. Both men finally relented, but the incident convinced Bunker that Alvim had to go, and he arranged to have the Brazilian general recalled. As a means of saving face for Alvim, Palmer was ordered home as well. Another Brazilian general assumed command of the IAPF, while Palmer's chief of staff moved into the deputy's position.[16] The unity of effort in evidence since the summer remained intact, despite the close call.

Legitimacy

If the perceived legitimacy of a peace operation is determined by the support it receives from the participating nations, the belligerents, and the people affected by it, one would have to conclude that the Dominican intervention lacked legitimacy in its early phases. The unilateral commitment of US troops and, despite public professions of neutrality, the open support they and the Johnson administration gave to the Loyalist faction alienated OAS representatives, several members of Congress and the media, Constitutionalist leaders and their armed followers, and undetermined portions of the Dominican public (although a good number of the latter expressed relief that the wholesale bloodshed of the civil strife subsided after the arrival of the US forces). Over time, the peace force in the Dominican Republic acquired a significant degree of legitimacy, although the process of reversing initial impressions occurred only gradually and fell far short of winning over all the critics. Extremist leaders on both sides, for example, could never accept a peace process that was expressly designed to exclude them from political power, even remove them from the country, and Dominican nationalists could never accommodate themselves to foreign troops on their soil. Outside the country, many Latin Americans refused to place anti-communism above their aversion to US intervention in hemispheric disputes, and within the United States, the Johnson administration's critics in Congress and the media continued to accuse it of displaying an "arrogance of power" and of creating a "credibility gap" between its actions and its public pronouncements.

Still, by summer 1965, the peace operation had gained in stature and had won over many of its early opponents. To begin with, the Johnson administration, in jettisoning its blatantly pro-Loyalist position, had made it possible for US forces to hold both sides to the conflict in check and to impose the "rules of the road" evenhandedly on all belligerents. Some rebels questioned US neutrality, while many Loyalists resented it, but after late May, neither side could find evidence that American troops were openly partial to the other. Various humanitarian activities carried out by US soldiers and Marines, such as the impartial distribution of food and the provision of medical supplies and basic urban services, mitigated the hostility many Dominicans felt toward them. Throughout the intervention, mass rallies and other civil disturbances would be staged to protest the presence of the foreign soldiers, but these events were usually contained by troops specialized in riot control methods designed to defuse potentially dangerous situations before they escalated into uncontrolled violence. Another means by which the US command sought to convey its good intentions was to take prompt legal action against individual Marines and soldiers who committed criminal acts against Dominican citizens or property. Strict rules of engagement were also enforced to minimize the chances of innocent citizens being wounded or killed during the course of military operations in a congested urban area. Finally, the arrival of the Latin American contingents of the IAPF and, after September, assigning them some of the more delicate tasks in enforcing the fragile peace agreement contributed to the perceived legitimacy of the overall operation.[17]

Getting the OAS to support the peace effort, to create the IAPF, and to take the lead in the peace negotiations also contributed to the intervention's legitimacy, both within the OAS and among the American and Dominican people. So, too, did the manner in which the peace settlement was negotiated and implemented. Ambassador Bunker was clearly determined to work out an accord that all but the extremist elements in Dominican society could live with, and the Act of Reconciliation contained concessions to both Loyalist and Constitutionalist demands. In helping to enforce the agreement, the IAPF generally acted evenhandedly, even when Alvim and Palmer, as previously noted, questioned the wisdom of certain moves that, in their opinion, seemed to enhance the stature of the radical left. Above all, the elections of 1966 legitimized the peace process, as power was transferred via the ballot box from the provisional government to that of President Balaguer.

Support to Belligerents

The rebel movement that coalesced as a result of the 24 April revolt attracted support from many quarters of Dominican society--disaffected workers, politicians, reformers and revolutionaries, businessmen, officers and enlisted men, middle class professionals, and so on. Those who took to the streets during the fighting in and around Santo Domingo armed themselves with antiquated US weapons located at friendly military bases or seized from unfriendly ones. In this respect, the revolt was home grown and, with some notable exceptions, confined to the capital city. External support was virtually nonexistent. Some of the rebels had received training in Cuba, and that country and the Soviet Union together voiced strong moral support for the Constitutionalist cause. Support of a more tangible nature, however, was not forthcoming. Once the intervention got underway, the United States mounted air and naval patrols of the Dominican coastline to block any attempts to infiltrate arms and men to the rebels. US Special Forces, dressed in civilian clothes, also fanned out into cities and towns around the country in a successful effort to monitor local support for the revolt and to gather information on possible outside assistance.[18] Paratroopers, MPs, and other troops in the LOC also interdicted the small number of locally procured weapons being smuggled to the rebels in Ciudad Nueva via automobiles and the city's sewer system. By the time peace talks began, the bulk of the rebels were surrounded and cut off from any potential source of external military assistance.

The Loyalist junta likewise enjoyed the initial backing of large segments of Dominican society and also possessed weapons received through US assistance programs. What external support the junta received came from US sources during the first weeks of the crisis. The Loyalist attack on the rebel provisional government on 25 April had the "reluctant" approval of the American embassy, and the Johnson administration acceded to the junta's urgent requests for communications equipment and, ultimately, US troops. When the first elements of the 82d Airborne Division arrived at San Isidro, General York and his staff worked closely with the Loyalist generals, keeping them apprised of pending operations and occasionally making use of their troops.[19] This ill-concead show of solidarity with the junta proved costly, however, as the news media charged US officials with duplicity and as many Dominicans came to view the American force as blatantly partial to one side. Clearly, Washington could not continue to support the Loyalists and, at the same time, hope to negotiate a lasting peace. Thus, once it became evident that communist elements within the rebel movement were not in a position to take over the country, and once GNR forces had cleared pockets of rebel troops out of northern Santo Domingo, the United States assumed a neutral posture. The switch came so suddenly in mid-May that US forces had to turn their guns against General Imbert's soldiers and pilots in order to prevent the stunned and incredulous Loyalists from mounting further operations against the rebels. Relations with Imbert's men deteriorated further when the IAPF on several occasions before and after the peace agreement accused the GNR of flagrant cease-fire violations. Finally, whatever lingering hopes for preferential treatment Loyalist leaders still harbored dissipated when several of their number were encouraged to leave the country, often with an IAPF escort.

Support Actions of Peace Forces

Together with the unity of effort forged by the United States and the OAS in seeking to resolve the Dominican crisis through a moderate, inclusive political settlement, the factor most critical to the success of the intervention was the determination of the US and Latin American participants to stay the course until the peace agreement could be negotiated, implemented, and secured. The sheer size of the IAPF served as a signal of this determination, as the belligerents in the civil conflict were made to realize that they did not possess the wherewithal to challenge the peace force militarily.

What may seem surprising from the perspective of the 1990s is that neither belligerent resorted to terrorism or propaganda in an attempt to undermine the American public's support for the continuing US presence in the Dominican Republic. Such present mindedness, however, must be reined in. In 1965, the use of terror tactics against armed and vigilant troops was not perceived as a pervasive or serious threat, despite Viet Cong activity in Vietnam (especially the February 6 attack on the US base at Pleiku) and the status accorded terrorism in Fidel Castro's schools for guerrilla fighters. Sniper fire, the occasional grenade, and the possibility of small-unit attacks--not rebel truck bombs--were what concerned Marines and paratroopers manning defensive positions in the LOC. As for the possibility of a terrorist act or an anti-imperialistic propaganda campaign undermining America's "will" to stay the course in Santo Domingo, the notion would have seemed ludicrous to Americans and Dominicans alike. When, four years before the intervention, President John F. Kennedy had proclaimed in his inaugural address that the American people would "pay any price, bear any burden, meet any hardship, support any friend, oppose any foe to assure the survival and success of liberty,"[20] the was merely reaffirming the Cold War consensus shared unquestioningly by the overwhelming majority of his countrymen. The Dominican crisis would create the first small chink in that consensus, but although the critics of President Johnson's so-called "arrogance of power" were vocal, they were few in number. The Cold War consensus would wither in the jungles of Vietnam, not in the streets of Santo Domingo.

With little pressure to "bring the boys home," with low casualty figures (27 Americans were killed in action during the year-and-a-half occupation), with criticism of the intervention confined to a limited number of voices in Congress and the news media, and with Cold War defense budgets at all time highs, the Johnson administration encountered no serious problems in sustaining the political and logistical support required to keep US troops in Santo Domingo as long as they were needed. At the time of the intervention, no party to the conflict was under any illusion that the troops would be withdrawn before they had attained their objective.[21]

Military Actions of Peace Forces

At its peak, the level of US troops in the Dominican Republic numbered nearly 24,000. The Latin American Brigade of the IAPF added about another 2,000.[22] Unlike Operation Just Cause nearly twenty-five years later in Panama, these numbers were not achieved within a couple of days through a lightning strike of a massive invasion force. Rather, the troop buildup in the Dominican intervention was gradual, not reaching its apex until mid-May. While this piecemeal increase of US and Latin American peace forces entailed several disadvantages, in that certain programs critical to the peace process could not be initiated until specialized units had arrived on the scene, the Marine contingent and the Army combat brigades that launched the intervention were, in fact, of sufficient strength to prevent either side, but especially the rebels, from mounting any concerted military resistance to their presence or, in the case of the Loyalists, from attaining any undue military advantage without US approval.

When US combat forces entered Santo Domingo in late April and early May, they found a city wracked by chaos and anarchy. Bodies were strewn in the streets, public services had ceased to function, the specter of hunger and disease hovered ominously, and effective government had come to a virtual standstill. In an effort to relieve the suffering they encountered, Marines and paratroopers shared their food with the Dominican people and provided what medical assistance they could. These initial efforts were ad hoc and poorly coordinated, but they did help to alleviate a desperate situation. More substantial and formal programs would begin once the first civil affairs, military police, and engineer units began arriving in the country, together with civilian officials experienced in running humanitarian and relief programs. As Dominican citizens lined up at food distribution points and medical stations, American MPs worked to create a semblance of law and order and to stop weapons smuggling across the LOC, US military engineers and civil affairs personnel labored to repair and restore power, water, sanitation, and communications to the capital, other civil affairs officers worked with those Dominican officials who were receptive to their help in getting government offices and financial institutions running again, and peace forces established a guns-for-money program. None of these efforts proceeded without friction: Army engineers balked at having to collect garbage, several Dominican administrators refused to cooperate with foreign soldiers and officials, US military and civilian specialists often found themselves duplicating one another's efforts or working at cross-purposes, and few belligerents turned in their weapons voluntarily, even for cash. Still, life slowly returned to normal in the capital, as US "stability operations" reduced the suffering, and as the presence of the IAPF eased fears of renewed conflict and raised hopes for a peaceful resolution to the crisis.[23]

To reinforce these expectations and to reduce chances that extremists within the belligerent camps might provoke an incident to derail the peace process, IAPF troops, often to their dismay, operated under strict rules of engagement and were ordered by their superiors to exercise restraint, even when confronted by snipers' bullets or demonstrators' bricks.[24] The peace force was also restricted in the type of weapons it could employ. Early in the intervention, the use of mortars and artillery was prohibited, for fear of igniting a conflagration in the capital. For the most part, the IAPF employed small arms and riot control devices, although a tank company was brought into the country at Palmer's request, primarily for its psychological, not its military, impact.

Not all US military personnel participating in the intervention performed their missions openly. As part of an operation code-named Green Chopper, US Special Forces, as previously noted, donned civilian clothes and took up residency in several dozen cities and towns throughout the country. Their reports reinforced what the CIA chief of station in Santo Domingo had been saying from the outset of the crisis: the countryside was for the most part quiet; the fate of the Dominican revolt would be determined in the capital city. Green Berets and Navy SEALs also operated in Santo Domingo, where they assisted in civic action programs, helped collect intelligence, and engaged in a number of clandestine activities, such as the sabotage of rebel communications facilities. In the mid-1960s, Special Forces were just beginning to be used for counterinsurgency and stability operations. Palmer, although not entirely comfortable with the unorthodox forces under his command, pronounced them "invaluable adjuncts" to the activities of the conventional troops.[25]

Military Actions of the Belligerents and the Peace Forces

The peace force that provided the military muscle in support of OAS initiatives in the crisis was, in general, a highly professional outfit. The participating US units were well trained and disciplined. If some of them were not wholly prepared for the kind of political-military situation they encountered, they learned quickly, if sometimes reluctantly, to adapt. The Latin American contingent to the IAPF presented a lesson in contrasts. The Brazilian troops that composed the bulk of the force were excellent, while the Honduran contingent arrived lacking many of the bare essentials for carrying out their mission. (The United States provided the required supplies and, where necessary, training.)[26]

What was critical for the successful outcome of the Dominican intervention was that neither belligerent could match the IAPF in professionalism, weapons, and numbers. Once Palmer received orders in mid-May to stop further Loyalist advances, the US command's erstwhile "allies" became decidedly less friendly, but limited their displeasure to mortar rounds fired at rebel positions (in cease-fire violations investigated by the Latin American Brigade). The GNR made no attempt to force its way through IAPF lines into Ciudad Nueva. The Constitutionalists in their small commando-type units also produced few martyrs. The rebels recognized their position of inferiority and, for the most part, confined their hostile activities to propaganda, street demonstrations, and sniper fire aimed at the IAPF. On the one occasion when a sniping incident escalated into a major firefight between US and Constitutionalist forces on 15 June, General York turned units of the 82d loose against key rebel positions and came within a few hours of pushing Caamaño's men into the Ozama River. Knowing that President Johnson desired a political settlement to the crisis, Palmer hastened to the scene of the fighting and, in an animated face-to-face exchange, ordered York to stop the attack. York, whose sympathies for the Loyalist cause were well-known, was recalled from the country soon thereafter, but in such a way that did not prejudice his career.[27]

The peace settlement called for the United States to take the lead in reintegrating, reforming, reorganizing, and, in short, professionalizing the Dominican armed forces, but the political tensions that afflicted the provisional government of García-Godoy stalled early steps in this direction, as did the growing US preoccupation with Vietnam by late 1965. Over the years, both the Dominican police and military would improve their performance, but not to the degree anticipated by the peacemakers.

Actions Targeted on Ending Conflict

In addition to the civic action, civil affairs, humanitarian and relief programs, military operations, and diplomatic initiatives already mentioned, the peace force in the Dominican Republic engaged in a variety of other activities that, each in its own way, contributed to the resolution of the crisis. When US troops first entered the country, military intelligence on the situation was virtually nonexistent. At the national level, the State Department, the Department of Defense, and the CIA set up crisis action teams for sharing information, but with the CIA busy compiling lists for the White House of communist participants in the revolt, intelligence officers on the scene began the painstaking process of collecting operational and tactical information. Aerial reconnaissance provided some material, but more would have to come from human intelligence (HUMINT), the networks for which were virtually nonexistent. This shortfall presented few problems with respect to obtaining information about the Loyalists, given the cooperation that existed with them in the first weeks of the crisis, but rebel informants would have to be identified, contacted, and debriefed. Facilities were also needed in which rebel "detainees" could be interrogated. All of this took time, but by mid-May, US commanders believed they had acquired fairly accurate orders of battle and other pertinent information about the opposing forces.[28]

As intelligence accumulated, the peace force was better able to anticipate problems, such as organized street demonstrations, and to mount psychological operations aimed at winning acceptance for the IAPF mission and the peace settlement. Essential in the battle for "hearts and minds" was the equipment--particularly the military vehicles mounted with loud speakers--provided by US PSYWAR units. Unfortunately, even the best equipment could not compensate for pamphlets, newsletters, and broadcasts whose content was heavy-handed and far from persuasive. Friction in the working relationship between PSYWAR officers and their civilian counterparts in the US Information Service added to the problem. Surveying the overall impact of the information war, Palmer glumly labeled the Americans "amateurs" in using propaganda as a weapon.[29]

Looking at the overall situation, however, one would have to draw a more favorable verdict on the way in which the US government, the OAS, and the IAPF combined diplomatic skill, the effective use of intelligence, fairly successful attempts to project a positive image, and a variety of humanitarian programs to lower tensions and to create the atmosphere in which a peace settlement could be negotiated and implemented. If some of these efforts took time to reach their full potential, the presence of overwhelming military force in the form of US and Latin American troops bought whatever time was needed.

Conclusion

The US intervention in the Dominican Republic in 1965 has been denounced as a blatant demonstration of neo-imperialist arrogance and praised as a peace operation that put an end to indiscriminate bloodshed and opened the door for political democracy and economic stability. There is some truth to both arguments. In ordering troops into the Dominican Republic, President Johnson pushed aside various commitments not to interfere in the internal affairs of other countries in the hemisphere and launched the first overt US military intervention in Latin America in over 30 years. By taking this action, however, he helped set the stage for an experiment in Dominican democracy that is still underway as of this writing. The goal of US policy during the intervention was to produce long-term stability in a noncommunist Dominican Republic. By that standard, the intervention was a success, at least from Washington's perspective, even though no one then or today would claim that progress in the political arena was matched by similar breakthroughs in alleviating the country's social and economic problems.

This essay has attempted to analyze how certain key factors--the "Max Factors"-- influenced the successful outcome of the Dominican intervention. Briefly stated, unity of effort, the use of overwhelming force, a commitment to stay the course, and the decision to seek a political settlement acceptable to a majority of Dominicans were crucial elements that shaped the course of events. If applied with caution, this information might be of use in formulating policy for future operations, so long as the uniqueness and complexity of the Dominican intervention (indeed, each and every politico-military operation) are not overlooked, and so long as expectations are tempered by the sentiment Dean Acheson evoked when he attributed the outcome of the Cuban Missile Crisis to "pure dumb luck."

Notes

[1] This essay is based primarily on material in my account of the Dominican crisis, *Power Pack: US Intervention in the Dominican Republic, 1965-1966*, Leavenworth Paper No. 15 (Fort Leavenworth, KS: Combat Studies Institute, 1988), and in a memoir published a year later by General Bruce Palmer, Jr., *Intervention in the Caribbean: The Dominican Crisis of 1965* (Lexington, KY: University Press of Kentucky, 1989). Further analyses of the crisis can be found in Piero Gleijeses, *The Dominican Crisis: The 1965 Constitutionalist Revolt and American Intervention* (Baltimore: Johns Hopkins University Press, 19780: Lawrence M. Greenberg, *United States Army Unilateral and Coalition Operations in the 1965 Dominican Republic Intervention* (Washington, DC: US Army Center of Military History, 1987); Abraham F. Lowenthal, *The Dominican Intervention* (Cambridge, MA: Harvard University Press, 1972); John Bartlow Martin, *Overtaken by Events: The Dominican Crisis from the Fall of Trujillo to the Civil War* (Garden City, NY: Doubleday & Co., 1966); Herbert G. Schoonmaker, *Military Crisis Management: US Intervention in the Dominican Republic, 1965* (Westport, CT: Greenwood Press, 1990); Jerome N. Slater, *Intervention and Negotiation: The United States and the Dominican Revolution* (New York: Harper & Row, 1970).

[2] Quoted material in this paragraph is taken from Telegram no. 1051, American Embassy, Santo Domingo, to Secretary of State, 25 April 1965, National Security Council History of the Dominican Crisis, Lyndon B. Johnson Library, Austin, Texas.

[3] Yates, *Power Pack*, 37-39, 41-43.

[4] Bennett had been in Georgia visiting his seriously ill mother when the crisis erupted. Upon receiving reports of the revolt, he traveled to Washington for consultations, then headed back to Santo Domingo. Regarding the events of Tuesday afternoon, he maintained then and later that he lacked authority to mediate the crisis.

[5] Yates, *Power Pack*, 46-53, 55, 65-69.

[6] Details of these initial military activities by US troops between 20 April and 3 May can be found in *ibid.*, 78-96.

[7] The exact number of communists involved in the Dominican revolt and the degree of influence they exerted over it has never been determined. Some recent assessments simply argue that communist involvement and influence was greater than conceded by the rebels and less than imagined by the Johnson administration.

[8] Quoted in David Wainhouse, *International Peacekeeping at the Crossroads* (Baltimore: Johns Hopkins University Press, 1973), 472.

[9] The IAPF was the first hemispheric multilateral peace force to be created and deployed by the OAS. Some US military officers and political advisers hoped that the IAPF could be institutionalized or, in the event of another crisis, resurrected. Both hopes proved unrealistic, in that many Latin Americans, in regarding the IAPF as an instrument that violated the principle of noninterventionism, had no wish to repeat the experiment. The administration of President Jimmy Carter found this out in the late 1970s when it proposed a new "IAPF" to oversee a post-Somoza transition in Nicaragua. See Robert A. Pastor, *Condemned to Repetition: The United States and Nicaragua* (Princeton, NJ: Princeton University Press, 1987), 145. It should also be noted, however, that multilateral forces containing hemispheric elements were employed by

the Organization of East Caribbean States in Grenada and approved by the OAS for use under the UN in El Salvador and Haiti.

[10] Palmer, *Intervention in the Caribbean*, 43-44; Yates, *Power Pack*, 86.

[11] Palmer, *Intervention in the Caribbean*, 73-75, 77-79; Yates, *Power Pack*, 149-54, 208 n15; Greenberg, *Unilateral and Coalition Operations*, 74.

[12] Palmer, *Intervention in the Caribbean*, 84.

[13] On contingency planning for US operations north of the LOC, see Yates, *Power Pack*, 114-15.

[14] Palmer, *Intervention in the Caribbean*, 57-58. A short summary of Bundy's mission can be found in Jerome Slater, "The Dominican Republic, 1965-66," in Barry M. Blechman and Stephen S. Kaplan, eds., *Force without War: U.S. Armed Forces as a Political Instrument* (Washington, DC: The Brookings Institution, 1978), 322-24. (Guzmán, it might be noted, was elected president of the Dominican Republic in 1978.)

In addition to presidential emissaries from the United States, diplomats representing the OAS were also busy in Santo Domingo. While they generally coordinated their activities with US officials, they, too, suffered from the fact that no one person or group among them was authorized to speak for all. Consequently, they enjoyed no more success in arranging a settlement than did their US counterparts during the first days and weeks of the crisis.

[15] Palmer, *Intervention in the Caribbean*, 86-88; Yates, *Power Pack*, 145-46, 161-62.

[16] Yates, *Power Pack*, 166-69; Palmer, *Intervention in the Caribbean*, 129-31.

[17] US humanitarian and peace-keeping operations are covered in detail in Yates, *Power Pack*, chapters 6-8.

[18] The Special Forces mission, Operation Green Chopper, is discussed in *ibid*, 107-8.

[19] As an example of the coordination that took place between the junta and US officers, the military operations undertaken by the Marines and paratroopers on Friday, 30 April, were briefed in advance to Loyalist officers at San Isidro on instructions from Ambassador Bennett. A small Loyalist force was with the paratroopers at the bridgehead Friday night, mainly for the purpose of patrolling the gap between the 82d and the Marine positions in Santo Domingo. The lack of fire discipline on the part of this force, however, led a US colonel to request that the men be sent back to San Isidro. *Ibid*, 78; Palmer, *Intervention in the Caribbean*, 36, 196 n5.

[20] President Kennedy quoted in Theodore C. Sorensen, *Kennedy* (New York: Harper & Row, 1965), 246.

[21] The perception that the United States would stay the course in the Dominican Republic may have changed, however, had the intervention continued beyond 1966. In 1965, US involvement in the war in Vietnam increased dramatically, and as that conflict escalated, it siphoned off more and more of America's military manpower. By 1966, US units in the Dominican Republic had set up areas in which they could train for what they would be called on to do in Vietnam in the likelihood they would be sent there.

[22] With the arrival of the IAPF, however, the Marines began to redeploy back to the United States. Furthermore, over the following year, there would be a gradual withdrawal of various US Army units no longer needed in Santo Domingo or required elsewhere.

[23] Yates, *Power Pack*, chapters 6-8.

[24] US troops in Santo Domingo generally understood why they could not use artillery, mortars, and other heavy weapons. They also accepted with equanimity some limits on their use of small arms. But as rules of engagement (ROE) became more restrictive, to the point of prohibiting US troops from returning sniper fire or from firing on "enemy" soldiers unless US positions were in danger of being overrun, frustration mounted, as did confusion over the proliferation of ROE. Political considerations determined much of the ROE, but so did the commander on the scene. Soon after his arrival in Santo Domingo, Palmer spent one night at a Marine strong point in the LOC. Listening throughout the night to what struck him as indiscriminate fire on the part of the Leathernecks, he became convinced of the need for strict ROE. By the end of his tour, he still upheld the necessity for rules of engagement, although he conceded that they might have been excessive in some cases. *Ibid*, 140-43; Palmer, *Intervention in the Caribbean*, 52-53.

[25] Yates, *Power Pack*, 128-33, 206 n16.

[26] *Ibid*, 147-49.

[27] *Ibid*, 158-59; Palmer, *Intervention in the Caribbean*, 80-83, 200 n11.

[28] Yates, *Power Pack*, 101-8.

[29] *Ibid*, 136-38

9

Peace Enforcement in Somalia: UNOSOM II

Thomas J. Daze & John T. Fishel

On 3 December 1992, the United Nations took an unprecedented step to resolve the problems of starvation, famine, and lawlessness in Somalia. It was significant in two regards. It was the first attempt by the international community to deal with the new post-Cold War phenomenon referred to as the "failed nation state." It has further significance in that the United Nations expanded its traditional role of Chapter VI peacekeeping operations to a more ambitious Chapter VII peace enforcement intervention authorizing participating states of the coalition to use "all necessary means" to execute the parameters of the Security Council mandates.[1]

By the Spring of 1993, what had begun as a mission to provide security for the delivery of humanitarian assistance was quickly evolving into one of nation building. However, the operation would undergo a major transformation in its structure and organization prior to taking on these new and substantially greater responsibilities. On May 4, 1993 the US led Unified Task Force (UNITAF) transferred civilian as well as military control of the Somalia operation to the United Nations. This transition was more than a change in leadership for it marked a planned turning point in the scope of the mission.

At transition the new mandate of UN Security Council Resolution (UNSCR) 814 came into effect. The narrowly focused mission of UNITAF, as executed by the Bush administration and its allies under UNSCR 794, had been to provide security for humanitarian relief efforts so that these endeavors could continue without further interruption and rescue a starving population. United Nations Operation in Somalia II's (UNOSOM II) stated mission in UNSCR 814 was not only to provide a secure environment for the continuation of humanitarian relief operations but also to provide the secure environment needed to allow the achievement of national reconciliation with the establishment of a transitional government as well as to advance economic rehabilitation. Significant tasks included the disarmament of the factions and the return of hundreds of thousands of refugees. These objectives implied a distinctly different end state from that of UNITAF with very different implications for the military forces committed to Somalia. UNITAF's short term mission ended with the successful delivery of humanitarian aid. UNOSOM II would end with the reestablishment of a functioning government.[2]

By its very nature, it was a mission which could place UN forces in direct opposition to one of the more belligerent clans which had been at war with each other for nearly two years. In particular, it would clash with Mohammed Farrah Hassan Aideed, a prominent clan leader who had his own political ambition for the end state of the nation, one that would establish him as head of the new government. Within a week following the transition of the mission to the UN, Aideed's militia skirmished with UN forces near the city of Kismayo. Three weeks later his militia initiated a deliberate ambush of UN forces in the capital, Mogadishu, resulting in the deaths of over thirty peacekeepers. This attack embroiled the UN in a protracted conflict that would ultimately end with the withdrawal of UNOSOM II from Somalia without accomplishing the mission given in its mandate.

This brief discussion sets forth the political and military context in which the UNOSOM II mission took place. The rest of this chapter explores that mission in terms of the several dimensions of the model. We begin with a consideration of Unity of Effort.

Unity of Effort

If a necessary but insufficient condition for achieving Unity of Effort is agreement on the objective of the operation among the parties to it, then UNOSOM II was in trouble from the beginning.[3] Although this operation had a clearer mandate than its predecessor, Restore Hope, it was plagued by the fact that the Clinton administration did not really know exactly what it had signed on to, any more than did the other participants. As the implications of the lack of analysis of the meaning of the mandate sank in, other players began to deny that they were, indeed, party to the agreement. The impact would only increase as time passed.

Lack of agreement about the meaning of the mandate was only compounded by the command relationships that structured UNOSOM II. It is instructive to point out the normal command relationships of a UN peacekeeping mission and then to address the way in which this operation deviated from the norm. United Nations operations usually employ a force under a single Force Commander appointed by the Secretary General with the approval of the Security Council.

The Force Commander reports either to the Special Representative of the Secretary General (SRSG) or directly to the Secretary General.[4] While this is the norm, if there is an SRSG, the Force Commander typically has a high degree of autonomy.[5]

UNOSOM II's first deviation from the norm was in the relationship between the SRSG and the Force Commander. At American insistence, the SRSG was the former Deputy National Security Advisor to the President of the United States, Admiral Jonathan Howe while the Force Commander was Lieutenant General Cevik Bir of Turkey, a NATO member. Moreover, the Deputy Force Commander was American Major General Thomas Montgomery who wore a second hat as Commander of US Forces in Somalia (COMUSFORSOM). This arrangement made for a much closer relationship among the principal leaders of the mission than usually is the case. Moreover, it gave a particularly strong leadership role to the SRSG and made the command relationships an American show in everything but name.

Below this level, the UNOSOM II Force Commander, General Bir, established operational and tactical control as the working command relationships for forces in Somalia. All national contingents were under the operational control of the Force Commander. He intended to exercise operational control of contingent forces through brigade commanders, each of whom had been assigned an area of responsibility. In practice, these command relationships and the UNOSOM II command and control structure proved ineffective. Some national contingents simply would not serve under the operational control of other contingent commanders. Instead, they would prefer to work "in coordination with" or "in cooperation with" other contingent forces.[6]

The multinational character of United Nations peace operations warrant particular attention. National interests and organizational influence may compete with doctrine and efficiency as well as the objective of the mission. Consensus building is difficult (and often contentious) and continuous, while solutions often are national in character. Commanders can expect contributing nations to adhere to national policies and priorities, which at times, can complicate the multinational effort.[7]

The command relationship between UNOSOM II and the US Quick Reaction Force (QRF), which was prescribed by the Commander in Chief, US Central Command and outlined in the Terms of Reference for US forces in Somalia (USFORSOM), illustrates the problem. The QRF, located in Somalia, was under the operational control of Central Command (CENTCOM). Tactical control of the QRF was delegated to the Commander, USFORSOM, for "normal training exercises within Somalia.... [and] in situations within Somalia that exceed the capability of UNOSOM II forces and required the emergency employment of immediate combat power for a limited period or show of force operations."[8] Any tasking for the.QRF outside these guidelines required explicit

CENTCOM approval. The terms of reference provided adequate flexibility for the UNOSOM II Deputy Force Commander to employ the QRF in emergency situations. However, to conduct critical, yet non-emergency, combat operations which exceeded the capability of UNOSOM II forces, the terms of reference proved to be quite inflexible.[9]

Thus, the American version of its grant of operational control of US forces to the Force Commander flew in the face of its own normal definition of operational control, which, in any case, was reserved by the CENTCOM commander. Needless to say, the grants of "operational control" by other force providers were similarly restrictive. As a result, when the mandate given by UNSCR 814 expanded due to the ambush of Pakistani peacekeepers on June 5, 1993 with the passage of UNSCR 837 the next day, several force providers indicated that they had not signed up for the capture of a factional leader. This was most true of Italy which maintained a unilateral, direct dialogue with the leaders of Mohammed Farrah Aideed's militia.

In short, Unity of Effort was not achieved by UNOSOM II as a result of two critical factors. First, whatever agreement on the objective that had existed broke down following the passage of UNSCR 837, largely due to the fact that the force providers were not consulted. Second, the command and control arrangements were flawed, especially with respect to US participation which was circumscribed by the American failure to support the very arrangements it had put in place.

Legitimacy

The dimension of Legitimacy in the analysis of UNOSOM II is closely related to Unity of Effort, especially with respect to the principle of the Objective. The fact that UNOSOM II's objectives were neither entirely clear nor agreed upon by all the force providers had significant impact on the operation's Legitimacy.

Legitimacy clearly is a matter of perception. It revolves around the degree of support for the operation and the Peace Force (PF) itself from the participating nations and the belligerents alike. As suggested, the community authorizing the operation needs to see its objectives as both worthwhile and capable of being accomplished while the belligerents and the people of the area of the operation need to see the PF as an impartial arbiter of their conflict. Moreover, the Legitimacy of the operation depends on the perception among the people of the operational area that the PF can provide the security required to begin the establishment (or reestablishment) of appropriate governmental functions.

In the case of Somalia, it appears that during Operation Restore Hope UNITAF met most, if not all of these requirements. UNITAF generally was perceived as an impartial arbiter of the conflict. It demonstrated the capability to provide security for the delivery of humanitarian assistance and to begin the reestablishment of governmental functions. Yet, its very success sowed the seeds of the potential delegitimization of its successor, UNOSOM II. Mohammed Farrah Aideed was the one factional leader who was unwilling to accept a restored Somalia under any terms but his own and was astute enough to see that he would have an opportunity to create a new reality as UNITAF transitioned to UNOSOM II.

In February 1993 Aideed had lost the southern city of Kismayo to the forces of another factional leader, Hersi Morgan (son-in-law of the deposed dictator), a loss which reinforced his already firm belief that there was no requirement for foreign intervention in Somalia and which became a festering wound to him. Thus, Aideed began, at this time, to regard the United States and the United Nations not as neutral humanitarians but as political adversaries.[10] However, he had not sought a direct confrontation with UNITAF which demonstrated an overwhelming military presence in the form of US and other western nation forces. He knew, though, that he could simply wait these forces out, all the while preparing military actions to be used against UNOSOM II should his political position deteriorate further during the continued UN intervention.[11]

On May 7 Aideed's forces attempted to seize Kismayo and, although they were defeated by the Belgian peacekeepers, the UN failed to eject them from the area. Two days later the Galcayo peace conference began. Although this was an Aideed initiative, it turned out to be a major political setback for him. The UNOSOM II political division successfully opposed Aideed's attempt to manipulate the conference, thereby leaving him extremely frustrated over his inability to control the political process in Somalia.[12] With his political stature threatened and having been defeated by a western military force in Kismayo, Aideed lashed out on June 5 against the Pakistani peacekeepers.

These events clearly set the stage for the contest for Legitimacy that would take place in Mogadishu, the other cities and towns of Somalia, New York, the capitals of the force providers, and over CNN. In Somalia, the issue of Legitimacy ultimately turned on whether the PF could provide the required degree of security in the face of Aideed's opposition. A critical part of UNOSOM II's problem was that to be effective it needed to be perceived as, at least, impartial and, at best, neutral in terms of the factional fighting. Without that perceived impartiality it lost consent. Aideed's grant of consent had been exceedingly tenuous and was completely withdrawn with the failure of his political plans at the Galcayo conference. Thus, from June 5 on, Aideed's actions were aimed at undermining the Legitimacy of UNOSOM II among the people of Mogadishu, and to the maximum extent to which he was capable, the people of Somalia. He also aimed at exploiting cracks in the coalition of nations and forces that made up UNOSOM II.

The juridical Legitimacy of UNOSOM II stemmed from UNSCR 814, that is from the agreement of the members of the Security Council in New York. The practical Legitimacy which flowed from that resolution was found in the terms of commitment by the force providers. For example, the US committed to provide significant forces on the condition that the SRSG was an American (with a military background), the Force Commander was from NATO, and the Deputy Force Commander was American. No nation committed its forces under the full operational control that the SRSG and Force Commander envisioned or desired, not even the US. Nevertheless, the terms of UNSCR 814 and the commitment of forces agreements set the practical and juridical limits of Legitimacy. The events of June 5 were to change that.

As a result of Aideed's ambush of the Pakistanis, the United Nations Security Council passed Resolution 837 (UNSCR 837) on June 6. The Resolution strongly condemned the unprovoked attack, the use of radio broadcasts to incite such attacks, and

> reaffirms that the Secretary General is authorized under resolution 814 to take all necessary measures against all those responsible for the armed attacks ... including against those responsible for inciting such attacks, to establish the effective authority of UNOSOM II throughout Somalia, including to secure the investigation of their actions and their arrest and detention for prosecution, trial, and punishment ....[13]

The resolution was written and passed overnight. While resolutions of the Security Council are supposed to be binding on all UN members, the Council depends on enforcement by force providers who may not be Security Council members. Such was especially the case of UNSCR 837. At American urging, the Council rushed the resolution through in order to demonstrate, "as one senior administration official put it, that the United Nations, engaged in a major multi-national peacekeeping mission, could not be 'pushed around by some renegade warlord.'"[14]

Even before the passage of UNSCR 837 the Italian ambassador to Somalia had expressed reservations to the Force Commander over the appearance of UNOSOM II's taking sides against Aideed.[15] As one of the force providing nations not consulted about UNSCR 837, Italy chose, essentially, not to participate in its enforcement. In a cable to New York the SRSG expressed Force Command's concerns regarding the "passive presence" of the Italian forces and the negative impact of a virtual Italian sanctuary for Aideed in Somalia.[16] The Italian case provides strong evidence of the rapid loss of Legitimacy within UNOSOM II.

Finally, the events of October 3-4, 1993 when 18 members of US Task Force Ranger were killed and 75 wounded, all shown live and in living color on CNN--including the dragging of the body of a dead American soldier through the streets of Mogadishu as well as the pictures of the wounded US helicopter pilot as Aideed's prisoner, raised serious questions with the American public over whether this peace operation was worth doing. When the Clinton Administration made no attempt to counter the impact of the view according to

CNN, the American public withdrew its grant of Legitimacy to the operation. At that point, the President announced a phased withdrawal of US forces and the end of American participation as of March 31, 1994. Both UNSCR 814 and 837 were dead. The peace operation in Somalia had lost its mandate and its Legitimacy.

Support to Belligerents

One of the complicating factors in the case study of UNOSOM II is the initial identification of the belligerents. The problem is analogous to threat analysis in conventional military operations with the caveat that all belligerents are potential allies of the PF as well as potential adversaries. To understand the belligerents requires a brief review of some of the major aspects of Somali society and the nature of the Somali state.

Somalia was made up of the fusion of British Somaliland in the north and Italian Somaliland in the south. Although the two had been separate colonies they were united by the Somali language and their Islamic religion. The Somalis are, however, a clan culture reckoning descent from six major clan families. While each major clan tends to control discreet territories within (as well as outside) Somalia's borders, there is significant overlap, more in the south than in the north.[17] Still more important is the fact that the clans further divide into any number of competing sub-clans. At the same time, political and militia organizations are overlaid on the sub-clans resulting in the potential (and often the reality) of conflict between the traditional and the "political" leadership. Ultimately, an oversimplified picture of the belligerents appeared around rivals from the same clan who held leadership in Mogadishu and loose alliances with other militia leaders, Ali Mahdi and Mohammed Farrah Aideed.

At the several peace conferences held in Addis Ababa and at Galcayo during the UNITAF and UNOSOM II interventions, 14 militia factions were recognized as participants in the peace process.[18] In effect, this recognition gave primacy to the militia factions, their "political" organizations, and the "warlords," over the traditional clan leaders. Moreover, it reinforced the picture of the belligerents as falling into two distinct political-military coalitions. The result of this process was two edged. As suggested in the previous section, it tended to isolate Aideed from the rest of the players but it also strengthened his hand by cementing his coalition of sub-clan leaders and supportive factional forces and militias.

While Ali Mahdi generally had supported UNITAF and later UNOSOM II, this support had not won him sufficient external support for his cause. Rather, the US and UN tended to treat him as simply the other factional leader, like Aideed, but a "good boy." In the end this left Ali Mahdi as isolated in fact as Aideed seemed to be. Yet, Aideed was not isolated. Rather, most of his sub-clan supported him; several other militia leaders did as well; so too did key economic leaders such as Osman Atto. As important as these supporters were, Aideed also received indirect external support from the Italians.

Soon after UNSCR 837 triggered UNOSOM II operations aimed at Aideed, the warlord struck back. On July 2 his militia ambushed Italian forces inflicting casualties of three killed and 30 wounded causing the Italian force to abandon several key strongpoints. Later that month the Italians negotiated with local elders from Aideed's clan to re-occupy those strong points. In effect, UNOSOM II forces were only allowed to operate in that portion of North Mogadishu at the discretion of Aideed's forces.[19]

Following the July 2 attack the Italian force commander virtually reverted his troops to a consensual peacekeeping status. In so doing, cordon and search operations and aggressive checks at strong points ceased. This was evidenced in Force Command's July 6 cable to the Under Secretary General for Peacekeeping Operations:

> National authorities and local commanders feel free to ignore direction and urging for aggressive action. ... [a national contingent] is insistent on further negotiations with faction elders who have no actual influence on the ... militia.[20]

This concern was also highlighted in a July 7 UNOSOM II Force Command Situation Report.

> [National] military officials have forbidden them [their national forces] to conduct indiscriminant violent reprisals against Aideed's forces. This prohibition places [their Brigade Commander] in a difficult position because he is required to negotiate before engaging in military operations against Aideed.[21]

This inaction on the part of the Italians had deeper effects on coalition operations. Many coalition partners were hesitant to share operational and intelligence data with the Italian forces fearing such matters would be compromised. Even within the headquarters, the UNOSOM II chief intelligence officer, an Italian, was excluded from the planning process on numerous UNOSOM II directed operations.

The situation clearly did not improve for UNOSOM II over time. Rather, the impact of Italian inaction (which amounted to de facto support for Aideed) simply strengthened his hand and increased the boldness of his subordinates as reflected in this discussion of an encounter with a Mr. Gullit, a clan elder supporting Aideed, near a strong point in north Mogadishu:

> [The operations officer commented that Gullit] was the leader and did most of the talking.... He stated that ... [Aideed's militia] would not accept any other contingent than the one (the Italian Brigade) that currently occupied the area and that they were ready to die before they would cooperate with UNOSOM....

> We killed seven Nigerians because they violated the occupation agreement established for the strong point by sending the reinforcing platoon of APCs....[22]

In short, the effective "defection" of Italy from the coalition and its *de facto* support for Aideed very much increased the capabilities of the latter by creating effective sanctuaries for him within the confines of Mogadishu. In these areas he could hold meetings in relative safety to plan his next moves. Moreover, his forces could use them to rest and recuperate as well as rearm. Because of the support available to him, both internal and external, Aideed became, over the several months between June and October 1993, increasingly more formidable. His increasing strength ultimately was manifest in the aftermath of UNOSOM II 's pyrrhic victory on October 3-4, when Task Force Ranger took 18 killed and 75 wounded in its attempt to arrest Aideed. The result, of course, was the US withdrawal from the mission and the collapse of UNOSOM II.

Support Actions of Peace Forces

The perception of the nature of the commitment controls this dimension; that being the case the commitment was stated as a mandate in a series of UN Security Council Resolutions. From the passage of the first, UNSCR 794, there was a dispute between the United States and the Secretary General over the meaning of the key words of the mandate, to "use all necessary means to establish as soon as possible, a secure environment for humanitarian relief operations." At a December 22, 1992 meeting with the Secretary General, Secretary of State Lawrence Eagleburger re-emphasized the US position of a limited mission in Somalia.

The Clinton Administration entered office determined to concentrate on domestic policies, and early on echoed President Bush's call for a rapid hand over to UNOSOM II. With the continued desire of the Secretary General to expand the mandate to one of nation building there was much disagreement as to the shape of UNOSOM II. The first indication of a major adjustment in the US position came on March 26, 1993 when the Security Council adopted Resolution 814 which outlined in detail the mission and tasks of UNOSOM II, to include disarmament and nation building. This resulted in relatively early indications that the international community had achieved a consensus to strongly support a complex peace operation. More importantly, these rhetorical indicators were backed up on the ground by the clear strength of UNITAF.

The core of UNITAF was the US Joint Task Force Somalia, organized around the I MEF (Marine Expeditionary Force), under the command of Marine Lieutenant General Robert Johnston. In addition, it included the US 10th Mountain Division (light infantry) with substantial support forces and a high degree of mobility due to significant numbers of helicopters. Precision firepower was available to the force from AC 130 Spectre gunships. Augmenting the Americans were allies, mostly from NATO nations and some others, including units of the vaunted French Foreign Legion. At its peak UNITAF numbered some 38,000 troops. Indicative of its effectiveness was the fact that its forces rarely were challenged by the militia of Aideed or any of his lieutenants and when they were, they defeated the challenge with hardly any friendly casualties.

When UNITAF transitioned to UNOSOM II on May 4, 1993, the UN force was programmed to be nearly as strong as UNITAF with some 28,000 troops. However, on transition day UNOSOM II numbered a mere 14,000 with few of the combat capabilities that UNITAF had shown. Instead of two US divisions as the core of the fighting force, UNOSOM II had only one infantry brigade of the 10th Mountain Division available as a Quick Reaction Force for emergencies. The principal combat forces belonging to Force Command were a number of battalions and brigades from Belgium, France, Italy, Malaysia, Nigeria, and Pakistan, all with incompatible equipment, different command and control commitments, and different levels of capability. The face the UNOSOM II force showed to Aideed was one of much less support from the world community than UN rhetoric and UNITAF had demonstrated.

The perception of the length of the commitment likewise was as mixed as the signals the international community sent. While the series of Security Council Resolutions indicated that the UN and its force supplying members were prepared to stay as long as necessary to restore civil government and society to Somalia, beginning with the dispute between the US and the Secretary General over the meaning of UNSCR 794 the clarity of the message was in doubt. First, the US made it very clear that UNITAF had a mission of limited duration. President Bush even speculated that US forces could hand over the mission to the UN by January 20, 1993, inauguration day. That, however, clearly was unrealistic. Still, an early transition to UNOSOM II was desired.

With the inauguration of the Clinton Administration, the appointment of Lieutenant General Cevik Bir (of Turkey, a NATO member) as UNOSOM II Force Commander, and the passage of UNSCR 814, it seemed like the goal of a seamless transition from UNITAF to UNOSOM II, on a schedule driven by events and not by time, was becoming a reality. Given the nature of the problem, the date of passage of UNSCR 814, and the time required to deploy forces and equipment, May 1993 appeared to be a realistic date for transition. This tentative "planning" date soon became very fixed in many minds.

As May approached, there was some concern in UN New York as to when Force Command would assume theater responsibility, and if it was premature to establish the command. All parties involved in the transition process had a position on the subject. UNITAF, seeing its mission as completed, wanted the transition to occur as expeditiously as possible.[23] It was the Force Commander's belief that UNITAF was "extremely aggressive in their insistence on a 1 May 1993 deadline for transition."[24] The UNITAF staff did not share an understanding of the constraints of the UN in terms of resource procurement.[25] UNOSOM II's position was that transition should occur based on the capabilities of Force Command to assume the mission and effect a seamless transition. The result of these apparently small discords rebounded, perhaps, giving the impression that the contributors to UNITAF (many of whom were also contributors to UNOSOM II) had lost their will to stay the course.

Later events such as the response of a number of force providers to the June 5 attack on the Pakistanis and the passage of UNSCR 837 reinforced the impression that the nations making up UNOSOM II lacked the will to stick out the fight. The events of October 4 and 5 where US Task Force Ranger took its large number of casualties simply confirmed the fact of the perception that Aideed had outlasted UNOSOM II.

The last element of this dimension involves the perception that the commitment of military forces will be consistent with the threat posed to the accomplishment of the mission. Rather than look at all the force providers to UNOSOM II it is instructive to consider the changing commitment of the United States to the mission. In UNITAF, the US led the military effort committing a Marine Expeditionary Force headquarters (the equivalent of an army corps), under the command of a three star general, a Marine division, an army division, and significant air and naval forces along with major sustainment elements. Equally important was the fact that the force commander controlled all the US forces. By contrast, under UNOSOM II, the US committed less than a single division and did so with reluctance. When it later increased its forces it did so unilaterally without giving any control to UNOSOM, thereby raising significant questions as to the depth of the commitment to the UN mission. Thus, by all three criteria, the Support Actions of the Peace Forces were found wanting.

Military Actions of Peace Forces

Force size is the first variable of this dimension. In a peace operation, particularly a peace enforcement operation, the PF need to be of sufficient size and strength to deter the use of force against them or their mission. A related factor is that they need to be introduced as a body and not piecemeal since the latter allows the belligerents to adjust to the new realities as well as giving them time to probe the PF for weaknesses at relatively low risk. UNITAF and UNOSOM II present a stark contrast with respect to both aspects of this variable.

First, UNITAF was a large force as noted above. Most of it arrived quickly, quite literally overnight. The Marines undertook a nighttime amphibious landing under combat conditions after having made a show of force with naval and Marine air in the days immediately preceding the landing. They were quickly followed by the 10th Mountain Division, French Foreign Legion troops, and the forces of the other contributing countries. Almost before anyone had realized it, UNITAF had reached its 38,000 peak and was reducing its forces to about 28,000, the level at transition. Even more than the numbers was the combat capability those numbers represented. UNITAF was an integrated combined arms force with infantry, mechanized, armor, attack helicopters, AC 130 gunships, F-14 and F/A 18 jet fighter bombers, and the ability to call for naval gunfire.

The contrast with UNOSOM II was striking. Planned for 28,000, on transition day the force numbered a mere 14,000. Its component combat elements would trickle in from May to September 1993. Beginning in the late summer, as new units from additional force providing countries arrived, units from countries already there withdrew, leaving the force somewhat below its optimal strength.

The combat capability of the UNOSOM II force also compared unfavorably to that of UNITAF. Most of UNOSOM's combat elements were in battalion strength, or less, from a variety of contributing nations with widely differing equipment, training, doctrine, and leadership. The US combat forces were reduced from two divisions with all their support to the brigade sized Quick Reaction Force (QRF) which was only under the control of Force Command during bonafide emergencies. Quality of other combat forces varied greatly.

The principal purpose of the PF is to contribute by its actions to the de-escalation of the conflict. To that end, the Force Commander undertook a series of show of force operations at transition. The intent of these operations was to show that a seamless transition had occurred between UNITAF and UNOSOM II and to demonstrate to the Somali people that the security for humanitarian relief and political reconciliation would continue and grow under the UN.

The effect of these show of force operations on the populace was uncertain. Less than 72 hours after the assumption of command from UNITAF, and in the middle of a show of force, UNOSOM II faced its first major confrontation with militia forces. It occurred, not in Mogadishu where it was most expected, but in the southern port city of Kismayo. During the late evening hours of May 6 and extending into the morning of May 7, 1993, a band of approximately 150 armed men attacked Kismayo where they engaged elements of the Belgian Parachute Battalion. During the engagement, one Belgian officer was wounded and an estimated 40 Somalis of the attacking force were either killed or wounded.[26]

A Force Command investigation team determined that the attack was conducted by forces allied to Aideed. Despite the fact that Belgian forces had soundly defeated the hostile militia, the Belgian commander's actions suggested to Force Command that he was unwilling to risk further casualties to his force. Indeed, his actions prompted Force Command to remind the Belgian commander that UNOSOM II, while operating under Chapter VII, found itself in the role of peacemaker, and "the intent is to aggressively establish and maintain a secure environment by force of arms, should the situation in your AOR become untenable."[27]

The failure from early in the operation to undertake military and associated diplomatic actions to de-escalate the conflict clearly increased Aideed's confidence that his intransigence and skillfully directed violence against individual national contingents of UNOSOM II would result in his ultimate victory. The UN Security Council and the SRSG played directly into his hand when, after the June 5 ambush of the Pakistanis, they pushed through UNSCR 837 without ever building a consensus for it among the force providers. In turn, this pushed the US into dispatching Task Force Ranger whose mission to capture Aideed only escalated the level of violence. The results became apparent in the October 3-4, 1993 firefight which left 18 members of the task force dead, 75 wounded, and some 300+ Somalis, not all of whom were militia fighters, killed and many more wounded. Since all out war was not what the Clinton Administration had in mind, these events prompted it to set a date certain for the withdrawal of US forces and the abandonment by the US of the mission. The US withdrawal, of course, doomed UNOSOM II to failure.

Military Actions of the Belligerents and the Peace Forces

Events developed this dimension in a particularly interesting way. As UNITAF gave way to UNOSOM II the military effectiveness of the PF deteriorated. Meanwhile, the tactical skills of Aideed's militia improved as did his effective employment of those skills. As militia professionalism grew, the tactical employment of the PF became significantly less resolute and more tentative. Thus, the relationship between the PF and Aideed's militia, in terms of their military professionalism, was an inverse one. Following the passage of UNSCR 837, Force Command initiated offensive actions to restore order and security in Mogadishu. The aim of the operations conducted from June 6 through August 31 was to re-establish a secure environment (including control of key facilities and supply routes) and to neutralize Aideed's militia and his radio station. It was critical for UN forces to regain control of the city for two reasons. First, the adverse effects on the morale of the PF that the June 5 attack engendered had to be negated. Second, the UN civilian staff, many nongovernmental organizations, and UN relief agencies had departed the country after the attack and would not return until a secure environment was restored.

One important operation was conducted on June 17 against what was called the Aideed Enclave. While this operation attained a tactical victory its positive effects were short-lived. The counterattack against Moroccan forces precipitated their withdrawal from the city and denial by their national authorities for future employment in Mogadishu.[28] The failure to secure a strong point in the enclave allowed militia infiltration back into the area. French forces were asked but were reluctant to retake the ground previously fought over and their government ordered them out of Mogadishu.[29] Italian forces, who had participated reluctantly in the operation, were not prepared to do so again.

Aideed's militia were not idle in these circumstances. On June 22 they began what became nightly harassment of UNOSOM II installations with small arms and rocket propelled grenade fire.[30] Weekly anti-UNOSOM II demonstrations were held at the soccer stadium near the Aideed enclave and the militia began erecting road blocks in areas they controlled on a number of key streets and roads in the city. Although Force Command initially saw the road blocks as harassment and protest, their tactical significance became apparent when Pakistani forces accompanied by US engineers were ambushed while clearing one.[31] Over the next few months, this escalation of violence by Aideed's militia became increasingly more frequent. Moreover, the ambushes fueled the reluctance of UNOSOM II units within the city to get out on the streets in lightly armored vehicles or on foot.

A unilateral operation in July raised the US profile beyond what the Clinton Administration desired. This resulted in greatly increased difficulty in getting US aviation assets approved for anything beyond force protection; it also resulted in significant limitation on the use of US ground forces in search operations other than those immediately adjacent to US facilities. This policy was in keeping with the original command intent to maintain a low signature in order that US combat forces could revert to an "over the horizon" mission by the end of summer. This policy of withholding US troops negatively impacted the coalition forces and their own willingness to place soldiers at risk. The Pakistani Foreign Ministry stated that without US attack helicopter strikes there would be "chaos in the country."[32] Attempting to prod coalition forces into action without continued use of US forces, especially attack helicopter assets, slowed any UNOSOM II follow-on action and effectively lost any initiative gained by the operation. This US policy (with the exception of Task Force Ranger and its unilateral special mission) would not change for the duration, despite the fact that levels of violence increased and success for the UN mission was significantly more at risk than it had been in May when the policy was first developed.

In contrast to some of the developments noted above, August brought an increased dedication of resources to capture Aideed and his senior advisors and Task Force Ranger was introduced into theater to carry out this mission.

Admiral Howe, the SRSG, had requested additional forces from the United States for this effort. He either saw the lack of initiative by the coalition or understood that there was no properly configured force in theater that could execute the mission to arrest, detain, and bring to trial those responsible for the armed attacks against UN forces. It was at this point that a US official noted that the Pentagon argued, "'...if it is us against Aideed, we might as well try to actually get Aideed' ... Howe...wanted more force and said 'you have approved the U. N. ... resolution to go after [Aideed] and you have to provide the forces to do it.'"[33]

After a series of unilateral operations in September, during which Aideed and his troops learned a great deal about the capabilities and tactics of US forces supporting Task Force Ranger, as well as their vulnerabilities, a major operation that would become the decisive event in the UNOSOM II mission took place. On October 3 the task force received information that a number of Aideed's senior advisors were meeting in a building in downtown Mogadishu. Task Force Ranger assaulted the area and quickly captured 24 detainees, including two senior Aideed advisors. Taking advantage of what had been learned in previous operations Aideed's militia shot down a Task Force Ranger UH-60 helicopter near the raid site. As Ranger ground forces moved to the crash site to recover survivors they came under a barrage of fire from surrounding buildings and streets, taking a number of casualties. This force formed a perimeter around the crash site. Two miles to the south, a second UH-60 (Blackhawk) was shot down. Although the US QRF had a back-up company ready to reinforce Task Force Ranger, if necessary, it was mounted in soft skinned vehicles and unable to punch through the hostile resistance and link up with the Rangers by itself.

As a result, the UNOSOM II reserve of a Pakistani tank platoon and two Malaysian mechanized companies were ordered into action. While it was ready to launch in less than an hour, Task Force Ranger notified headquarters that its forces had fortified several buildings as strong points and were not in danger of being overrun. Force headquarters therefore slowed the rescue operation in order to implement a fully developed tactical plan that made use of the capabilities of the US QRF and the Pakistani and Malaysian armored vehicles. After encountering heavy resistance, the rescue column reached the two crash sites and evacuated the Rangers. In the course of the action 18 US soldiers were killed and 75 wounded; three Malaysian armored personnel carriers were destroyed, one soldier killed, and ten wounded; and two Pakistani soldiers were wounded. Estimates were that between 300 and 500 Somali militia were killed and some 700 wounded.[34]

Clearly, the events of October 3-4, 1993 amounted to a major armed clash between the US and UNOSOM II forces on one side and Aideed's militia on the other. Although there was no lack of professionalism on the part of the coalition forces who, in fact, achieved a significant tactical victory, the events indicated just how far Aideed's forces had come. They now had the capability to make any effort to subdue Aideed extremely costly--more costly, as it turned out than the US was prepared to pay.

Actions Targeted on Ending Conflict

Of the actions comprising this dimension one, intelligence, represents classical military thought. As the ancient Chinese sage, Sun Tzu, put it:

> Now if the estimates made in the temple before hostilities indicate victory it is because calculations show one's strength to be superior to that of the enemy; if they indicate defeat, it is because calculations show that one is inferior. With many calculations, one can win; with few one cannot. How much less chance has one who makes none at all![35]

By contrast, the other actions, population and resources control, psychological operations, and civic action, often get short shrift from the warriors and in Somalia, at least, received the sobriquet of "mission creep." In any event, this discussion asserts that lack of preparation and attention to the actions of this dimension in UNITAF, carried on into UNOSOM II, contributed in significant ways to the failure of the latter mission.

First, a lack of what is sometimes called "basic intelligence"--that is the political, cultural, and social nature of the society--created obstacles to success from the beginning of UNITAF. Where that basic intelligence was strong, in the US Liaison Office of Ambassador Robert Oakley, it was not responsible to nor required by the UNITAF Force Commander, Marine Lieutenant General Robert Johnston.[36] Thus, UNITAF largely worked in the dark at the strategic level. Moreover, as the Army forces stated in their after action report, "National and Strategic systems were unable to provide detailed information prior to deployment."[37]

Second, US forces at the tactical level also had serious problems. Although the Marines had a relatively effective tactical intelligence collection system that relied on human sources, the army's intelligence units generally were not organized to operate in a human source environment. "...commanders must task some units, other than intelligence, to perform detailed collection tasks. The units tasked often do not have the background or training...[needed]. As a result, reports sometimes lack detail and leave gaps in the collection plan."[38] As a result, army forces relied heavily on the intelligence capabilities of the special operations forces, especially army Special Forces. Although they certainly would have made use of the intelligence capabilities of Civil Affairs and psychological operations (PSYOP) personnel, these were in short supply resulting in a lack of basic intelligence useful at the operational and tactical levels.

The transition to UNOSOM II did not improve the picture either. UN resistance to the notion of intelligence in a peace operation was compounded by the fact that Force Command's U2 was an Italian, who because of his government's policy, was excluded from staff planning of UN operations. Although tactical intelligence support for the hunt for Aideed was relatively effective in that it was able to locate specific, high priority human targets for capture, it never did identify the fact that Aideed's militia had developed effective tactics to make aviation operations increasingly costly affairs.

Although UNITAF clearly rejected the larger mission of nation building it did undertake a significant number of activities that could fall under such a rubric. Among these were road building and the establishment of local governments and police. US officers tended to speak somewhat disparagingly of these efforts as "mission creep" but they were clearly inherent in the UN Secretary General's perception of the mandate. This was, of course, the definition prescribed by UNSCR 814 that was to be executed by UNOSOM II.

Early in May, the UNOSOM II political staff forwarded a paper to Force Command which outlined what they perceived to be an opportunity for early commitment of forces to the Central Region of Somalia, outside Mogadishu. It offered an assessment of multiple factions awaiting UNOSOM II deployment which represented both a challenge and an opportunity to place a permanent force in the town of Galcayo to ensure its demilitarized status.[39]

Rather than being seen as simply one logical course of action for a unified effort by all the agencies, the document became an implementation policy for the political staff and the SRSG. Plans for a methodical, controlled buildup of forces gave way to guidance to determine how soon a deployment could be made into the Central Region. Expansion was becoming a time driven process rather than being driven by events or capabilities.

A related shortfall in the establishment of a coordinated strategy to end conflict was the lack of a humanitarian relief policy. Feeding sites were scheduled to be closed at the end of May 1993--a phasing out of UNITAF's humanitarian mission. Yet, follow on funds and a plan for their investment required to rejuvenate the Somali economy were lacking. To be successful the UN needed a coordinated military, political, and economic strategy. A secure environment needed to be established in order that local political structures could be re-established. These structures, including police, judiciary, schools, and public administration, required initial economic support. Once basic government services were restored, local economies could develop and become self-sustaining, thus ending the need for major continued humanitarian assistance. Such a strategy never developed. Efforts made to correct this situation in the late summer failed. This resulted in the political and economic instruments of power becoming dependent on the military strategy for dealing with hostile militia forces. Complementary strategies never were developed nor were the appropriate mix of capabilities--including Civil Affairs and PSYOP forces--emplaced to address the hostile clans nor to capitalize on those areas where peaceful reconciliation was progressing. Thus, the limited success in establishing district and regional political councils did not translate into similar successes in restoring basic government services.

In short, the focus of both UNITAF and UNOSOM II in terms of their actions was much too narrow to end the conflict. UNITAF discounted the need for basic intelligence on Somalia and saw the necessary nation building activities as mission creep. While UNOSOM II recognized the need for effective intelligence, the effort was so compartmented that it failed to achieve the required degree of synergism. It also fell afoul of the political disagreements among the force contributing nations. UNOSOM II had neither the military organizations--Civil Affairs and PSYOP--in sufficient numbers, nor more significantly the civil development organizational capabilities to produce or implement a coordinated plan for the restoration of civil government and society to Somalia. As a result, the entire process reverted to guerrilla warfare of Aideed's militia against the UNOSOM II forces.

Conclusion

This chapter has applied the seven dimensions of the paradigm to the first post Cold War peace enforcement operation, Somalia. It clearly demonstrates the applicability of each dimension as well as all seven together. The analysis, dimension by dimension, fairly screams of a doomed operation, one which by its failure to address appropriately the several variables making up each dimension, as well as the whole, ultimately had no chance of success.

The chapter shows that, after a promising start in UNITAF, Unity of Effort foundered on the shoals of a flawed command and control structure, lack of coordination and cooperation among the agencies making up UNOSOM II, and, escalating from a relatively minor problem in UNITAF, the profound lack of agreement on the objectives of UNOSOM II among the force providing nations. The lack of Unity of Effort both influenced and reflected the ebbs and flows of the Legitimacy of the operation. Where UNITAF had a high degree of Legitimacy due, in part, to the agreement among all parties on the objective of humanitarian relief, resulting in a degree of consent from the belligerents--however grudging, UNOSOM II rapidly lost its Legitimacy as, first, consent was withdrawn by one faction and, then, agreement among the force contributors on the objectives of the operation slipped away.

The loss of consensus among the members of the coalition was soon reflected in the tacit and overt support given to Aideed by Italy. This, in turn, further weakened the strength of the UNOSOM II coalition as the various contributors reassessed their support. The changing degree of support for the operation was reflected in the military actions of the PF as UNOSOM II sent mixed signals regarding the strength and focus of the effort. The inverse relationship between the increasing professionalism of Aideed's militia and the decreasing professionalism of the several UNOSOM force contingents reflected especially the nature of the support Aideed was receiving both from Somali clans and factions and from the Italians as well as the PF weaknesses in the other dimensions.

Finally, the inability of the several components of UNOSOM II to identify clearly the actions required to end the conflict--a problem which developed during UNITAF between the US and the UN Secretary General--greatly contributed to the failure. When the SRSG and Force Command finally did identify the required actions, they could not get the other components to deliver what was needed in a timely fashion. It was, in a cliche, too little and too late.

Notes

1 US Forces Somalia, After Action Report, "Executive Summary," US Army Peacekeeping Institute, Carlisle, PA, 1994.

2 Ibid., p. 4.

3 See John T. Fishel, "Achieving the Elusive Unity of Effort," in Max G. Manwaring (ed.), *Gray Area Phenomena: Confronting the New World Disorder*, Westview Press, Boulder, CO, 1993, pp. 109-127.

4 US Department of the Army, FM 100-23, *Peace Operations*, Washington, DC, 1994, p. 23.

5 Interviews with officers who have served in UN peacekeeping operations over a number of years.

6 U.S. Forces Somalia, p, 2-3.

7 FM 100-23.

8 Terms of Reference (TOR) for US Forces in Somalia, April 1993.

9 Ibid.

10 Jennifer Parmelee, "Relaxing in Ethiopia, Unrepentant Aideed Finds Time For Envoys," *The Washington Post*, 26 December 1993, p. A41, and Alex Shoumatoff, "The Warlord Speaks," *The Nation*, 4 April 1994, p. 444.

11 Walter S. Clarke, "Testing the World's Resolve in Somalia," *Parameters*, Carlisle, PA, winter, 1993-94, p. 53.

12 Ibid.

13 UNOSOM II Fax from the Under Secretary General for Peacekeeping Operations to the Special Representative to the Secretary General, Subject: "Draft Resolution on Somalia, S/25889," 6 June 1993, pp. 2-4.

14 Michael Elliott, "The Making of a Fiasco," *Newsweek*, 18 October 1993, p. 36.

15 UNOSOM II Memorandum from Force Command to the Special Representative to the Secretary General, Subject: Trip Report to Italian Brigade, 27 May 1993, p. 2.

[16] UNOSOM II Code Cable from the Special Representative to the Secretary General to the Under Secretary General for Peacekeeping Operations, Subject: Additional Concerns of Force Commander, 18 July 1993, p. 1.

[17] Terrence Lyons and Ahmed I. Samatar, *Somalia: State Collapse, Multilateral intervention, and Strategies for Political Reconstruction*, Brookings, Washington, DC, 1995, pp. vii-13.

[18] Ibid., pp. 44-49.

[19] UNOSOM II Force Command Special SITREP to UN New York, 3 July 1993, pp. 1-3and UNOSOM II Code Cable from the SRSG to the Under Secretary General for Peacekeeping Operations, Subject: "Additional Insights re Situation in Mogadishu," 16 July 1993, p. 2.

[20] UNOSOM II Code Cable from Force Command to the Under Secretary General for Peacekeeping Operations, Subject: " Security Situation in Mogadishu," 6 July 1993, p. 2.

[21] UNOSOM II Force Command SITREP to UN New York, 7 July 1993, p. 9.

[22] UNOSOM II Operations Division Memorandum for Record, Subject: "Occupation of Strong Points 19, 42, and 207," 10 September 1993, p. 2.

[23] F. M. Lorenz, "Law and Anarchy in Somalia," *Parameters*, Winter 1993-94, p. 37.

[24] UNOSOM II Memorandum from Force Command to the Special Representative to the Secretary General, Subject: "UNOSOM Transition Process," 18 April 1993.

[25] Ibid.

[26] UNOSOM II Fax from Commander Belgian Brigade to the Force Commander, Subject: "Situation in Kismayo," 7 May 1993.

[27] UNOSOM II Fax from force Command to Commander Belgian Brigade, Subject: "Current Operation Within AOR Kismayo," 11 May 1993, p.1.

[28] Daze, Field Notes, 22 June 1993.

[29] Letter form the Chief of the French Defence Staff to Force Command, 14 June 1993.

[30] UNOSOM II Force Command SITREP to UN New York, 22 June 1993.

[31] UNOSOM II Force Command SITREP to UN New York, 28 June 1993.

[32] Keith B. Richburg, "Criticism Mounts Over Somali Raid," *The Washington Post*, 15 July 1993, p. A21.

[33] Thomas W. Lippman and Barton Gellman, " A Humanitarian Gesture Turns Deadly," *The Washington Post*, 10 October 1993, p. 3.

[34] This account is taken from UNOSOM II Force Command SITREP to UN New York, 3 October 1993 and US Quick Reaction Force, Falcon Brigade, 10th Mountain Division, Summary of Operations on 3 October 1993.

[35] Sun Tzu, *The Art of War*, translated by Samuel B. Griffith, Oxford University Press, London, 1963, p. 71.

[36] Interview with a member of Ambassador Oakley's staff, 1994.

[37] US Army Forces Somalia, 10th Mountain Division (LI), "After Action Report: Summary," 1994, p. 31.

[38] Ibid., p. 30.

[39] UNOSOM II Interdivisional Memorandum, Subject: "Galcayo as Keystone," May 1993.

10

The US and the UN in Haiti: The Limits of Intervention

Thomas K. Adams

a whisper of hope in a camouflage uniform

By the end of August 1996, soldiers from the US led Multinational Force (MNF) and its successor, the United Nations Mission In Haiti (UNMIH) had been present for more than two years. During that month sporadic, escalating violence climaxed with a series of attacks beginning August 19th when a group of former Haitian soldiers attacked the capital's central police station and nearby Legislative Palace with rocket launchers and automatic weapons.[1] On the 21st of August, two prominent politicians were assassinated and on August 22nd shots were fired into the national television building followed by telephone death threats against television and radio executives and workers.[2]

Despite strenuous efforts by the United States, the United Nations and others including nongovernmental organizations, to restore political stability, incidents such as these make it questionable how much has actually been achieved. The Haiti case raises a basic question - in a situation of near total economic and political collapse, what can an intervention force reasonably be expected to do? The answer is that a military force in a peacekeeping role has distinct limits on what it can be expected to achieve.

Using the Manwaring or SWORD model, this chapter suggests that, by the parameters of the model, the military intervention has been very well conducted. SWORD, however, is a long-term model. It does have short term components in the sense that there are some sets of tasks, mostly military, that must be accomplished early in order to facilitate success in the other, long-term variables. These short term components are: Military Actions of the Peace Forces, Actions Targeted On Ending Conflict and Military Actions of the

Belligerents and Peace Forces. There are also three long-term components: Legitimacy, Support to Belligerents and Support Actions of the Peace Forces. Finally the dimension termed called Unity of Effort can be thought of as both a long and short-term component.

The MNF and UNMIH mandate was based on a operation of short duration. The MNF's job essentially was to pave the way for the UN Mission in Haiti. UNMIH's role was to midwife local and national elections and the installation of a new government by January 1996. The UN force was to be expeditiously withdrawn after that. Nevertheless, the UN found itself compelled to extend its mandate at least two more times as the old patterns of political violence that drew in the MNF and later the UN reasserted themselves.

To begin, it is useful to review the circumstances of the intervention and its goals. On the night of September 18, 1994, with a U.S. Navy task force steaming off the Haitian coast, a high level negotiating team led by former President Jimmy Carter convinced Haiti's "de facto government" led by Haitian Lieutenant General Raoul Cedras to accept a United Nations mandate. Cedras allowed the multinational intervention force peacefully ashore and relinquished power to the country's elected leader, President Jean Bertrand Aristide.

Although further negotiations occurred between U.S. Ambassador William Swing, LTG Hugh Shelton (commander of JTF 180) and General Cedras, "the discussions were one sided". All 20,000 US and Caribbean soldiers were on the ground within two weeks and LTG Shelton "made it quite clear that he was willing to use them" if the Haitian leadership proved uncooperative.[3] The presence and threat of military force had successfully "taken" Haiti without bloodshed. It remained to be seen what that force could do now that it was there.

Beginning a few days later, the original intervention force, consisting of the Army's XVIII Airborne Corps and a Navy carrier task force with added Marine and Special Operations elements, was gradually replaced by the Army's 10th Mountain Division and elements of the 3d Special Forces Group. Largely for public relations purposes, the intervention force included small elements from various Caribbean states and was officially known as the Multi-National Force or simply "the MNF". Although the MNF included more national contingents over the next six months, among Haitians the MNF was clearly identified as an American force and the presence of other foreign troops seen as some sort of odd American quirk.

After a little more than six months, the MNF was replaced by UNMIH, a truly international force. Although the Americans provided the largest contingent by far (over 1700 soldiers) other nations were also major contributors. Bangladesh provided 847 soldiers, Canada 446, Nepal 409, Pakistan 844 and CARICOM 266 while still others were small force contributors.[4]

On March 31, 1995, US President William Clinton delivered his verdict on the MNF and Operation Uphold Democracy,

> A 30-nation Multinational Force, led by the United States, entered Haiti with a clear mission--to ensure the departure of the military regime, to restore the freely elected government of Haiti, and to establish a secure and stable environment in which the people of Haiti could begin to rebuild their country. Today, that mission has been accomplished--on schedule and with remarkable success.[5]

The UN Mission, like its predecessor, took its principal mandate from SCR 940. UNMIH defined success as "the conduct of free and fair parliamentary and presidential elections in the context of a secure and stable environment, culminating with a peaceful transition to the newly elected government in February 1996."[6]

Defined in these terms there is no question that UNMIH and the MNF were successful. The elections were accomplished despite some difficulty and the new government successfully installed in February, 1996. However, this is a minimal definition of success. It is problematic how much real difference these outcomes will make in troubled Haiti. The point of the mission, in the minds of most observers, was to restore legitimate popular government to Haiti. The military mission was a part of this larger political objective. The country remains in very serious straits politically and economically and the rule of law has not yet been successfully established.

There is no argument that Haiti is a political and economic basket case. Overpopulation, deforestation, abysmal public health, a dysfunctional government, wildly skewed wealth distribution and bleak economic prospects offer little hope for significant improvement in the conditions most Haitian's live under.[7] The crux of the problem is that Haiti suffers from a predatory culture. This fosters exploitation, corruption, injustice and economic stagnation. Moreover, there is no experience and little understanding of the nature and function of democratic institutions. The social results include pervasive apathy, distrust, violence, vengeance, class hatred and xenophobia. While these may be survival adaptations to Haiti's chronic political and economic chaos they make it difficult or impossible for an effective government to emerge.[8]

To correct this situation at a basic level, there was and is a need to create a social contract that extends outside immediate family and supporters to the more general society and the institutions of government. This ought to begin with the creation of legitimate and effective institutions of government worthy of loyalty, beginning with an effective police force and justice system. Without establishing these institutions it is questionable that any outside intervention in Haiti can have a serious or lasting impact. Moreover, the creation of a police force was part of the UN mandate for the intervention, so a civilian police element, called CIVPOL, was part of the civilian structure of UNMIH. Unfortunately, the creation of an effective, nonpolitical police force is the work of years, not months.

Realistically it is probably outside capabilities of the United States or the United Nations to create democratic institutions in Haiti without a lengthy and extensive presence there. Nevertheless the MNF and UNMIH both understood the need for such measures and attempted to accomplish them within their very limited capabilities. Parallel, cooperative bilateral efforts were also separately undertaken by the US including a Department of Justice training program to train the new police force and American military civil affairs officers were briefly posted as "ministry support teams" to help the government of Haiti. However, in practice, the MNF mission reduced to "create a secure environment for handover to UNMIH" and UNMIH's mission came down to "field a police force and hold elections".

Both forces acted on the belief that the key to political legitimacy lay in the mandated 1995 elections - the June legislative and municipal elections and the presidential elections in December. The unresolved problem was not that it was impossible to hold a reasonably open election. In Haiti the difficulty is to hold an election whose outcome means something. The intimate, reciprocal relationship among legitimacy, public order and free, unintimidated elections was implicitly recognized in the mandate when it set for the purposes of the intervention as assist with the elections, a new police force and government transition. However, this is not an easy dynamic to create under the conditions in Haiti. Days before President Clinton's arrival for the turnover from MNF to UNMIH political violence erupted with the murder of Mirelle Durocher Bertin, a former Cedras supporter and political organizer.[9]

An early problem arose from the dissolution of the FAd'H. Once the police forces had been dissolved, criminal gangs began to emerge and claim territory, presenting the Interim Public Security Force with a continuing challenge to their authority. There was also a rise in "citizen self-help" (vigilante) activity resulting in several deaths.[10]

When the UN forces, including the large American contingent, began to draw down after February 1996, the number of peacekeepers fell from almost 6,000 to about 1,300 and violence seemed to increase. Haitians, including Senator Jean-Robert Martinez voiced concern that disruptive elements now in self-exile could return when the UN departed. Furthermore, street crime had become a serious problem.[11]

Actually, due to controversy in the Security Council, the UN provided only 600 peacekeepers after March 1996. The additional 700 were Canadian soldiers sent at Canadian expense under a bilateral agreement with the Haitian government. Although technically not part of UNMIH the Canadians functioned as a fully integrated part of the force. In fact, a Canadian officer,

Brigadier General J.R. Pierre Daigle, was the commander of the UNMIH force from April through July of 1996.

As feared, an apparent pattern of intimidation and deliberate assassination of political activists continued in March 1996 with the shooting death of Haiti National Police (HNP) agent Christine Jeune, an opponent of Aristide's and Preval's crime policies.[12] Deliberate targeting of the new Haitian police force seems to have begun about that time. By mid-June, 1996, a total of twenty-six officers of the fledgling police force had been shot down and others wounded. Accusations were made that officers had responded with the summary execution of the alleged culprit.[13]

All in all, the new police force has suffered serious growing pains. In addition to the August 1996 police station assault, there has been a rising incidence of harassment attacks (as opposed to attempted murder) against off-duty HNP officers. On February 21, 1996 police apparently panicked at an incident during Carnival festivities in Port-au-Prince, killing two persons and wounding several others including six HNP officers. This was followed by a bloody March shoot-out between police and well-armed gangs in the Cite Soliel slums. Several bystanders were reported wounded in an incident on July 1, 1996 when two off-duty policewomen supposedly "shot it out" over a boyfriend in the town of Corail.[14] Because, in the author's view, Haiti's recovery depends most crucially on the fielding of a capable, effective police force the following discussion will touch on police affairs within several of the categories below.

Unity of Effort

Unity of effort can be regarded as both a short and long-term dimension. Unity must be obtained early in order to ensure success but must also be sustained in the long-term. The concept of unity of effort is related to the military principle "unity of command" and conceptually has two principle components. One is the common understanding of the desired end state among the participants in a mission. The other is the effective coordination of available means to achieve this end state.[15] Operations such as the intervention in Haiti differ from conventional military operations in that the desired end state is a political condition, rather than a success defined as military victory. As pointed out by the newest draft edition of the Army's manual on *Stability and Support Operations*, "There will seldom be real unity of command when many agencies and forces engage in common effort."[16]

Unity of effort was clearly on the minds of those involved in the MNF and UN operations in Haiti. LTG Hugh Shelton's initial orders to the MNF intervention Task Force were clear and simple, "create a safe and secure environment by any means possible." In his statement of "Commander's Intent" Major General Joseph Kinzer, UNMIH Force Commander, stated plainly that "interagency cooperation and unity of effort" were the keys to success.[17] The follow-on UN Mission was tasked by UN mandate to continue supporting this stable environment and further assist the government of Haiti by creating an "environment conducive" to the conduct of free and fair elections.[18] Unity was considerably advanced by the simplicity of the objectives in UN Security Council Resolution (UNSCR) 940, operationalized by UNMIH as "field a police force and hold elections".

The cause of unity on the military side was aided by the unique dual status of the Force Commander as commander of both US and UN forces in Haiti. Not all US forces in Haiti (including a US only task force) were under the operational control of UNMIH. However, General Kinzer, in his dual role, had command of all military forces in Haiti.[19] This relationship served to provide unique unity of effort and to quiet those vocal critics in the US (including members of Congress) who were adamantly opposed to US soldiers serving under foreign "command".

The disparity in size between the 20,000 man MNF and UNMIH's 6,000 man force raised concern for the ability of the UN to effectively accomplish the mission. To validate the force reduction and facilitate the shift to UNMIH, the MNF reduced its size to 6,000 troops and maintained that force level for a period of approximately 90 days before replacement by UN forces. This preparatory period enabled a "seamless" transition from one commander to another that was virtually transparent to the Haitian population. To a large degree, the transition meant that in place US forces simply changed their headgear, trading kevlar helmets for UN blue berets. Short-term unity of effort, operationalized as general agreement on broad goals and general means was successfully achieved. Sustained unity of effort proved more difficult.

As is typical in UN missions, the Special Representative of the Secretary General had little authority over the various UN agencies whose charter derives from the General Assembly (via the Economic and Social Council) rather than from the Security Council. There were at least ten major groups, organizations and agencies to coordinate: UN Headquarters, UN Development Program (UNDP), MICIVIH (*Mission Civile en Haiti*, human rights monitors), International Electoral Commission (election advisors), American Embassy in Haiti, US Interagency Working Groups, US Agency for International Development, US Atlantic Command, numerous NGO/PVOs, and the government of Haiti. UNMIH itself included military, civilian police (CIVPOL) and civilian development/assistance components. Late in the UNMIH portion of the mission, the new Haitian National Police were added to the list.

The only unifying thread from the standpoint of UNMIH was the identification of the SRSG as the single authority for all UNMIH. The SRSG, however, lacked any staff mechanism to coordinate the activities of the various components, particularly between the military and civilian elements. Early questions about the exact nature of CIVPOL's mandate, particularly regarding their direct involvement in law enforcement, also inhibited teamwork. Without an entity to coordinate mission activities, close liaison became critical.

In an effort to coordinate the efforts of various nongovernmental relief efforts by international organizations the MNF established a pair of Civil Military Operations Centers (CMOCs), one in Port-au-Prince and the other in Cap Haitien. These centers were continued under UNMIH. Obviously the CMOCs had no overt control over the various nongovernmental relief groups and depended largely on persuasion for their influence. Nevertheless, they were an important step forward in coordinating the development and assistance efforts of various players in Haiti.

The lesson here is that unity of effort can be achieved only when appropriate structures and means are available. Lacking these structures, UNMIH depended primarily on effective personal leadership by the SRSG and Force Commander and the generally cooperative attitude of the various entities involved in the assistance effort. This was effective for the military side of the UN Mission and reasonably so for the internal operations of the Mission as a whole.

Legitimacy

Legitimacy, defined as the willing acceptance of and support to political authority is the single most important dimension of the model in cases such as Haiti. Within the SWORD model, legitimacy is a long term dimension concerned chiefly with the public perception of the peace force. However, in a situation of near governmental collapse, the real issue is the restoration (or creation) of faith in government. But at least a modicum of legitimacy must be achieved quickly by the peace force for itself in order to lay the basis for longer term success. In general, the force enjoyed legitimacy throughout the mission at every level. Initially, General Shelton's forceful attitude toward the despised Cedras government and that government's obvious deference contributed enormously to the perceived legitimacy of the force among most Haitians. The desired result, however, was not only the legitimacy of the MNF and UNMIH but also that of the new Haitian government. It remains to be seen how much of this legitimacy (which was clearly attached to the discernible achievements of the Mission) can be transferred to the new government. To coordinate these parallel threads, legitimacy for the peace force and for civil government is a challenge. An important determinant of legitimacy for both in Haiti was the ability to suppress endemic violence.

There were at least three principal areas of concern with regard to legitimacy. These were the legitimacy of the force in the eyes of the Haitian people, before the international community and, perhaps most important, in the eyes of the American public without whose support the operation would quickly have become impossible. In addition to the international legal legitimacy provided by UNSCR 940, the MNF undertook effort to promote both its own legitimacy and that of the Haitian government as the sources of progress. The MNF brought in a variety of specialized unit commanders before the press and Haitian officials to talk about what their units were doing to help Haiti's legitimate government "get back on its feet".[20] Given the peaceful nature of the intervention, the international media quickly lost interest. By the time of the March 1995 transition from the MNF to UNMIH, US media outlets had decided that the story was over in Haiti. Apparently operating on the principle that "no news is good news" the American public took little further interest in the operation.

UNMIH also drew its initial legitimacy from UNSCR 940 and the later UNSCR 975, which authorized it to conduct operations in Haiti. The UN Mission made a sustained effort to stay within the mandate, respect local Haitian laws, and understand the legal and political ramifications of its actions. As with the MNF, individual training and discipline played a very important part. Incidents at the tactical level could have severe operational and strategic consequences, a fact that was continuously impressed upon all members of the force.[21] UNMIH's military contingent also took up the mantle as a source of immediate progress and completed hundreds of civil affairs and humanitarian assistance projects such as community based building projects and medical training for local health workers. In their report of January 31, 1996, UNMIH reported 853 completed civil affairs projects and 108 on going. These ranged from sanitation and reforestation to NGO convoy security and public sanitation. Because of resource constraints most of these were limited, local projects.[22]

The campaign to communicate improvements in the electoral process, the Haitian National Police, local governing councils and other government functions was part of a conscious effort to change the population's traditional view of government institutions and processes as inherently exploitative and oppressive.[23]

The relationship between the intervention force and the FAd'H may have, to some degree, have worked against the cause of long-term legitimacy. The general population of Haiti had expected that the US led intervention force would hunt down and destroy the hated FAd'H and then assume the role of a public order force until a new Haitian system could be created. Initially, this had also been more-or-less the expectation of American planners. The FAdH however, being inept rather than stupid, never had any real attention of fighting the invaders. Cedras quickly came to terms with the Carter mission and then began to bargain for the most advantageous possible exit. This left the intervention force in the unenviable position of visibly cooperating with the single most hated element of Haitian society and may have tainted further efforts to build a new police force.[24]

One important step to legitimize the governing and especially the electoral process would have been for the Aristide government to preside over secure, well-run elections. Still, no one expected trouble-free elections and their expectations were rewarded. The June elections were delayed, plagued with organizational problems and occasional fraud and violence that combined to jeopardize their legitimacy in the eyes of many Haitians. Rather than creating a democratic society, the election produced a legislature so thoroughly controlled by Aristide's Lavalas Party that the effective result was a one-party state.[25]

The weeks following the elections saw an increase in political violence, most of it against those associated with the Cedras regime or the widely hated FAd'H. The second round of legislative elections occurred in October with fewer administrative problems although the level of violence continued to simmer. Then in November the long-standing character of the political climate in Haiti seemed to reassert itself when two newly elected legislators (one a cousin of Aristide) were assassinated. The President called on his supporters to disarm the *attaches* (FAd'H paramilitary thugs) believed responsible. The rioting that followed killed at least ten persons. Dozens of homes were looted and burned.[26] Shortly afterwards apparently unrelated rioting broke out in Cite Soleil (Port-au-Prince's worst slum) leaving three dead.[27]

On December 17, Haiti held a reasonably calm Presidential election. Although its credibility may have been harmed by a spare voter turnout (estimated at 15-28 per cent) the process selected Aristide's first Prime Minister, Rene Preval, to succeed him. On February 7, 1996 President Preval was inaugurated, marking Haiti's first peaceful transition of national power in living memory.[28] However, the increasing violence of July and August of 1996 called into question the degree to which the legitimacy achieved by the MNF and UN peace forces has managed to attach itself to the new government.

Support to Belligerents

Support to belligerents is a long-term dimension which seeks to evaluate the military effectiveness of the combatants, other than the peace forces. In Haiti, there were no combatants, per se and little potential for widespread belligerency outside the FAd'H and its auxiliaries. As noted earlier, armed resistance to the newly installed government seems sporadic and criminal in nature and not the product of an organized belligerency. The departing Cedras government had no international support and little internal support of any consequence after the intervention.

The most important potential bellicose elements were, as noted, the FAd'H and their auxiliaries, the so-called *attaches*. The FAd'H, however, in its role as a police force was at least supposedly cooperating with the intervention until replaced by the interim police. The intervention force confiscated virtually all of the FAd'H's heavy weapons and most or all of the weapons maintained in the various military armories. This removed much of the potential for large-scale military mischief.

pite widespread rumors of threats from FAd'H dissidents who had fled to the Dominican Republic, no large-scale resistance materialized.[29] Had an internal resistance developed, MNF and later UNMIH control of the western side of the island was complete enough to make it impossible for such a resistance movement to receive useful outside support.

While there has been little or no popular support for the former FAd'H, it is clear that they have retained a supply of arms and remain capable of damaging activities against public order and the democratic government. The issue of disarming the ex-FAd'H then becomes critical and will be examined in another section, that dealing with actions targeted on ending conflict.

Support Actions of Peace Forces

The dimension, support actions of the peace forces, is another long term dimension. Its chief components are the perceived length and strength of the peace force commitment. Although, the SWORD model places psychological operations (PSYOP) under the dimension "actions targeted on ending conflict", since the major activity of these elements was directed at ensuring the perceived legitimacy of the force and the new democratic government, they will be considered under the dimension of support actions.

UNMIH's pre-mission analysis determined that the strategic center of gravity for Haiti was President Aristide and the operational centers of gravity were control of Port-au-Prince and Cap Haitien.[30] UNMIH's operational concept emphasized force presence in Port-au-Prince and Cap Haitien, rural patrolling to bolster the US Special Forces teams in the countryside and an information campaign using Military Information Support Teams (MIST, a.k.a. PsyOps) to communicate with the population. The force also maintained a well-armed quick reaction force (QRF) capable of rapid response by ground or air. The nine legislative departments (or provinces) of Haiti were organized into six operational zones. Each of the UN Zone Commanders had responsibility for all forces and activities in his zone with additional support on-call as needed. Wisely, the zone headquarters were deliberately placed in areas with a history of unrest, and the remainder of the force positioned to respond rapidly throughout its area of responsibility. The principal activity of these forces was to patrol their territory and provide stability through presence among the populace. Lastly, a full-time security element was organized to the protect the President and ensure his safety as the visible symbol of Haitian sovereignty.[31] In the short-term these measures probably contributed to the legitimacy of the intervention force and certainly were helpful as support actions in ending conflict during the UN presence.

A deliberate decision was made that the US military would not become involved in "nation-building" in Haiti. However, as noted earlier, Haiti's infrastructure had suffered greatly the past several decades making economic recovery problematic at best. Nevertheless, restoration of the Haitian economy was desperately needed even though not a part of the Force's mandate. Despite the limited mandate and lack of funds, the MNF and the UN both took on a great number of sorely needed infrastructure restoration and repair measures under the rubric of "operational necessity".[32]

The UNMIH SRSG and the Force Commander made several efforts to "cobble together" money from various sources, including US$1 million allocated for repair projects that affected military operations. This was successful in limited projects including the partial restoration of electrical power to Port-au-Prince and Cap Haitian and repairing one of three hurricane damaged bridges near Jacmel but was simply not sufficient for the kind of major, long-term structural rehabilitation required.[33]

Public safety continued to be an issue. The discredited Haitian military/police forces were widely considered to be corrupt, abusive and untrustworthy. Their abrupt dismissal by President Aristide, coupled with the general ineffectiveness of the Interim Public Security Force (IPSF), left the country with hardly the semblance of a law enforcement and criminal justice system while prisons were crowded to overflowing. This ineffectiveness was rooted in the general hatred among the Haitian people for the FAd'H both as an institution and as individuals. These feelings transferred to the IPSF and the general populace very often simply refused to accept the authority of the former FAd'H members reincarnated as the IPSF.

Although the Interim Public Safety Force (IPSF) was widely criticized, it was still the only available solution to the police problem until the Haitian National Police could be fielded. Essentially the IPSF was the product of a US Department of State sponsored program. It was created by removing the worst of the old Haitian police and providing the remainder (about 3,400) with a six-day course in the basic law enforcement techniques, ethics, responsibility and conduct in a democracy.[34] The strategic planners might have benefited from the Panamanian example where, in 1990, the US retrained members of former Panamanian Defense Forces as police. The result was a considerable loss of legitimacy for the newly democratic Panamanian government and the cause of public order in general.[35]

The very real threat of prison riots and wanton lawlessness in the streets led UNMIH to introduce a military presence in the prisons and police stations. Without effective local law enforcement, it was obvious the secure and stable environment established under the MNF could continue only as long as the UN contingents were in place, providing support to the Haitian government. The solution to this was to be the creation of the new Haitian National Police (HNP). The new Haitian National Police force had to recruit and train an eventual total of 7,000 officers who would replace the IPSF. Both of these forces were monitored and assisted, first by the MNF's International Police Monitors (IPM) and then UNMIH's Civilian Police (CIVPOL) element. However, the recruitment, training and equipping of an entirely new police establishment was not a quick or easy undertaking.

Military Actions of Peace Forces

This is a short term dimension whose major components are the size of the peace force and the types of activities it engages in. In a military intervention such as Haiti, it might be expected that the most intensive military action would occur early in the operation. But in the Haiti case, the overwhelming size and capability of the intervening force and the lack of significant armed opposition would have made the initial entry of the peace forces relatively unopposed even without the Carter agreement that allowed the MNF permissive entry into Haiti. The MNF's "enemy" had been identified before the mission as the FAd'H. However, after the Carter mission, the ragtag Haitian Armed Forces/police, at least on paper, became collaborators with the intervention force. In fact the FAd'H had never posed a significant military threat to the intervention.

In the last analysis, there were few purely military operations conducted by the MNF after the initial incursion and almost none by the follow-on UNMIH force. Even the quick reaction force launched by UNMIH's Canadian peacekeepers to counter the August 19, 1996 attack against the Port-au-Prince central police station met little opposition as the perpetrators fled.

For the most part, the conventional military mission, to deter violence by any potential belligerents, was achieved by the mere presence of the force. Both the MNF and UNMIH took care to insure that this presence was made obvious and real by a continuous patrolling, especially in the capital and Haiti's trouble prone second city, Cap Haitien. Other than this, "military actions" often were really more closely related to support functions than actual military activity in the pure sense of defeating or deterring an organized enemy. Despite this, both the MNF and UNMIH clearly demonstrated the advantages of using military capabilities in support of limited political objectives.

Public order issues reared up again in an ugly incident early in the intervention when US soldiers stood by while FAd'H beat Haitian civilians, killing one within a few feet of the US position. The problem lay with the MNF's original rules of engagement (ROE) which were too restrictive and resulted in an incident.[36] Reporters quickly raised this as an issue of effectiveness, centering on apparent contradictions in ROE for US troops. The JTF staff judge advocate held a news conference within 24 hours explaining essentially that there had been some confusion between the initial "forced entry" ROE and the alternative, "peaceful occupation" ROE resulting in the writing of a third set of ROE to cover the "hybrid" situation that resulted from the last minute deal with the Cedras government.[37] The initial report of the US 16th Military Brigade highlighted this as a deficiency which was quickly corrected in the full glare of publicity. The MP brigade commander went on to demand a meeting with the FAd'H Chief for Port-au-Prince and demand a halt to the abuses while advising him that US military would now intervene to protect local citizens.[38]

The inability of the Haitian government to communicate with its own constituents, the Haitian people, was a serious problem. The potential to further such communication lay with the US Army's Psychological Operations Forces (PSYOP). But, suspicion as to the nature and methods of as well as the capabilities and functions of these forces made UNMIH's civilian leadership reluctant to include them as part of the force. When it finally became clear that these elements were no more than militarized public relations and media units the UN became more willing to take advantage of their capabilities. A clear explanation of the their valuable capabilities helped create confidence in these units while renaming them Military Information Support Teams (MIST) increased the comfort level of UN leaders in Haiti as well as in the Department of Peacekeeping Operations (DPKO) at UN New York.

The MISTF (Military Information Support Task Force a.k.a. Psychological Operations Task Force) developed and executed the UNMIH information campaign. In addition to developing information products (i.e. radio/loud speaker messages, hand bills, posters, and videos), it worked extensively with various government ministries and agencies, to assist them in improving their ability to effectively communicate with the population and prepare them to assume these tasks upon the departure of UNMIH. Tactical dissemination teams (TDTs) were deployed throughout the AOR, to provide general support to the zone commanders. They coordinated with local radio stations, used loud speakers, and conducted face-to-face communication to disseminate information to the Haitian population.[39]

Surveys conducted by the TDTs were valuable in assessing the current attitude and perceptions of the Haitian people. Also, TDT's were extensively used throughout the country to disperse demonstrations and quell unrest. The information programs and activities were a very effective military activity that contributed directly to maintaining the secure and stable environment. The success of MIST is measured by the appreciation of their work expressed by both the UN and the Haitian government during the mission.

Military Actions of the Belligerents and the Peace Forces

This dimension deals chiefly with proficiency and aggressiveness of the belligerent forces. As noted earlier there were no belligerents per se in Haiti and no significant military actions by any potential belligerents. The current violence within Haiti, however troubling, does not seem to have a larger political purpose. Although it has proved impossible to substantiate, it is widely believed in Haiti that at least some former FAd'H leaders self-exiled to Santo Domingo are simply awaiting the departure of the UN forces. If this leadership exists and can command a degree of loyalty from the armed ex-FAd'H the combination could be very worrisome. For this reason, failure to disarm the ex-FAd'H may have serious long-term consequences. However, events to date have still not justified referring to the ex-FAd'H activity as "military" despite the potentially damaging consequences.

Actions Targeted on Ending Conflict

This short-term dimension is concerned with those immediate actions taken by the peace forces to reduce or eliminate the general level of violence. Arguably it is here that the military intervention forces enjoyed their greatest, though least durable, success. The conflict in Haiti was never importantly military. The only significant military opposition, the FAd'H, was both inept and incapable and concerned chiefly with the individual survival of its members. Conflict in the form of widespread political and criminal violence (along with endemic corruption) was, however, a root cause of the civil violence that had nearly destroyed Haiti both politically and economically.

The issue of disarming the population was reportedly raised on several occasions in interagency working groups before the operation and among operational commanders, Haitian officials and the US Embassy after it began. However, it is impossible to point to a single discrete decision that no widespread disarmament of the population would be attempted. It was just something "everybody knew" was probably impossible and almost certainly counterproductive. BG Richard A. Potter, Special Forces commander for the MNF remarked, "If we were going to reinstate the rule of law, we couldn't begin by kicking down doors all over Haiti."[40]

But, the MNF did confiscate some weapons during Operation Uphold Democracy. As described by General Potter, "All visible weapons were confiscated throughout Haiti. If anyone appeared on the streets with a weapon it was confiscated on the authority of the Task Force Commander." In addition, stocks of FAd'H weapons were taken under MNF control and, for the most part, destroyed (including crew-served and automatic weapons in police stations and a large cache discovered at Adm. Killick Naval base). The MNF rejected a wide-spread weapons confiscation program in favor of a weapons amnesty and "buy-back" program.[41] In its evaluation of the countrywide MNF weapons-buy-back program the 3d Special Forces Group (whose teams handled much of the program) termed it "marginally successful".[42] By the time of the turnover to UNMIH most of the *attaches* had not been not disarmed and few of the weapons in the general population were seized. (Estimates are that about 30,000 of the estimated 175,000 small arms in circulation were confiscated). Under UNMIH, another weapons "buy-back" program was instituted but it also met with very limited success. It did tempt numerous former FAd'H members who still had older weapons to turn these in for cash.[43]

Special Forces teams also confiscated weapons as part of the activity of the 17 Special Forces detachments spread throughout the country. Each of these reported locating one or two weapons caches but most of the recovered weapons were rusted and unserviceable.[44]

Major General Kinzer stated that he was constantly aware of the potential to build a "house of cards," which would crumble upon the UN's departure. Preparing the Haitian government to take charge of its own destiny began at the outset of the mission. While focusing on mission accomplishment, the force wanted to preclude the government and people of Haiti from becoming overly dependent upon it. General Kinzer reported only indifferent success in his continuous efforts to "energize" Haitian government preparations for the UN's departure. Most Haitian officials did not seem to truly believe that the international community, in particular the UN, would leave them to their fate.[45]

Under pressure from China (which objected to Haiti's tentative relationship with Taiwan) and Russia, the UN Security Council agreed on 29 February 1996 to reduce the UN mission in Haiti and to reduce the time the UN force would remain. Mission strength was planned for 1,900 soldiers and 300 international police officers after Canada volunteered to send 700 soldiers at its own expense.[46] With the March 1996 reduction of UNMIH forces, a multitude of tasks were transferred to the Haitian government and other international agencies. Demonstration of military perseverance continues in Haiti today with the continuation of UNMIH and the US Support Group, Haiti, a bilateral cooperation agreement between the US and Haiti.

Conclusions

Applying the SWORD model to the Haiti case in any useful way presents a basic difficulty. The model was devised for application to long-term efforts. In particular it is not designed to accommodate an intervention which is limited to a short, pre-specified period. The expectation of the designers is that any very short-term effort will simply be avoided by the opposition which can afford to "wait it out" for a period of months until the intervention force departs.[47] This may be what will occur in Haiti.

Some of the factors of the model treated here, notably Unity of Effort, are short-term in the sense that successful accomplishment of the elements underlies long-range success. However, it should be noted that the statistical validity of the entire model is significantly greater than that of the various component factors taken individually. This mitigates against any attempt to separate out long-term factors from short-term ones and apply the short-term ones to the Haitian situation.

The underlying rationale of the model is that "success" is defined in general terms as the creation of a safe and stable civil situation in which development continues to occur and the people are willing to accord sufficient legitimacy to the government for it to operate. The model then seeks to determine if the factors are present which can reasonably be expected to bring about this situation. It should also be noted that, in the words of Professor Manwaring, "the model does not acquiesce to policy" - a policy informed by the model would have been aimed at a much longer process aimed at fundamental reforms with the purpose of restoring popular legitimacy to the Haitian government.[48] Elections, in this interpretation, would be seen as a necessary, enabling step but not an end in themselves. Although it is too soon to state whether or not there has been a "success" in Haiti, the military establishment of a safe and stable situation is an important milestone on the road to "success". It is however, only a milestone.

The foregoing discussion returns again to the a basic question raised at the beginning of this chapter - in a situation of near-total economic and political collapse, what can an intervention force reasonably be expected to do? There is only so much that can be accomplished by such limited, specific, measures, however skillfully done or well-intentioned. When it came to the larger issues of restoring the economic functioning of Haiti, there was simply nothing the military force could do, given its resources and authority.

In larger terms it is hard to escape the conclusion that the strategic planners, both in the US and at the UN either seriously underestimated or were never prepared to deal with the sheer difficulty of producing anything like a lasting democracy in Haiti. The basic requirement seems to be a need to fundamentally reform the relationship between the state and civil society in Haiti. There was never a serious attempt made to perform widespread "social engineering" in Haiti. This was not the intention of the UN mandate and never a part of the mission of either MNF or the UN force. Nevertheless, in order to achieve lasting peaceful reform in Haiti social engineering was exactly what was required. The most significant concrete step, police reform, has fallen on difficult times with the withdrawal of most international police support (reduced from 900 CIVPOL in January to 300 in June). Mr. Brahimi's successor as UNMIH SRSG, Enrique Ter Horst, stated specifically in May 1996 that the HNP could not ensure a "stable environment" without UN assistance.[49] What remained in August 1996 was a reduced UNMIH CIVPOL component confined to Port-au-Prince and a handful of trainers under a US Department of Justice program. Neither of these agencies can provide what the HNP desperately needs - leadership, field supervision, internal order and discipline.

These types of problems were much on the mind of Kinzer when he stated "We did what we could do. Turning on the lights in Port-au-Prince is an example of a measure within our mandate and our capabilities and a useful action for long and short term reasons. It provided a tangible benefit for ordinary Haitians by reducing street crime and taking a step toward a return to normal conditions. Likewise, the elections were part of our mission and were accomplished despite difficulties and provided an opportunity for better government. That's what we could do."[50]

To argue as some have that restoration of political stability to Haiti was not the military mission is probably correct. However, to have conducted a two year exercise in political symbology was not the purpose either. The growing level of internal violence underscores these failure of symbolic support and piecemeal measures.

The key to stability and progress in Haiti is popular acceptance and support of the Haitian government, otherwise referred to as "legitimacy". This in turn depends on a majority belief that the government is operating according to their desires and on their behalf. This cannot be achieved by any foreign intervention, military or otherwise. Nevertheless, the MNF and the UN, by their intervention made an implicit promise that this intervention was for the benefit of the Haitian people. Certainly it was perceived that way by many Haitians. While it is true that the MNF and UNMIH cannot produce legitimacy for the new Haitian government at the same time it does have an obligation to conduct those unpalatable but basic support measures, such as disarming the ex-FAd'H and continuing to support the HNP, that will enable the new government to achieve general acceptance. That will stem from the ability of the government of Haiti to sustain and improve on these advances. In the last analysis, the problems of Haiti may simply be too deeply rooted for any military intervention to resolve. In this regard it is well to note the final sentence in the January 1996 UNMIH Command Briefing's discussion of the UN mission's impending transition. "The Haitian government must take charge of its future."

> Then came a whisper of hope in a camouflage uniform, the controversial US military action ordered by President Clinton. Initially they were greeted by the chaos and horror that Haiti had become, but soon the troops gained control of the streets, and there seemed a palpable lifting of fear. Haiti is a land of extremes with a long history of turmoil. Whether this tenuous calm is only a temporary respite, whether the joy now felt will leave only a bittersweet taste of peace, remains to be seen.[51]

Notes

[1] "Gunmen Open Fire on Haitian Buildings", Washington Post August 20, 1996, pg. 14.

[2] Michael Norton, "Political Turmoil Hits Haitian Media" Washington Times, August 23, 1996, pg. 17

[3] LTC Colonel Timothy Vane, spokesman, XVIII Airborne Corps, FT Bragg NC, correspondence with the author dated May 10, 1996.

[4] UNMIH, Command Briefing, January 31, 1996, courtesy of HQ UNMIH.

[5] President William Clinton "Haiti: A Time of Peaceful Transition", Remarks at UN Transition Ceremony, Port-au-Prince, Haiti, 31 Mar 1995, U.S. Department of State Bureau of Public Affairs Dispatch (Vol 6, No 15) April 10, 1995; Pages 283-285.

[6] "UNMIH Overview", pg. 8; provided by HQ UNMIH, Port-au-Prince Haiti, March 5, 1995.

[7] See for example - World Peace Foundation, Haiti: Prospects for Political and Economic Reconstruction, WPF Report No. 10 (conference report) November 1995; Gabriel Marcella, Haiti Strategy, Strategic Studies Institute, US Army War College, October 1994; Ernest Preeg, The Haitian Dilemma, Center for Strategic and International Studies, 1996.

[8] This has been commented on by numerous scholars over the years, perhaps most cogently in recent years by Donald E. Schulz and Gabriel Marcella, Reconciling the Irreconcilable: The Troubled Outlook for U.S. Policy Toward Haiti (Carlisle, PA: The Strategic Studies Institute) 1994. See also Michel-Rolph Trouillot, Haiti: State Against Nation, (New York:Monthly Review Press) 1990 and James Leyburn, The Haitian People, (New Haven:Yale University Press) 1966.

[9] Amy Wilentz, "Trying to Pin Down Elusive Death Lists", Los Angles Times, April 9, 1995, p.M-1.

[10] Johanna McGeary, "Did the American Mission Matter" Time Magazine, February 19, 1996, pp. 36-38, p. 37.

[11] National Public Radio, "Haiti Faces New Challenges with Fledgling Police Force" All Things Considered, February 11, 1996.

[12] As reported by the expatriate newspaper Haiti Insight, Aristide regarded the gangs as much as political phenomena as a criminal one and sought to promote "a dialogue between HNP and the well-armed civilian gangs. See J.P. Slavin, "The Haitian Police: Struggling With Inexperience" Haiti Insight, April/May 1996, p. 4.

[13] Sandra M. Garcia "Murder of Police Frightens Haiti", Miami Herald International Edition, June 4, 1996, pp. 1A and 3A.

[14] Telephone interview with Prof. Bryant Freeman, University of Kansas, July 2, 1996. A fluent Creole speaker and long-time observer of Haitian affairs, Dr. Freeman monitors the Haitian Press on behalf of the U.S.-based Haitian Institute. He was a civilian member of UNMIH and an election observer for Haiti's December 1995 elections.

[15] For a further discussion of this issue see John T. Fishel's "Achieving the Elusive Unity of Effort" in Gray Area Phenomena, Max G. Manwaring Ed., (San Francisco:Westview Press) 1993.

[16] US Army, FM100-20, Stability and Support Operations, Final Draft, April 1996, pg. 2-8.
[17] MG Kinzer, "Memorandum for the United Nations Mission in Haiti", dated Dec 28, 1994, courtesy of General Kinzer.
[18] UNSCR 940 (1994), text courtesy of the U.S. Mission to the United Nations, NY, NY.
[19] "Success in Peacekeeping", UNMIH After Action Report (AAR), US Army Peacekeeping Institute, Carlisle Barracks, PA pg. 6. This report was prepared by General Kinzer's staff in May and June of 1996. Hereafter cited as UNMIH AAR.
[20] LTC Colonel Timothy Vane, spokesman, XVIII Airborne Corps, FT Bragg NC, correspondence with the author dated May 10, 1996.
[21] MG Kinzer interview, Carlisle PA, 10 May 1996.
[22] UNMIH Command Briefing, 31 January 1996, courtesy of HQ UNMIH.
[23] MG Kinzer interview, Carlisle PA, 10 May 1996.
[24] For an account of post-agreement maneuvering by the FAd'H leadership, see Larry Rohter, "Haiti's Military Peruses the Fine Print", New York Times 22 September, 1994, p. A14.
[25] Freeman interview, University of Kansas, July 2, 1996.
[26] Foreign Broadcast Information Service (FBIS), Daily Report: Latin America, November 14, 1995.
[27] Art Pine, "Haiti's Stability Still in Doubt" Los Angles Times November 25, 1995, p. A22.
[28] Larman Wilson "Trying to Give Intervention a Good Name" Freedom Review (Vol 27) 3 January 1996, p. 28.
[29] UNMIH Command Briefing, 31 January 1996, courtesy of HQ UNMIH.
[30] Haiti AAR, pg 8.
[31] Haiti AAR, pg 9.
[32] Kelly Klemens, Captain, US Army, "Joint Engineer Operations in Haiti", Engineer (Vol 24: No. 1) 4 January 1995 pp. 36-42.
[33] MG Kinzer interview, Carlisle PA, 10 May 1996.
[34] Fishel characterized the effort to retrain FAd'H members as IPSF as "too much in too short a time with significantly less than was required in human resources". John T. Fishel, "The Intervention in Haiti", in Civil Military Operations in the New World Order Praeger, Westport, CT; 1997.
[35] John T. Fishel, "Haiti Ain't Panama, Jack", unpublished conference paper, courtesy of Dr. Fishel.
[36] Rick Bragg "GIs Angry Over Orders to `Stand By', New York Times 22 September 1994, p. A14.
[37] LTC Timothy D. Vane, telephone interview, 02 March 1996. LTC Vane was the Public Affairs Officer for JTF 190.
[38] 16th Military Brigade (Airborne) briefing, undated but provided to the author c. Jan 20, 1995. Courtesy of MNF/JTF 190, Port-au-Prince Haiti.
[39] Haiti AAR, pg. 9.
[40] Interview with BG Richard A. Potter (USA, ret), 6 March 1996, Carlisle Barracks, PA; Brigadier General Potter commanded Task Force (TF) Black, the initial Joint Special Operations Task Force under JTF 180. He subsequently commanded TF Raleigh, the Army Special Operations Force remaining in Haiti after the departure of JTF 180. UNMIH officers point out that disarmament was not specified in the mandate.

[41] 16th Military Brigade (Airborne) briefing, undated but provided to the author c. Jan 1995. Courtesy of MNF/JTF 190, Port-au-Prince, Haiti.

[42] 3d Special Forces Group (Abn), "Unconventional Operations Report", 11 Dec 1994, pg. 27.

[43] Ibid.

[44] Potter interview, March 6, 1996.

[45] MG Kinzer interview, Carlisle PA, May 10, 1996.

[46] Barbara Crossette, "UN Mission to Haiti is Reprieved" New York Times, March 1, 1996, pg. A8.

[47] Interview with Max G. Manwaring, Carlisle, PA, June 14, 1996.

[48] Interview with Max G. Manwaring, Carlisle PA, July 26, 1996.

[49] "UNMIH to Stay Until 1997", International Peacekeeping News (Vol 2, No 2) May-June 1996, pp. 11-12.

[50] MG Kinzer interview, Carlisle Barracks PA, May 8, 1996.

[51] Bob Shacochis, "Letter from Haiti..", Vol. 34, Columbia Journalism Review, January 7, 1995; pp. 26.

Conclusion

11

Lessons that Should Have Been Learned: Toward a Theory of Engagement for "The Savage Wars of Peace"

Max G. Manwaring and Kimbra L. Fishel

He who dedicates himself to the dignity of mankind, and dedicates himself to the earth, reaps from it the harvest that sows its seed and sustains the world again and again.

The Rebel
-Albert Camus

Since the end of the Cold War, the nature of the international security system and the verities that shaped US and Western national purposes, policies, strategies, and priorities have undergone fundamental changes. In place of the predictable Cold War international structure we now have a world of dangerous uncertainty and ambiguity in which time-honored concepts of security and the classical military means to attain it are no longer completely sufficient to address current threats.

In this connection, we find that George Kennan's containment theory of engagement no longer serves to inform where security efforts will and will not occur, or for what purposes.[1] No equivalent alternative structure has taken its place. Lacking an architecture for when, how, where, and why to use the instruments of national and international power, the United States and the rest of the international community are forced to consider security problems on a case by case basis. In this situation, the only criterion for evaluation seems to be nothing more than "uniqueness." We are left with vague entreaties that foreign policy and military management must serve the amorphous "national well-being" and "democracy" in a piecemeal and ad hoc crisis management manner.

Given the anarchical nature of the international security system, there is nothing to check a world political actor except the power of other actors. The hard evidence over time and throughout the world indicates that violence is all too often considered an acceptable option in attempting to achieve personal, subnational, transnational, and national goals as well as international objectives. The stark reminders of the strengths of tribalism, feudalism, religious fundamentalism, racism, and the ubiquitous obstacles to change such as lack of awareness, absence of political competence, inadequacy of commitment, corruption, and retention of privilege for a few, are all very much a part of the cultures in many areas of the world.

The unstable "peace" of the post Cold War era is manifest by myriad instabilities. They include: human starvation, widespread disease, refugee flows, illegal drug trafficking and organized crime, extreme nationalism, irredentism, religious fundamentalism, militant reformers, ideologues, demagogues, civil and military bureaucrats, terrorists, insurgents, warlords, and ethnic cleansers. All these phenomena, and associated political actors have at their disposal an awesome array of sophisticated conventional and unconventional weaponry to use for their own narrow purposes. For many, violence is a normal and accepted way of dealing with problems--changing what a given agenda decrees is to be changed, or keeping things the way they always have been. The consequences are seen in the form of environmental devastation, lack of political and socioeconomic justice, and "wars of national debilitation, a steady run of uncivil wars sundering fragile but functioning nation states and gnawing at the well-being of stable nations."[2]

In this security environment, the United States, other powers, the United Nations, and other interested regional and non governmental organizations have become increasingly involved in some form of direct or indirect intervention in pursuit of unilateral national security or humanitarian interests, or in pursuit of multilateral "collective security" interests. The politically correct argument is ambiguous: "the magnitude of the human tragedy constitutes a threat to international peace and security." A more cynical argument is straightforward: "stability creates national and international well-being; instability creates chaos." At a practical level, the assertion of a national or international obligation to intervene in an internal situation to achieve a desired level of stability and peace redefines the purposes and means by which "peace operations" might take place. This assertion also leads to a peacekeeping environment in which multilateral political considerations rather than unilateral military considerations dominate.

If the peacekeeping environment is itself multifaceted, then a peacekeeping operation must acknowledge and understand the particular type of conflict it faces and the key elements necessary for success. These key elements provide the basis for a theory of engagement. In defining these elements, this book turns to the SWORD model. By analyzing peace operations through application of the seven dimensions of the SWORD model, we strive to determine if the SWORD model can provide the framework now needed to support a theory of engagement. Clearly, the cases elaborated in this book and others illustrate the fact that, although every conflict is situation specific, none is completely unique. There are analytical commonalties in each case that define relative success or failure. What do these cases tell us about the application of the SWORD model to peace operations? Do they support the paradigm as it currently stands, or is some modification from the initial study as discussed in Chapter One now needed?

To begin with, what these cases do **not** demonstrate is a contradiction of the SWORD model. These cases actually show that whether by pure "dumb luck," or some more deliberate attempt to apply the common sense aspects of the SWORD model, the level of success in contemporary peace operations is determined by the the degree to which the application of the seven strategic dimensions apply. This finding suggests that the model constituted by these dimensions can be used to understand and deal with the contemporary "peacekeeping" phenomena. In general, when we identify all the factors of the SWORD model in any given peace or stability operation, we can see greater chances of success. When those factors are weak or absent, we can see greater chances of failure. Equally important, however, are the dimensions themselves, how they intertwine and overlap, and how two dimensions in particular, Legitimacy and Unity of Effort, emerge from these cases with a special significance.

Traditional Peacekeeping

The traditional peacekeeping environment is one in which all parties involved in the conflict seek an outside party such as the United Nations to come into the conflictive area and help implement a formally agreed upon accord. Resolution of underlying political problems is the key element for long term success to the peace operation. It is also the most difficult goal to achieve, even in the most "friendly" environments conducive to traditional operations.

When the cases illustrated in this book are analyzed, Unity of Effort and Legitimacy emerge as the two most critical dimensions to explaining the strengths and weaknesses of traditional peacekeeping. Unity of Effort, as demonstrated, exists on several levels: an international level, a regional level, an organizational level, and an internal or local level. In the ideal case, Unity of Effort exists at each level as well as among the different levels as a whole.

The Cyprus case shows that there existed initially a strong international Unity of Effort backed by the United States and Great Britain. The ten UN sponsored proposals beginning in 1965 attest to the international Unity of Effort. However, because there was no Unity of Effort between the Greek and Turkish Cypriot communities themselves, the proposals were rejected. As demonstrated by Swan in Chapter Two, the regional key players, Greece and Turkey, had conflicting interests which defied a Unity of Effort. Thus, when UNFICYP was established there was no supported history of UN proposals on which a Unity of Effort could be based and which could provide the framework for de jure legitimacy.

In contrast, the Salvadoran case presents a good example of the different levels of Unity of Effort and the linkages among the levels. This type of unity however is context dependent, as Fishel and Corr have demonstrated in Chapter Three. International Unity of Effort was made possible by the end of the Cold War, and all parties involved internationally, regionally, and locally were truly committed to peace. Unity of Effort between the Salvadoran government and the FMLN was made possible once revolution was no longer a viable goal for the FMLN. Thus, ONUSAL's traditional operation commenced on a solid framework that President Jose Napoleon Duarte began nearly a decade before. The Salvadoran case stands in contrast to Cyprus in that Unity of Effort was achieved based on a strong commitment to peace and a single goal among all levels whereas in Cyprus, Unity of Effort suffered due to conflictive interests among major parties, most notably the regional players of Greece and Turkey.

Finally, the Ecuador-Peru case examined by Fee in Chapter Four, is perhaps the most traditional peacekeeping operation of the three cases examined as the major problem revolves around a border dispute between two countries rather than internal unrest. It presents an international Unity of Effort for MOMEP based upon a long standing agreement, the 1942 Rio Protocol. Also, the 1995 Peace Declaration of Itamaraty is supported by the regional parties, Peru and Ecuador, although for different reasons, and there is an underlying legitimacy present. Thus, MOMEP enjoys international, regional and internal support. Organizational Unity of Effort within the US government is also demonstrated by the Departments of State and Defense and allowed for the rapid deployment of the US support element, as explained by Fee.

Traditional operations enjoy a degree of Unity of Effort on at least one of these levels. However, real Unity of Effort is impossible without an underlying de facto Legitimacy for the mission. In Cyprus, de facto Legitimacy was initially lacking for the operation. De jure Legitimacy for UNFICYP was created, as indicated by Swan, through negotiations among the UN Secretary General, the Guarantor Powers, and the Cypriot communities. In contrast ONUSAL and MOMEP enjoyed both de facto and de jure Legitimacy. It is interesting to note that the creation of de jure Legitimacy in Cyprus eventually acted to undermine the Unity of Effort of the operation. As de jure Legitimacy turned to de facto Legitimacy within the Cyprus communities, responsibility and resolution of political problems shifted from Cyprus itself to the United Nations! Thus, Legitimacy in this case is a superficial construct rather than an inherent part of the operation.

Unity of Effort and Legitimacy create the conditions in which the other dimensions, Support to Belligerents, Support Actions of Peace Forces, Military Actions Of Peace Forces, Military Actions of Belligerents and Peace Forces, and Actions Targeted On Ending The Conflict, operate. Cyprus received long term political and military Support to Belligerents, notably from Greece and Turkey, which acted to impede Unity of Effort and indicated a lack of de facto regional Legitimacy for UNFICYP. However, in the 1970s, UNFICYP was able to overcome some of these problems by gaining international and local support through Support Actions of the Peace Forces such as the civilian police, thereby enhancing its Legitimacy. In addition, UNFICYP was able to learn from its mistakes and enhance the Unity of Effort as shown by Swan, although the long term future of UNFICYP is problematic.

The Salvador case represents a shift in the Support to Belligerents dimension which both strengthens Unity Of Effort and Legitimacy for ONUSAL and reflects the underlying presence of these two dimension in the operation. All military actions and support actions as well as Actions Targeted On Ending The Conflict were undertaken in an environment in which the end goal of peace gave the mission Legitimacy as well as Unity of Effort. The commitment to peace was so strong that ONUSAL's own faulty actions, such as the investigation of the UN Truth Commission, could not overturn the peace process. MOMEP entered a situation in which there was no major external support to the parties. Unity of Effort and Legitimacy were further reinforced and maintained through integration of former belligerents into the peace forces. Legitimacy was bolstered through Military Actions as explained by Fee, and the main challenge to MOMEP is the ability to maintain a long term commitment to resolution of the border dispute.

Traditional peace operations show several important elements of the peace keeping process which will be salient in both wider peacekeeping and peace enforcement operations. Legitimacy is paramount. With this in mind, it is vital that the operation define what it seeks to accomplish. If the goal is to prevent war and invoke long term political and social change leading to or maintaining a democratization process, it is vital that there is agreement among the conflictive parties on these objectives else any outside efforts are almost sure to meet with failure. What the UN accomplished in El Salvador it did based on a political context and setting established by the Salvadorans themselves. This type of understanding and agreement is strongly lacking in Cyprus. Thus, if the goal in Cyprus is the same as the goal in El Salvador, than UNFICYP's mission falls short indeed. However, if the goal in Cyprus is simply military peacekeeping in a more restricted sense - keep the opposing parties from killing each other - UNFICYP was able to learn from mistakes and improve its execution. However, UNFICYP's superficial Legitimacy will surely come back to mar its long term process for future success. Primary responsibility for resolution of problems must remain among the combatants themselves, something the Salvadorans had come to grips with before ONUSAL set foot in country.

Wider Peacekeeping

Wider Peacekeeping may simply be explained as traditional peacekeeping taken one step further. It is in this context that the concept of traditional peacekeeping begins to shift from the idea of monitoring agreements between a relatively few sovereign, consenting, and responsible parties to a considerably larger number of more difficult and ambiguous tasks outlined in Chapters VI and VII of the United Nations Charter.

In Wider Peacekeeping, the critical dimensions of Unity of Effort and Legitimacy are much more difficult to attain and maintain. As Vacarro notes in Chapter Five, the Cold War context did not allow for international Unity of Effort in the Congo crisis, and the Legitimacy of the UN mission was severely subverted by external actors. Conversely, an absence of this same Cold War environment allowed historic hatreds to violently surface in the former Yugoslavia, leading to a breakup of the country through ethnic conflict including ethnic cleansing.

The UNPROFOR case is especially noteworthy. In Chapter Seven, MacInnis demonstrates the difficulty encountered by an intervening force faced with a situation such as UNPROFOR1 found in Croatia. Unity of Effort is impossible unless the intervening powers understand the situation with which they are faced. As MacInnis indicates, there was no "politico-strategic guidance" in the UN mission. No single aim or agreed upon set of goals united the parties to the conflict among themselves or with the peace forces. Without this basic framework of agreement and commitment, the other dimensions of the paradigm lose effectiveness. Similarly UNPROFOR2 in Bosnia-Herzegovina lacked Unity of Effort on all levels.

The Legitimacy dimension was never truly present in either of the UNPROFOR missions. Although de jure Legitimacy of the mission did exist on an international level, the UN mission lacked de facto Legitimacy among many factions on the ground. Without de facto Legitimacy, it is practically impossible for a peace operation to effectively perform many of the functions necessary to ending conflict such as demilitarization, demobilization, and the attempted establishment of responsible local law enforcement and other institutions as was done in El Salvador. It may be argued that such measures were not within

UNPROFOR's vague mandate and that the operation was only humanitarian in nature, but perhaps this brings us back to the critical point of understanding the situation in which the operation becomes involved and the limits placed on outside intervention. Can an outside power successfully intervene in an environment such as that experienced by UNPROFOR and be only humanitarian in nature? Can it, without the critical dimensions of Unity of Effort and Legitimacy, seek a greater goal than humanitarian relief? Is it possible to "build peace"?

Peace building intervention requires responsible states and/or international organizations to mount a coordinated humanitarian - political - economic - psychological - military - effort to create or reestablish the conditions that can lead to the emergence of legitimate traditional problem solving mechanisms. This is true in all levels of peace operations, but is especially apparent and most difficult to realize in wider peacekeeping and peace enforcement operations. UNPROFOR had no true sense of peace building when it began its operations. It is impossible for an intervening force to engage in a peace operation with the long term goal of definitely ending conflict without the means of peace building. This concept, however, strongly revolves around the Unity of Effort dimension and, especially, the Legitimacy dimension. Thus, UNPROFOR cannot be faulted too much for its inability to engage in such activity as the underlying requirements for such an effort, de facto Legitimacy and Unity of Effort among the conflictive parties, were not present.

The ultimate obligation to create or restore legitimate civil society must be that of indigenous peoples. Nevertheless, sufficient outside support and monitoring must be applied to permit the development of local institutions and infrastructure. As a consequence, political solutions leading to conflict resolution must be a part of the "endgame," and military operations must directly support that agenda. Because UNPROFOR's Legitimacy was substantively nonexistent and Unity of Effort was lacking, only a vague humanitarian agenda was present in an international environment which sought an effective end to the conflict. It was therefore impossible to design effective military operations to meet any agenda. Had UNPROFOR attempted such peace building efforts, it would have moved clearly into the realm of peace enforcement as did the effort in the Congo and UNPROFOR's successor, IFOR.

Peace Enforcement

A peace enforcement situation normally reflects deep-seated historical, ethnic, racial, religious, or other hatreds that are not amenable to rational cost benefit analysis. The probable mandate for the application of military force in such a case is to <u>aggressively take control of a contended area, stop any escalation of violence, enforce law and order, and impose an acceptable level of</u>

security and stability. Few, if any, of the contending parties to the conflict is likely to consider any of these peace enforcement measures to be in its best interest. Thus, an intervening force is not likely to be at all welcome by many factions, and the combatants may attack the peacekeepers as well as each other. It is particularly important that peace enforcers be capable of offensive military action as well as force protection.

This kind of situation is intensely political-psychological and involves sub-state and/or transnational factions attempting to gain control of a government or attempting to dismember a nation state for their own purposes. In either case, peace enforcers will probably find no specific territory to control, no definable military force to threaten, no single part of society on which to concentrate, and no totally legitimate government with which to work. This is analogous to an insurgency situation and peace enforcers may find themselves in an extremely difficult political-strategic predicament.

Because peace enforcement operations take place in a highly complex political-strategic environment, peace enforcers must be particularly sophisticated. They must understand and deal with ambiguity; they must understand the complete political-strategic nature of their tactical and operational actions; they must understand ways by which force can be employed to achieve political and psychological ends; they must understand ways political considerations affect the use of force; they must understand how to communicate and deal with a diversity of peoples and cultures; they must understand and deal with the global media; and they must understand how to cooperatively plan and implement interagency, international nongovernmental, and combined military operations.

The Somalia case, as discussed by Daze and Fishel in Chapter Nine, illustrates the difficulty involved in meeting these criteria and is a good example of what not to do in a peace enforcement situation. Somalia represents a peace enforcement operation gone wrong as end goals transform from an initial humanitarian operation under the Bush Administration, UNITAF, to a more arduous goal of nation building during the Clinton Administration, UNOSOM II. Unity of Effort and Legitimacy, initially present to a certain degree during UNITAF were fundamentally lost during UNOSOM II due to lack of agreement among the force providing countries as well as the conflicting factions on the desired goal or end state. This loss of the two vital dimensions as demonstrated by Daze and Fishel resulted in UNOSOM IIs inability to satisfy the five other dimensions necessary for successful operations.

However, Unity of Effort and Legitimacy provide only the framework for successful peace enforcement. With enough resources and complete Unity of Effort at the strategic level, it is possible to restrain the combative actions of parties to a deep seated, hate oriented conflict. Nevertheless, without legitimizing political-diplomatic conflict resolution measures, peace enforcement operations risk becoming limited military occupations. The Haiti case, as discussed by Adams in Chapter Ten, is a case in point. The US was prepared to intervene in Haiti to restore a democratically elected leader to power. Fortunately, an invasion by force was averted, and US forces were able to land in Haiti relatively free of resistance. The ability of the United States to invade Haiti was never questioned; the difficult stage was the attempt at nation building that was surely to follow. The political end goal was not sufficiently conceived before the military operation took place. It can be argued that intervention in Haiti was vital to US national interests due to Haitian refugees streaming onto US shores. However, integration of non military measures as discussed above with the military option undertaken is vital to long term stability and success. The consolidation of democracy in Haiti remains a highly questionable outcome. Again, an enforced peace can only provide the beginning environment from which to begin a political reconciliation process.

The cases examined in this study demonstrate that Unity of Effort and Legitimacy are the key dimensions around which all other dimensions revolve. Unity of Effort and Legitimacy are easiest to acquire and maintain in a traditional peacekeeping environment. As peace operations move toward wider peacekeeping and peace enforcement, both dimensions become more problematic. Because of the importance of Unity of Effort and Legitimacy, we find that the common denominator for all contemporary peace operations is political. For long term peace operations which seek to end conflict and promote democratization, all seven strategic dimensions must work to reinforce the central political goal - that of establishing a legitimate government. Any hope for successful execution of such an operation involves an understanding of the sources of current conflict which invoke peace keeping operations and the type of environment in which these conflicts are occurring.

The Central Strategic Problem: Legitimate Governance

Analysis of the cases in this study along with a large number of cases since the end of World War II[3] shows that instabilities generated by reformers, separatists, insurgents, and opportunists in all parts of the world are based on the moral Legitimacy of competing political forces. Nation states whose governments have achieved moral Legitimacy are relatively invulnerable to destabilizing actions. By contrast, governments that are perceived as lacking in moral correctness are prime targets for virtually anyone with a cause.[4]

The results of such moral incorrectness or malfeasance can be seen in governments unwilling or unable to provide basic services, to maintain decent roads, education, health, and public services for all segments of its population. It can been seen in the inability or unwillingness of governments to provide basic security and functioning legal systems that protect civil rights, and a sense of societal equity. Illegitimate governance is also seen when disparate ethnic, religious, or other political groups in a society become insistent on establishing separate identities, and government reacts with thuggish and brutal violence.

These instabilities generate further disorder, violent internal conflicts, and mushrooming demands by various groups for political autonomy. These legitimacy issues translate themselves into constant subtle and not so subtle struggles for power that dominate life throughout much of the world today. What these grievances have in common is that they are generated and complicated by misguided, corrupt, insensitive, and/or incompetent governance. Sooner or later, the spillover effects of national and regional instabilities place demands on the international community, if not to solve the problems at least to harbor the victims.

The implacable challenge in pursuing a legitimate governance theory of engagement is one of accepting the responsibilities of political leadership that the international security environment imposes. The general task is to apply the theory on the basis of realistic calculations of ends, ways, means, gains, risks, and core interests.

Once the international security environment and central strategic problem have been examined, the final step in developing an appropriate response to the multidimensional problems of contemporary security within the context of the seven dimensions of the SWORD model is to revisit the most salient lessons learned. These lessons include: the relationship of legitimate governance to stability; the relationship of development to security and stability; and the relationship between Legitimacy and the political competence to generate the capability to sustain political, economic, and social development. National and international security depend on international and domestic policies that provide for political competence, economic progress and social justice, and personal and national security (i.e., legitimate governance).

1. ***The Relationship of Legitimate Governance to Stability***
   Political Legitimacy is based on the moral right of a government to govern--and the ability of the government to govern morally. Popular perceptions of corruption, disenfranchisement, poverty, and lack of upward social mobility tend to limit the right, and the ability, of a regime to conduct the business of state. Until and unless a population feels that its government deals with these and other issues of political, economic, and social injustice fairly and effectively, the potential for internal or external factors to destabilize and subvert a government is considerable.
2. ***The Relationship of Security and Stability to Development*** The international security dialogue is focusing on national development. That requirement equates to a holistic national capability building effort. The generally uncoordinated, piecemeal, and ad hoc approach

to socioeconomic development must be brought to an end. Unless solutions to development problems are addressed on a coherent and long-term basis, there will be no self-sustaining national development. National development provides the capability for the nation state to develop the political and economic strength to provide internal order and progress. National development also provides the capability for the state to protect and enhance its interests in the international security arena. Thus self-sustaining national development provides both security and stability.

3. ***The Relationship between Legitimacy and Political Competence.*** Another lesson that should have been learned that helps define appropriate response to the problem of illegitimate governance and its associated instability threat is that of the relationship between Legitimacy and political competence. Legitimacy is necessary to generate the capability to effectively manage, coordinate, and sustain political, economic, and social development. This capability implies the political competence to develop legitimate governance and a resultant national and international purpose and will to which a citizenry can relate and support. This capability thus implies the competence to legitimize and strengthen national political institutions. The degree to which this political objective is achieved at home will determine the level of influence that can be exerted abroad. It will also define, more than anything else, progress toward viable national security and well-being.

Toward a New Stability Equation

We have demonstrated the core importance of the two dimensions, Unity of Effort and Legitimacy, through case analyses as well as the interrelationships among all seven dimensions of the paradigm. When this analysis of the SWORD model is considered in conjunction with the current strategic threat, the problem of legitimate governance, we find that peace operations through use of the seven dimensions are most successful, such as in the Salvador case, when the overall result attains the fulfillment of a holistic legitimate governance and stability imperative consisting of three principal elements. These elements are necessary to strengthen government through substantive, coordinated improvement in the civil and military bureaucracies, the economy, and the society. They are a basis for understanding a holistic legitimate governance theory of engagement, and a realistic and pragmatic approach to stability.

The three elements of a new stability (S) equation that must be developed based on the cases examined are: 1) the military police capability (M) to provide an acceptable level of internal and external security; 2) the economic ability (E) to generate real security and socioeconomic development; and 3) the political competence (PC) to develop a type of governance to which a people can relate and support.

The security and the socioeconomic components of stability are generally well understood. Clearly, however, the key political competence element is not as well understood, developed, and operationalized as the other two. The United States and the international community, generally, have emphasized economic development and military security under the assumption that social and political development would automatically follow. That has not happened.

It is heuristically valuable to portray the relationships among the three components of stability in a mathematical formula: $S = (M+E)\ PC$. The authors are aware that this mathematical equation is a vast oversimplification of what is a complex, dynamic system. But the illlustration nonetheless demonstrates the importance of political competence. The political competence element of the equation is so critical that it means that the sum of the whole can be substantially altered by the elements that constitute national political competence. The ultimate value of the economic and security elements of the equation can be reduced to nothing or nearly nothing if the political competence component is absent or weak--for example, $100 \times 0 = 0$.

Governments that have not been responsive to the importance of the political competence reality find themselves in a "crisis of governance." They face growing social violence, criminal anarchy, and overthrow. Thus, the development of political competence upon a foundation of moral Legitimacy is a challenge that governments must meet to survive the growing international anarchy.

Conclusion

Analysis of the problems of governance and stability which lead to peacekeeping operations as articulated in this book takes us beyond providing some form of humanitarian assistance or refugee assistance in cases of human misery and need. It takes us beyond traditional monitoring of bilateral agreements; protecting a people from another group of people or from a government. It takes us beyond compelling one or more parties to a conflict to cease human rights violations and other morally repugnant activities, or repelling simple aggression. Analysis of the problems of governance and stability takes us back to where we began. The core strategic problem is legitimate governance in the post-Cold War world. Foreign policy and military asset management must address this central challenge. This is best done through use of the seven dimensions of the SWORD model.

Nevertheless, no regime, group, or force can legislate or decree moral Legitimacy or political competence for themselves or anyone else. Legitimation and stability derive from popular and institutional perceptions that authority is genuine and effective, and uses morally correct means for reasonable and fair purposes. These qualities are developed, sustained, and enhanced by appropriate actions or behavior over time.

In the short-term, however, a fragile regime will likely require outside help in developing these qualities. Probably the best an outside power or coalition of powers can do is to help establish a temporary level of security that might allow the carefully guided and monitored development of the ethical and professional political competence underpinnings necessary for long-term success in achieving a relatively better quality of national and international stability and well-being. But, again, the enormity and logic of the peace building solutions required for the achievement of legitimate governance and stability demand a carefully thought out, phased, long-term planning and implementation process for sustainable political development.

The primary implications of this analysis are clear. The ability of "fragile" and menaced governments to control, protect, and enhance their stability and well-being is severely threatened in the contemporary security environment. A theory of engagement that is focused on Legitimacy and political competence by the employment of the seven dimensions of the SWORD model empowers a realistic response to the injustices, insecurities, and instabilities generated by corrupt, incompetent, and/or misguided governance.

The conscious choices that the United States and the international community make about peace operations now and in the future will help define the processes of national reform, regeneration, well-being, and thus relative internal and international peace. Success in countering the new world disorder and in fulfilling the hope for a better international peace will be constructed on the same pillars that supported favorable results in the past,[5] including a theory of engagement derived from the SWORD Model. This is nothing radical. It is basic foreign policy and military asset management, which, in the end, must rest upon the foundations of Legitimacy and Unity of Effort.

Notes

1 X (George F. Kennan), "The Sources of Soviet Conduct," *Foreign Affairs*, July 1947, pp. 566-582.

2 Leslie H. Gelb, "Quelling the Teacup Wars," *Foreign Affairs*, November-December, 1994, p.5.

3 See Max G. Manwaring and John T. Fishel, "Insurgency and Counterinsurgency: Toward a New Analytical Approach," *Small Wars and Insurgencies*, Winter 1992, pp. 272-305.

4 Ibid.

[5] See *Managing Contemporary Conflict: Pillars Of Success*, Max G. Manwaring and Wm. J. Olson, editors. Westview:Boulder, 1996.

12

Winning "The Savage Wars of Peace": What the Manwaring Paradigm Tells Us

David Last

The aim of this chapter is to examine the relevance of the paradigm and case studies for evolving military doctrine. First, the Manwaring paradigm is significant in the context of historic and contemporary doctrine, and the widely accepted principles of peacekeeping. It also sheds light on some gaps in the way we interpret military doctrine, particularly in our concepts of the enemy and victory. To work in complex, multidimensional operations, peacekeeping doctrine needs to be international and multidisciplinary, encompassing the social, political and economic dimensions of the conflicts it is trying to address. Second, the paradigm and case studies illustrate the continuity of the spectrum of force, and the need for a peace force to have a coherent force structure with clear division of responsibilities. Only by distinguishing among police, gendarme and military actions can a peace force assist the parties to the conflict to bring the instruments of violence under effective and appropriate control. The relationship between use of force and legitimacy is fundamental to success in peace operations. Finally, the case studies illustrate basic lessons about training and peace operations. Combat skills are a necessary but not a sufficient condition for success. Sometimes adequate strength can reduce the need to use force, but strength without contact skills and communication can be ineffective.

Relevance of Contemporary Doctrine and Its Historical Context

Doctrine provides a framework for analysis, not procedures and solutions. Peacekeeping doctrine is drawn empirically from the diverse experiences of several armies (mainly those of developed, western countries). Peacekeeping is seldom linked to its intellectual heritage, which comes from three very different sources. The most obvious source is direct experience of peacekeeping. This has been shaped by the evolution of military thinking about war fighting. More subtle has been the influence of the military response to revolutionary pressures for change; peacekeeping has drawn on the internal security and colonial policing traditions European armies. A counterweight to this influence has been the peace research tradition, reflected in Nordic and UN thinking about peacekeeping. The Manwaring paradigm occupies an important place at the juncture of these different influences on peacekeeping doctrine.

Experience and Principles

Chapter One described the evolution of US doctrine for peace operations. Other countries' doctrines have evolved based on their own experience. These are reflected in the principles to which each subscribes. There is broad agreement on the most important of these principles, as Table 1 shows. The Manwaring factors also relate directly to principles, as described in Chapter One.

Most of the experience underlying these principles was gained during peacekeeping and UN Observer missions carried out between 1947 and 1989. The logic of missions like UNFICYP, IAPF and ONUC was to prevent conflicts from escalating to superpower confrontation. Thus, even when they dealt with intrastate conflicts, they were set in an environment of traditional interstate politics. Table one shows the Principles of Peacekeeping.

Table 1: Principles of Peacekeeping[1]

UN	Nordic	UK	Canadian	US
consent and cooperation of the parties	host government authority	consent	mutual consent of belligerents	legitimacy
impartiality	impartiality	impartiality	impartiality	unity of effort
minimum force (self defense only)	avoid use of force	minimum force	force as a last resort	restraint
clear mandate	clarity of intentions	transparency	clear and enforceable mandate	maintain objective
support of international community	firmness	legitimacy	freedom of action and movement	security
freedom of movement	anticipation	credibility	attainable political settlement	perseverance
international composition	integration	mutual respect	mutual respect	
under UN command			negotiations	
			empathy	

Since 1989, United Nations peacekeeping has had to evolve to handle more intractable intrastate conflicts. Ideas about policing and internal security have had an impact on armies with internal security roles and colonial histories, such as Britain and France.[2] Table one indicates a much broader agreement on principles than military experience alone might suggest. The binding factor is an understanding that the use of force must be constrained. This is most evident in UN and Nordic documents. At the time of its publication in 1992, an International Peace Academy paper on the non-use of force[3] represented a consensus in New York, despite arguments that more forceful action would be appropriate in missions like Northern Iraq and former Yugoslavia.[4]

Most remarkable has been the divergence of national doctrine and the official UN approach to use of force. Boutros Boutros-Ghali's original *Agenda for Peace* left considerable room for assertive international action.[5] Kofi Annan's controversial article on "induced consent" advocated more coercive measures under international control.[6] While these trial balloons reflected both frustration and growing confidence, they have not met with the approval of the major powers which have become increasingly active in peace support operations. The permanent members of the Security Council may acknowledge that traditional peacekeeping is increasingly blending with low-intensity conflict, but they seem unwilling to see the UN take the leading role in applying force. This echoes the debates of the 1960s, as Dag Hammarskjöld tried to manage ONUC.[7] The UN can hold the ring, but applying force in pursuit of objectives remains a national prerogative, and stems from a long heritage of war-fighting doctrine which is well-established in large and middle powers.

War Fighting

Doctrines of organizing military force to win wars for the state come down to us from Machiavelli through the German-American tradition of Clausewitz, Moltke, Schlichting and the systems theorists of the Second World War and its aftermath. The idea of a dialectic of offensive and defensive action originates with Moltke and Clausewitz, who had divergent views about the primacy of policy. Moltke believed in unequivocal military leadership once the decision to go to war had been made, while Clausewitz believed that war was always subordinate to politics.[8] Schlieffen and Schlichting were instrumental in developing the idea of the operational level of war as an instrument for orchestrating the application of force to achieve war aims.[9] This evolution of war-fighting doctrine reached a peak in the Second World War, when the resources of whole societies were subordinated to military ends. The evolution continued during the Cold War confrontation, with increasingly sophisticated armies facing each other across a potential European battleground against a background of strategic deterrence and theater nuclear weapons. The increasing sophistication of European doctrine was ill-equipped to deal with the brushfire wars of decolonization or anti-communism in the Third World.

The problem with Cold War doctrine was that it focused on military victory, while the problems faced in the periphery were economic, social and political. Fired by the rhetoric of the Old World's own liberation ideologies (liberal and socialist alike) insurgents all over the world confronted forces of the *status quo* to build a just society. The "enemy" was changing, but ideas about offensive operations remained unchanged.

Building a Just Society

While military doctrine evolved to pursue the interests of the state, another tradition emerged which ran counter to states' interests. These were ideas about establishing a just society by attacking the instruments of state control through revolution and insurgency. They descend from the French and American Revolutions, the "year of revolutions"(1848)[10], and through the work of Marx, Engels, Lenin, Mao, Guevara, and the new revolutionaries of the urban era (Sanguinetti and Debray).[11] Each wave of social unrest met with an establishment reaction, informed by the military thinking of the day. There were also efforts to address the causes of the unrest, but techniques of control and repression predominated. The principles of free speech enshrined by the French Revolution soon gave way to press restrictions, censorship, and Napoleon's elaborate national police structure under Fouché, supported by a centrally controlled *gendarmerie*.[12] The nineteenth Century saw the further broadening of European control to Africa and South-East Asia. Military force was a principle means for incorporation of the periphery. Gunboats and garrisons were followed by missionaries and merchants.[13] Operating far from their capitals, soldiers like Lyautey and Galliéni found themselves acting as colonial administrators, using a combination of military force, economic incentives, and alliances with local elites to retain control.[14] Peacekeeping missions in the Congo, Namibia, and Cambodia are legacies of this era.

Marx, Engels, and Lenin justified class violence as a means of achieving legitimate social objectives. Mao and Ho applied revolutionary principles to the agrarian "third world". Castro and Guevara brought Lenin and Mao to Latin America. Debray and Sanguinetti brought the violent fight for social justice into the context of the media society and urban lifestyles. At each step, ideas about social relations and economic power were used to legitimize violence against the state. The state's clumsy and heavy-handed reaction often added to the legitimacy of counter systemic movements, encouraging new groups to use terror to advance their causes.[15]

The idea that injustice leads to violence has been prominent since the American Revolution (if not since Plato's *Republic*). It was in the 1960s that it began to be supported by empirical studies. American behaviorists identified the correlates of anomic and organized social violence.[16] The idea had more appeal as part of a coherent philosophy, and the work of European peace researchers gained increasing acceptance in the 1970s and 1980s. This was especially true in UN circles, where Johan Galtung's ideas about structural violence[17] resonated with Ráoul Prebisch's ideas about *dependencia*--the unjust exploitation of the Third World--and with the political ideas of the Non-Aligned Movement.[18] The military thinking of major powers was out of step with these developments. American military doctrine for "Foreign Internal Defence and Development," for example, acknowledged no link between concentration of land ownership and the insurgencies of desperate peasants whose actions were attributed to Soviet and Communist influence.[19] Yet at about the same time, *The Peacekeeper's Handbook* included a definition of Galtung's term "structural violence," and the warning that, "Conflict is an illness, and like any other illness it requires the correct treatment to cure it."[20]

Armies and the Just Society

How have armies responded to the social need to control violence? After prolonged and intractable religious violence, the Peace of Westphalia established the religion of the sovereign as the religion of state, thus embodying a state's legitimacy in its Sovereign. War became the sport of kings, and armies began to professionalize. The Concert of Vienna made the legitimacy of a state further contingent upon established boundaries. It was not until the Twentieth century that the principle of self-determination came to be the defining test of legitimacy, and it is one with which we are still struggling in cases where states dispute their boundaries, or are not in control within them, as several case studies show.[21] At each of these stages, armies were instruments of control. Peace operations are part of the evolution of the role armies have played in the pursuit and preservation of social order--sometimes for the better, sometimes for the worse.

Armies have dealt with revolutions and domestic disturbances through internal security and police actions. These actions form the closest parallel with peacekeeping, because they demand considered and restrained force, within a framework of law, rather than maximum force. To respond otherwise is to undermine the popular consent, the legitimacy, on which both governance and the instruments of power must rest.

The traditional response of state forces to social unrest has been suppression, sometimes with retaliation or reprisals. When silk workers in Lyons rebelled against low wages in 1834, government troops bombarded the city and stormed the barricades. The Paris insurrections of 1834 were brutally put down, and pressure built towards the Revolution of 1848.[22] The French administration of Algeria under Bugeaud (1840-1842) developed the *razzia*, brutal scorched earth raids on towns, to control the hinterland. This quickly stirred local opposition to French rule. Colonial experiences, however, also produced new insights into techniques for controlling peripheral areas through inducements and coopting elites. Colonialism provided a unifying theme about which national political, economic and military policy could coalesce. The French colonial ministry of Jules Ferry (1880-1886) articulated clearly the link between industrialization, protection of markets, and colonies. Paul Bert, resident general of Annam and Tonkin (1886), accomplished three things for Ferry: he rallied the commercial middle classes, redirected military efforts to focus on support to natives against pirates and bandits, and instituted reforms to garner both popular and mandarin support.[23]

This brief historical digression illustrates three points. First, most of the low intensity conflict with which armies have had to contend has been economic, social and political in nature; the same is true for the cases discussed in this book. Second, standards of "legitimacy" are derived from the context of the conflict, which changes as the fight progresses; Soldiers fought in Algeria and Vietnam, to find themselves reviled for it at home. The IAPF in 1964 operated in a different international environment from that facing UNMIH in 1994. Third, international intervention can catch intervenors in curious historical echoes. Jules Ferry and Paul Bert succeeded in Tonkin, within the orthodoxy of Nineteenth Century colonialism. The children of the commercial middle class they helped to build were receptive to the same ideas which had inspired the silk workers of Lyons. If the structure which confers legitimacy is flawed or collapses, then the intervention is unlikely to bring long-term stability. We cannot completely divorce doctrines of peacekeeping from the inegalitarian structure of the Security Council which authorizes missions--whether the missions are traditional peacekeeping, wider peacekeeping, or peace enforcement. "Legitimacy" must, therefore, refer to more than just the approbation of the current players, if it is to be an indicator of sustainable peace.

It is significant that the Manwaring paradigm is situated at the convergence of modern American war fighting doctrine and efforts to defeat violent social change (Figure 1). It began life as a paradigm for success in low intensity conflict, specifically counterinsurgency . It is now being applied to the problem of preserving and enhancing peace through the intervention of impartial third parties.[24] The central role of legitimacy is one of its most important insights. Legitimacy defeats an insurgency because removing the sources of illegitimacy can remove the sources of the insurgency. In the same way, the peacekeeping paradigm can be rephrased; peaceful change defeats violence. This means that doctrine for peace restoration needs to be an integration of military doctrine

Figure 1: Context of the Manwaring Paradigm

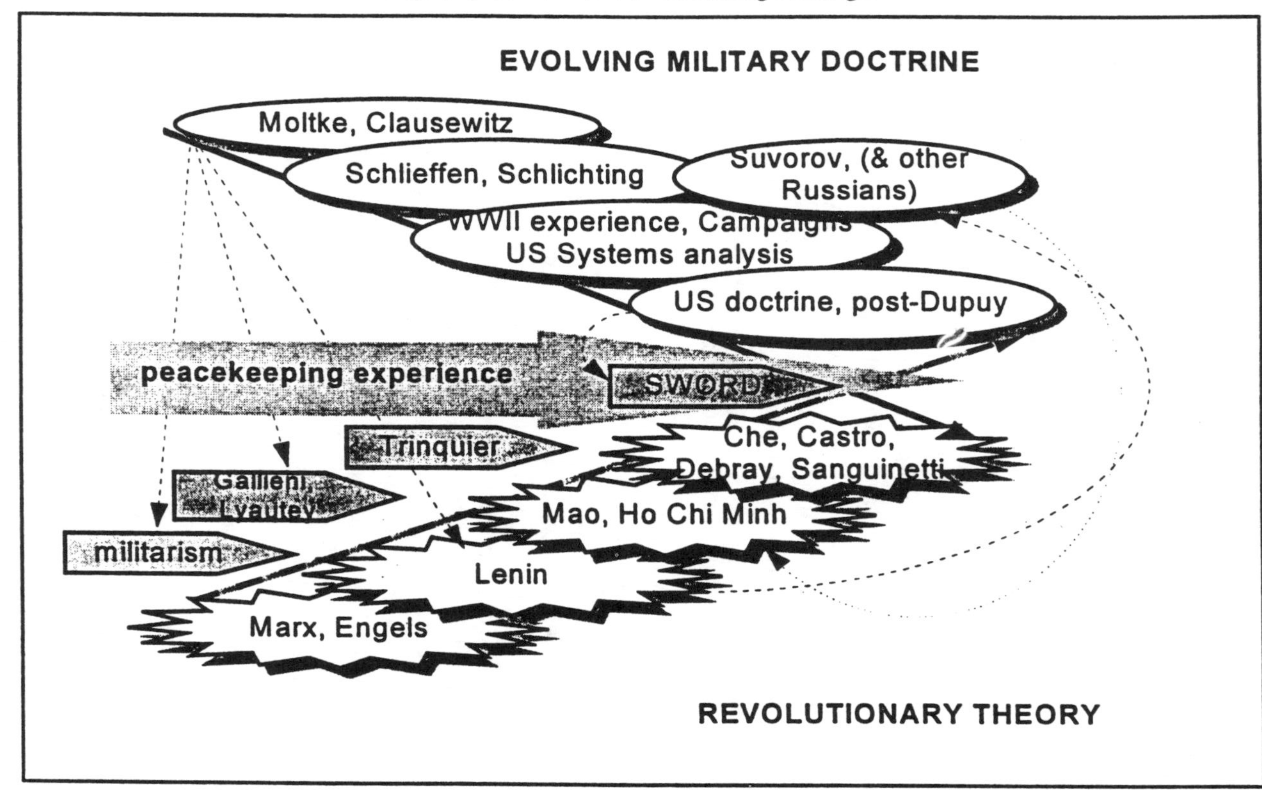

and its political and economic counterparts which have inspired social violence in the past. If progressive peacekeeping doctrine becomes a vehicle for peaceful social and economic transitions, it could be the next step in collective thinking about global security. But if wider peacekeeping and peace enforcement are only vehicles for managing conflict in the interests of established powers, they will fall short of their full potential.

Gaps in Doctrine and the Insights of the Manwaring Paradigm

That is the historical context of peacekeeping doctrine and the Manwaring paradigm. There are critical gaps in contemporary peacekeeping doctrine which the insights of the case studies can help us to fill in. Doctrine for the offense in conventional war is built on assumptions about the nature and behavior of the enemy; peacekeeping doctrine today does not help us to understand the "enemy". It places too much emphasis on what the third party should do, and too little on understanding the parties to the conflict. Finally, peacekeeping doctrine does not present a clear vision of what constitutes "victory," or at least an acceptable end state.

Understanding the "Enemy"

The enemy in peacekeeping operations is violent conflict. The contribution of the Manwaring paradigm is to describe specific steps toward controlling the violent aspects of a conflict, including isolating belligerents from support, peace forces taking effective military action, and taking early action to undermine the sources of violence. But much of this stops at "defensive" action. If we have a more sophisticated understanding of the ideas, the social and economic forces which underlie the urge to violent conflict, we can take genuine offensive action early in an intervention. Much of this will not be military action at all, although it may need to be coordinated with military action.

Unity of political, military, and economic efforts, and a common approach by all third parties is a necessary prerequisite to effective action. It requires an understanding of the nature of the violence being confronted. The UNOSOM case study illustrates the minimum requirements for unity of effort: there must be agreement on the objectives to be achieved, and there must be clear and effective measures for command and control. Italy and the United States had divergent understandings of the nature of the clan warfare in Somalia, and consequently of the objectives to be achieved. The command and control arrangements did not allow this divergence to be resolved before it undermined the mission.[25] Similarly, the lack of will to address the economic dimension of the Katangan secession movement undermined the UN's efforts to control secession and resolve the conflict within the Congo.[26] On the contrary, the example of UN-NATO cooperation over air strikes in August 1995 represents extraordinary unity of effort, clearly articulated objectives and effective command and control. Nevertheless, the future remains as uncertain as Somalia and the Congo. The air strikes helped to achieve the Dayton Accord, but did not address any of the causes of violence.[27]

Once there is agreement on the nature of the enemy, defensive action can focus on stopping the parties from shooting and moving against each other, and offensive action can follow up by attempting to remove the social, economic and political causes of the violence. While most of the dimensions of the Manwaring paradigm focus on defensive, mainly military actions, almost a third of the individual variables can be more political than military, and have economic or social components to them. This is particularly true of variables in the dimensions "Unity of Effort," "Legitimacy," and "Actions Targeted on Ending Conflict". It is within these dimensions--particularly the last--that attention must be focused to devise effective offensive techniques.

Understanding Our "Allies"

If the target of third party action is violence, then the parties themselves are necessary allies to defeat it. If their behavior remains the source of violent conflict, it must be changed by working with both sides. In counterinsurgency operations, one party is supported and the other is attacked; in peace operations, both must be treated as allies. Any move to delegitimize the interests of one of the parties in favor of the interests of the other will undermine the intervention, because it removes the basis for the consent of the parties, and paves the way for escalating violence. The more the peace force systematically targets one party, the more likely violence will target the peace forces. Two examples from the case studies illustrate the danger of delegitimizing core interests, and one example illustrates the concept of belligerents as cooperative allies.

The international community acknowledges the Greek Cypriot regime as the legitimate government of Cyprus; only Turkey recognizes the so-called Turkish Republic of Northern Cyprus. Turkish Cypriots have reasonable fears for their security under a Greek Cypriot regime. Unconditional acknowledgment of the Greek Cypriot government legitimizes Turkish occupation of North Cyprus in the name of Turkish Cypriot security. In fact, the Turkish army refers to the 1974 invasion as a peace operation, and it *was* from the point of view of Turkish Cypriots threatened by the Greek-sponsored coup of 1974. The legitimacy problem extends below the strategic level to confidence-building measures at the lowest level. A recent youth soccer match was canceled after

Greek Cypriot officials referred to "occupied Nicosia" and Turkish Cypriot officials demanded a retraction.[28] The different status of the two parties has become the major barrier to intercommunal communications, as each party maneuvers for regime advantage.[29]

In the case of Bosnia, it is easier to pick a good side and a bad side, but just as dangerous to do so. A common view in the West is that nationalist Serbs started a war of expansion, and used brutal ethnic cleansing to push out minority Croats and Muslims. The obvious sufferings of the Muslims have been used to obscure the legitimate fears of Serbs and Croats which underlie resistance to refugee return. Prior to 1992, the checks and balances of the Yugoslav federal system gave guarantees to Serbs and Croats that their identity would not be expunged in a Muslim state. The referendum and recognition of Bosnia removed this guarantee, and raised the stakes for ordinary Serbs and Croats. The Bosnian President, Alija Izetbegovic, is a proponent of Islamic rule.[30]

Failing to recognize and accommodate deep Serb and Croat fear of Islamic domination has played into the hands of extremist leaders, aided and manipulated by Belgrade and Zagreb.[31] The war fighting potential of the Federation Army (VF) and its major component, the Bosnian Army (ABiH) are increased by the American-led Train and Equip program and by bilateral deals with Islamic countries. Meanwhile the Bosnian Serb Army (VRS) continues to decline both in absolute terms, and relative to the VF.[32] It is possible to recognize the security dilemma this imbalance poses and deal with the interests of Serbs, without recognizing the leadership of the Bosnian Serbs.

In the cases of Cyprus and Bosnia, it is unlikely that confidence can be built at lower levels while one party's interests are delegitimized at the highest levels. The Military Observer Mission in Ecuador and Peru (MOMEP) provides an illustration of how confidence is fostered when third parties deal impartially with the interests of both parties. The Guarantors of the Peace Declaration of Itamaraty treated the border claims of Peru and Ecuador with strict impartiality, and observers supervised the verification flights without prejudice. Fee's anecdote about a Peruvian Major dispensing with nationality is unlikely in the context of Cyprus or Bosnia.[33]

There *are* spoilers in peace processes. Some leaders, groups, and individuals will consistently undermine the process of intercommunal reconciliation.[34] Extremists are likely to target moderates in their own community in order to undermine the peace. Too often, third parties are oblivious to this process. UNFICYP actually received orders not to report on strife within the Greek community which preceded the 1974 coup; intracommunal events were beyond the mandate.[35] A constant policy issue for those preparing campaign plans is the question of inclusion: How far to go to keep spoilers involved in the process, or when and how to cut them out of the process? An impartial third party cannot eliminate one of the parties or leaders, as the US attempted to do to Aideed. Even attempting to marginalize radicals and support moderates can backfire, as did Carl Bildt's support for the Moderate Serb Rojko Kasagic in Bosnia in June 1996. When a third party brings pressure to bear on one of the belligerents, that belligerent is likely to perceive the third party as an adversary. Worse, the use of force by the third party may irreversibly damage the image of impartiality.

There is a doctrinal solution to this dilemma. Third parties do have to pressure the belligerents. They sometimes have to use force against them, particularly in wider peacekeeping and peace enforcement. The use of force is not the end of impartiality. The solution lies in understanding the core interests of the belligerents, and communicating effectively as part of the strategy of applying force. The British doctrine of wider peacekeeping describes how consent for the broad objectives of the mission actually frees the mission to use force at the tactical level to overcome specific obstacles.[36] The crucial step in making this work is to communicate support for core interests at the same time as using force to attack those who damage the peace process. Where core interests are incompatible, as were those of the leftist constitutionalists and rightist loyalists in the Dominican Republic, the message is that these interests must be reconciled through a nonviolent political process.[37]

Understanding "Victory"

In thinking about the "savage wars of peace," we need a model for victory. How do we know when the war is won? Is Cyprus a win, loss or draw? With hindsight, we can see peacekeeping missions at several historical junctions. ONUC is to Colonialism what UNPROFOR is to the Cold War; each was an attempt to put together a state dismantled by political entrepreneurs under the cover of an uncertain transition. Both are unfinished. In contrast, new security arrangements in Europe after the Second World War led to comparative stability and prosperity. We need to think in terms of action to end a conflict, the subjugation of violence, and indicators of what might restart it. This leads us to some deductions about the type of doctrine which we need to guide us to "victory". How can endemic violence be subjugated? How do third parties know when it is safe to leave? What sort of doctrine will help us achieve elusive "victories" in the savage wars of peace?

The counterinsurgency version of the Manwaring paradigm implies a narrow interpretation of "Actions Targeted On Ending The Conflict". Civil affairs, civic action, and psychological operations are all military faces of a much broader process. The evolution of IFOR/SFOR's civil affairs tasks offers an interesting example. In March 1996, guidance on involvement in civil tasks listed engineering projects, mine clearance, transport, medical support, and telecommunications.[38] In June 1997, civil tasks included an active search for civilian partners and additional resources to take over some coordination functions of G5 cells and Civil-Military Cooperation (CIMIC) Centers.[39]

The case studies illustrate the limitations of purely military action. ONUC and UNPROFOR demonstrate the necessity for state-building as part of a peace operation. When weak institutions result in disputes being militarized, strengthening institutions is a step towards conflict prevention.[40] Intelligence and psychological operations are significant not for their military contribution, but because they can inform broader political and economic efforts. After the shooting stops, the most valuable information begins to be about factors like communities and crops, employment and attitudes. Analysis requires detailed local knowledge, and follow-up action is likely to be by teams of civilian specialists.[41]

There is a risk that third parties might see the enemy as violence initiated by one side, leading them to the belief that an end-state with that party weakened will serve to stabilize the situation. In protracted conflicts, this is unlikely to be so. Weakening one party may tempt another party to initiate the next round in a predictable window of opportunity. States which manage internal divisions without violence have developed regulation mechanisms based on a variety of political structures. Nordlinger identifies six conflict regulating practices which might be part of a stable end-state: stable coalitions, the proportionality principle, depoliticization, mutual veto, compromise, and concessions. Relying on majority rule may make conflicts worse. Trying to create national identity quickly will probably lead to violence and repression.[42] Social conflict is a chronic condition in many parts of the world, with acute episodes. It is easy to get involved during an acute spell, but it takes patience and long term commitment to support the evolution of conflict regulation mechanisms. Slow progress on the political front, unrealistic timelines, or the private agendas of third parties can all serve to wear down patience at the operational level.[43]

When is it safe to leave? Third party involvement in nurturing a settlement may take decades, but there are many alternatives to military presence. Diplomatic engagement and support for the economy are equally important.[44] Major powers have some leverage over the economic interests which may conspire to perpetuate the instability. The International Monetary Fund's conditionality and bankruptcy triggering mechanisms, for example, can exacerbate poverty and dependence which makes countries susceptible to further violence at the very time when they need prosperity to consolidate a tenuous peace.[45]

Military planners would like to have a definable end state, and a date by which the commitment will terminate. Few of the savage wars of peace lend themselves to this certainty. Gideon Rose has argued that rather than "exit strategies," we should prepare successive "transition strategies," along with contingency plans for the most likely sources of derailment.[46] If "victory"is definable, it consists of at least four elements: the absence of physical violence;

mechanisms for peaceful change to overcome structural violence (this usually entails democracy, but not always simple-majority elections); a sustainable economy with prospects for improvement; and freedom of information and association which will allow civil society to emerge with time. The absence of physical violence can be set as a military objective (though it requires police and sometimes gendarmes to support it). The other three elements must be set as political, economic and social objectives. In each sphere, the "allies" must lead the way.

The Type of Doctrine Needed

The US Army is well placed to understand and manage the complexities of wider peacekeeping and post-conflict transition. It has specialized civil affairs and psychological operations units. It is a well educated army, with a sophisticated intellectual and analytical establishment which is closely linked to operations. From the days of the Marshall plan and military government in Japan, through the years of "foreign internal defense and development" doctrine to today's concepts of "stability and support operations," there has been flexibility and ingenuity in American doctrine. However, it succeeds in incorporating many cultures by becoming a monoculture, often out of tune with its surroundings and neither aware of nor sympathetic to cultural differences. It is extraordinarily susceptible to domestic pressure, allowing belligerents to influence activity through US-based lobbying. Other armies have analogous but different problems. France and the UK have a colonial heritage, and continuing military presence in many areas. (France launched its the independent *Opération Turquoise* in Rwanda, and was rejected by the Central African Peace Force.) Russia has problems in the near-abroad, and baggage from the COMINTERN years. African and Asian countries often have to contend with racism. Each of these factors becomes a source of operational friction.

All this suggests that moving a conflict toward peaceful resolution requires multinational effort--the coordination of strengths and weaknesses from many national contingents. It is unlikely that any one country will have all the necessary attributes. Most will be prepared for only a limited national commitment. The nature of victory also requires a sophisticated combination of military and nonmilitary interventions, linking all instruments of influence. Effective staff structures can be used to reduce some of the tensions of an international command, as General Alvim was able to do in the IAPF.[47] But there will always be limits to the subordination of units, as there were in Somalia.[48] The more fragmented the command, the greater the importance of similar doctrine, to provide a framework for cohesive action--both military and civilian.

Peacekeeping doctrine needs to be internationalized, to allow countries to work together for peace, exactly as NATO doctrine allowed former enemies to work together. It must also be multi-disciplinary and transparent to all--neither confined to the military, nor even driven by the military. A coherent NATO framework for peacekeeping operations is beginning to emerge.[49] Since the International Peace Academy's first *Peacekeeper's Handbook*, various manuals intended primarily for soldiers have included sections on civilian police and UN civilian agencies. A new generation of handbooks is now being produced for multi-disciplinary audiences. Many recent titles deal with problems of civil-military coordination.[50] Neil Wright's handbook on Humanitarian emergencies produced for the UNHCR explains that organization to soldiers.[51] John Mackinlay's *Guide to Peace Support Operations* is the closest thing to a keystone manual for multi-functional operations which is on the market today, and has been published in three of the UN's six languages.[52] A *Guide to Peace Support Operations* may show the way for military and civilian peacekeeping doctrine.

Force Structure and the Use Of Force

Legitimacy, consent, and the use of force are the central themes in peacekeeping doctrine. But use of force is not a purely doctrinal matter. It depends fundamentally on the structure, armament and skills of the forces deployed for peacekeeping duty. Soldiers with side-arms and soft-skinned vehicles are not capable of "robust"action, regardless of their rules of engagement; Mechanized units with tanks and infantry fighting vehicles are not equipped for effective crowd control or urban policing. At either extreme, degree of support for the peace force will rapidly erode if it is incapable of the tasks required. A peace force's ability to deliver security depends largely on its structure and capacity for appropriate use of force. A different approach to force is required at various places in the spectrum of conflict.

Conflict and the Spectrum of Forces

Figure 2 illustrates a spectrum of security forces. At the left, police forces have a comparatively low capacity for organized violence, operate individually or in small groups, and deal mainly with individual civilians within a framework of civil law. At the right, military forces have a high capacity for organized violence, train to deal with similarly constituted forces, and operate within a framework of military and international law. The term *Gendarmes* comes from the French, meaning a paramilitary body charged with policing and administration of an area, support to army and navy (*armées de terre et de*

Figure 2: Spectrum of Forces

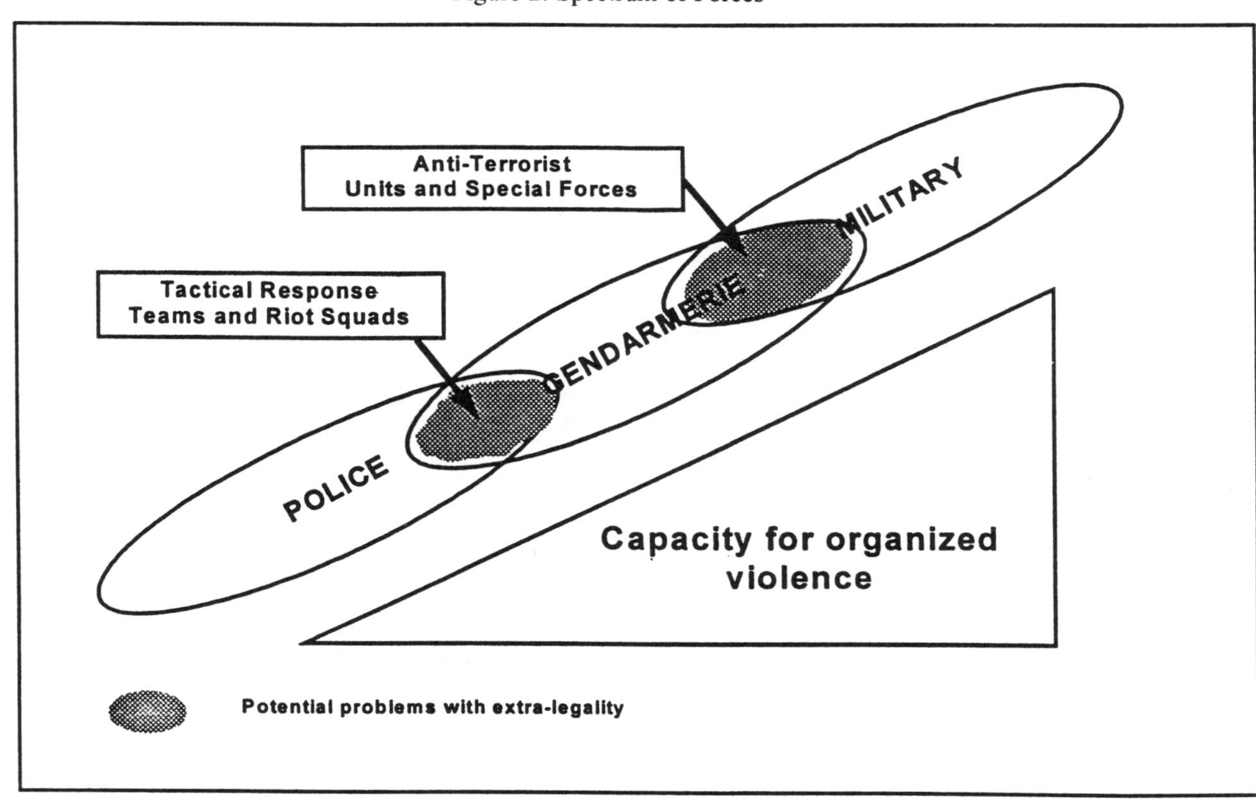

mer) and cooperation with judicial police. *Gendarme* forces generally operate in small units (platoons and companies). They may have heavy weapons and light armored vehicles, and they deal with internal threats to social order such as riots, insurgency, and organized crime.

There are abundant examples of good and bad forces in each of these categories. The common denominator of good police, *gendarme* and military forces is that they are under civilian control which is accountable to the communities they serve. Their actions are supported because they are perceived to act for the common good. They are capable of effectively and efficiently carrying out the tasks assigned. In a word, they are legitimate forces. Transparency, public oversight, and a framework of law are the essential tools to achieve this legitimacy. The amount of force which is permissible, the circumstances under which it can be used, and the legal framework for accountability is a function of the type of organization and its place in the spectrum.

Even in a country at peace with itself, the overlap between these types of forces can be a source of legal and operational dilemmas. Police SWAT teams, tactical response teams and riot squads have to operate at the extremes of the legal framework for police operations. When police operate in secret, wear masks, and target specific individuals or groups, these are danger signals. The same is true of anti-terrorist units and special forces who may operate outside the normal chain of military accountability. These special structures may be necessary responses to extreme circumstances, but can be abused both in a domestic context and in an intervention. Problems of special forces are magnified in a country at war, particularly a civil war. A force may be "legitimate" to its own constituency of extremists. The Haitian FAd'H had supporters. The Serb police in Bosnia continue to obstruct return of Muslims, with the approval of many Serbs who actively assist through gang violence.[53]

The challenge for peace force doctrine is to build a seamless framework of security to manage the full spectrum of violence: from organized military acts, through large-scale demonstrations and organized crime, to individual acts of political and social violence. Far from being a peace force problem, this whole spectrum must eventually be taken up by the belligerents, as they assume their own responsibilities for domestic and national security.

Police, Gendarme, And Military Actions

Doctrine should guide peace force actions, relations between the peace force and belligerent parties, and division of responsibilities. Whenever possible, functions should be civilian rather than military and local rather than international. Military forces are the least durable international commitment, except where strategic interests are concerned. Where functions must be assigned temporarily to military or international forces, the peace force campaign plan needs to address their eventual transfer. Doctrine should acknowledge that the spectrum of forces is continuous, although the organizations may be discreet, and may have little interaction in Western countries. We can see this continuity in peace operations.

UNFICYP offers an example of unhelpful evolution towards an imposed military division of the island. In 1964, the Greek Cypriot and Turkish Cypriot police at community level became the nucleus of the militias involved in inter-communal fighting. UNFICYP troops established security with the help of UN Civilian Police who supervised local police in their communities. After 1974, however, UN Civilian Police were effectively limited to policing in the Buffer Zone.[54] Even limited to the Buffer Zone, civilian police can help to demilitarize shooting incidents by conducting civil investigations.[55] This works because each party consents to UN mediation for incidents in the Buffer Zone, but it does nothing to resolve the broader issue of a divided society.

UNFICYP, IFOR and the UN Transitional Authority in Eastern Slavonia (UNTAES), Croatia, have all had to deal with civilian demonstrations designed to pressure the peace force and affect international opinion. In UNFICYP, unarmed troops conduct crowd control in the Buffer Zone, while the parties provide police controls outside the Buffer Zone. The UNCIVPOL role is limited to arresting civilians in the Buffer Zone and handing them back to their respective authorities. IFOR and SFOR have resorted to armed troops and armored vehicles in the Zone of Separation, with the International Police Task Force (IPTF) supervising the local police in their crowd control responsibilities. This has not been helpful, because demonstrations are sponsored by the authorities, and police in plain clothes are involved in fomenting them.[56] Because local police authorities have been unhelpful, UNTAES has resorted to the services of a Polish riot control unit which has been effective in managing staged demonstrations. In the meantime, a lot of effort has been invested in creating a joint Croat-Serb police force for Eastern Slavonia which will eventually take over the functions of communal policing.[57]

If a peace force lacks legitimacy amongst the parties to the conflict--if they do not consent to its presence or functions--then the importance of tactical concentration increases. Dispersed ONUC battalions operating in the Congo early in the mission were ineffective and at risk, as were UNPROFOR battalions in Bosnia. Replacing six battalions with a brigade in ONUC, and forming divisional areas and a Rapid Reaction Force in Bosnia improved the situation. This works for military formations, but what does it mean for police functions? IFOR matched IPTF patrols with protective platoons of mechanized troops to assist in the removal of road blocks, when armed local police opposed IPTF rulings.

Effective policing is executed at the level of the patrol--a small number of police or even an individual. Policing is only part of a justice system which also needs unbiased courts and a humane corrections or penal system. Monitoring the justice system effectively requires the consent of the local authorities, and reforming it to reflect international policing standards requires national will. In the absence of cooperation and the will to reform a judicial system, police actions may become *gendarme* or military actions. In ONUC, rounding up foreign mercenaries might have been carried out as a police action, but became a military operation by default.[58] If belligerent authorities are not in control, a military peace force presence is likely to be required. Supporting local civilian control through effectively structured police, gendarmes and military forces under legitimate civilian authorities is one of the services peace forces must plan to provide.

Lack of transparency and inadequate controls can be an acute problem with special forces at the junction of police, *gendarme*, and military forces. At their best, SWAT teams and counter-terrorist units are elite squads which attract the most effective and dedicated members of the force. At their worst, they embody the illegitimate use of force by coercive regimes. Some countries' international training programmes in the past have encouraged human rights abuses and bad practices by special forces.[59] Control is most difficult when there are shadowy unofficial forces operating, or squads of off-duty police or soldiers taking matters into their own hands. Regularizing irregular forces, imposing discipline within accountable structures, and using the civil courts to try and convict offenders are all techniques for controlling the excesses of special forces.

Force, Legitimacy and Consent

The relationship between use of force, legitimacy, and consent has been alluded to. Whether a peace force is engaged in peacekeeping, wider peacekeeping, or peace enforcement, its ability to "win" will ultimately depend on its "allies"--the belligerents. From the very outset of the mission, the full range of instruments at the disposal of the peace force should be concentrated on gaining the consent and support of the belligerent parties. Three relationships are important. The first is the relationship between the belligerent parties. The second is the relationship between the peace force and each belligerent party. The third is the relationship between use of force by the peace force and behavior of the belligerent parties.

The relationship between the belligerent parties is a crucial variable affecting decisions about the use of force. Independent of the presence of a peace force, there may be many tacit agreements or areas of *de facto* cooperation between the parties. These may relate to division of territory, black market operations, movement of people across confrontation lines, or levels of violence acceptable in a limited war. These represent a shifting balance of common interest between the parties, which can be supported or undermined by the actions of the peace force.[60] Settlements in civil wars often include provisions for the disarmament of factions, and some have argued that disarmament is an essential prerequisite for stability and the transition to political conflict resolution.[61] Defenselessness, however, may breed nervous aggression between the parties. Military balance and transparency measures such as those in place under MOMEP may be a surer path to stability.[62]

When a third party enters a conflict, the belligerents will attempt to influence its actions to gain advantage. The more powerful the force, in wider peacekeeping and peace enforcement missions, the more the parties have at stake in gaining its cooperation. Events may be staged, information manipulated, and coercive measures used to control the third party. The dilemma for a peace force is that it needs to be closely engaged with its "allies" to affect change, but the more closely it becomes engaged, the more susceptible it becomes to entanglement and manipulation. At one point, the IAPF risked becoming an enforcer for the "Loyalists". UNPROFOR and then IFOR risked becoming the agents of a Muslim minority. To the extent that special interests are served by the actions of the peace force, it will undermine its legitimacy. Legitimacy amongst local interests, however, can change as the tactical situation changes. When NATO airstrikes destroyed Bosnian Serb command and control assets in the August-September 1995 air strikes, they paved the way for huge gains of territory by the Federation. Despite this, Bosnian Serbs welcomed NATO's IFOR deployment, because the alternative was further loss of territory.[63]

The third important relationship is between the use of force and its effect on the behavior of the belligerents. Most peace forces operate with fewer military resources than the belligerents. Even when they have superior weapons, they are often outnumbered and have tenuous lines of supply. Only in the peace enforcement cases (IAPF, UNOSOM II, and UNMIH) has use of overwhelming force been a realistic option. Even IFOR's strength of 60 thousand seems insecure in a country with half a million well armed soldiers. The degree of consent or legitimacy enjoyed by a peace force varies inversely with the potential usefully to escalate the level of force used in a given situation. This relationship is illustrated in Figure 3.[64]

When local and international support for the mission is high, then the use of high levels of force will be perceived as unnecessarily coercive, and will erode legitimacy. This situation is normal in traditional peacekeeping missions; restraint is expected of peacekeepers, and any breach of the constabulary role would elicit protests by the belligerent parties. As the degree of belligerent consent declines in wider peacekeeping or peace enforcement missions, the use of limited force by a third party is likely to cause the belligerents to escalate violence to achieve their objectives. In ONUC, for example, "The UN force was not able to accomplish its purpose by force until it was strong enough to dominate the forces of the local actor concerned."[65] Limited use of force may be

Figure 3: Force and Consent

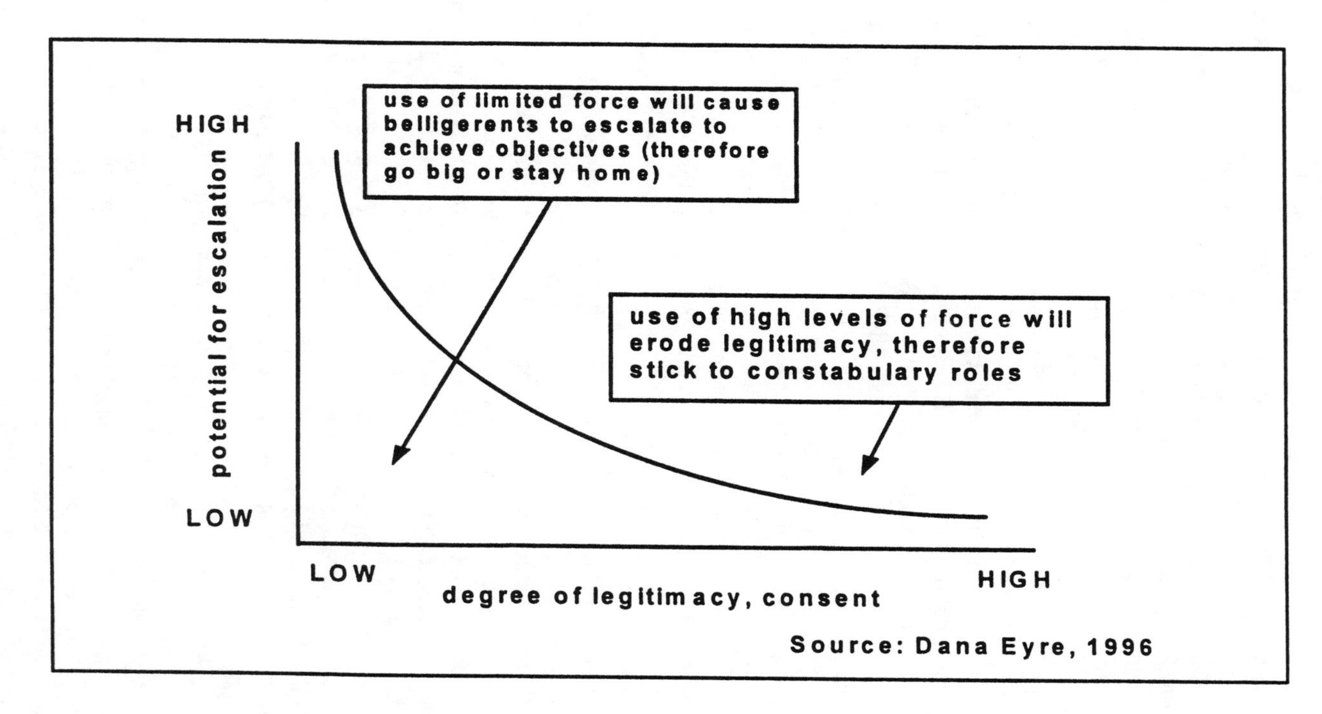

provocative and counter-productive, depending on the motivation and capabilities of the belligerent forces. When consent is limited and conditional, peace forces should be prepared to "go big or stay home".

The continuum illustrated in Figure 3 is descriptive, not prescriptive. It is possible to describe the points along the continuum. It may not be possible to choose a point at which to operate, and control the variables of consent and legitimacy. This dilemma is illustrated in recent American doctrine:

> The need to employ force may begin a cycle of increasing violence; therefore, the commanders must be judicious in employing forceful measures and must understand the relationship between force and the desired end state. Of the three variables [force, impartiality and consent] the level of force is the only one over which the commander can exert dominant influence. . . [66]

In fact, the peace force commander controls only the level of force *he* is using, not necessarily that of his allies--the parties to the conflict.

The three groups of case studies are distinguished by the balance between force, impartiality and consent, all of which affect legitimacy as Manwaring defined it. Peacekeeping and observer missions (like UNFICYP and MOMEP) enjoy a high degree of consent to their limited mandates, and exert minimal force. Wider peacekeeping missions like ONUC and UNPROFOR have experienced problems as they attempt to exert force. Where there is support at the strategic level, and at least a "modicum of in-theatre consent," they have been able to use force at tactical level.[67] Enforcement missions, like IAPF and UNOSOM II, can theoretically dispense with consent and operate according to the principles of war.[68] In practice, they do not do so. Peace enforcement operations are distinguished from war by the effort to control and de-escalate violent conflict. Targeting the enemy (violent conflict), and building the consent and support of the allies (belligerent forces) is therefore as important in peace enforcement as in peacekeeping. Any sudden change in the amount of force used therefore becomes a danger point for a mission, belying the theoretical curve of Figure 3.

Training and Operations for Peace

In the first part of this chapter, I argued for doctrine which takes account of the historical context of peace operations, and which is international and multi-disciplinary. For soldiers, a central debate about peacekeeping doctrine and training is the relative importance of military and nonmilitary skills in preparing peacekeepers. When the Manwaring paradigm is applied to case studies of peacekeeping, wider peacekeeping and peace enforcement, three sets of conclusions stand out about military skills, training and operations for peace. The first concerns the importance, and limitations, of war fighting skills. The second concerns the size and structure of peace forces. The third concerns special skills which need to be more effectively incorporated in peace operations.

War Fighting Skills and Peace Operations

All three groups of case studies demonstrate that combat skills are essential. In 1974, UNFICYP found itself in the middle of a shooting war. In traditional peacekeeping, and observer missions like MOMEP, peer group credibility and mutual confidence comes from the technical military competence and professionalism of the participants. Wider peacekeeping, missions like ONUC and UNPROFOR saw the use of heavy weapons and air forces. In peace enforcement missions, the size and complexity of the force alone demands strong professional military skills. Forces cannot be deployed for combat unless they possess the full range of combat skills; to do so would be irresponsible. Strong combat capabilities reduce the risk that the force will threatened, isolated, or endangered, as were Dutch peacekeepers in Srebrenica. Reducing the military risk increases political freedom of action. War fighting skills allow commanders to manage the inherent risks of a transition within a mission.

Force and Strength

Numerical strength is a factor in the dimension, "support to actions of the peace force". British internal security doctrine, referred to in Chapter One, advocates maximum *strength* (i.e. show of force) in order to minimize the use of *force* (i.e. application of coercive violence). In the context of internal security, a large force can afford to withstand a crowd, while a smaller one might be compelled to violence in self-defense. Does this dynamic work in peace operations? Aggregate figures for the total strength of a force are unlikely to provide a useful answer. The ONUC case illustrates the importance of tactical concentration. The total strength of the mission did not change, but its vulnerability decreased significantly when individual battalions were replaced by a coherent brigade. UNPROFOR's Rapid Reaction Force, a coherent NATO formation with an operational headquarters, was capable of operations which could not be contemplated by the "white" units of UNPROFOR. Homogeneity improves the strength and effectiveness of a force.

Force And Skill

Weak forces may resort to inappropriate violence, but strong forces with inappropriate skills may also be a problem. This is evident in the distinction between contact and combat skills. Contact skills are those which permit effective communication with the parties to the conflict (liaison, negotiation, mediation, and so on) while combat skills (shooting, patrolling, entrenching, and so on) are those which permit coercive force.[69] Aggressive patrolling, for example, is one of the ways peace forces control space. If they fail to control a buffer zone, the parties will encroach and tensions will escalate (as examples from UNFICYP show). But even the simple act of controlling space through patrolling must be balanced by the effective use of contact skills to control and de-escalate individual incidents. When a confrontation occurs, quick deployment of countervailing force may prevent further escalation, but meetings and negotiations permit de-escalation. Combat skills and contact skills are to peace operations as fire and movement are to combat operations.

Strong, effective forces with limited contact skills may be equipped to conduct a good *defense* against violent incidents. They are not well placed to undertake an *offensive* against violence--establishing trust and confidence between the parties to the conflict. This requires a range of additional contact skills, including professional consultation, mediation, problem-solving workshops, and so on. A broader view of "actions targeted on ending the conflict" would include these actions. These tools need to be used "aggressively" to control the psychological space of the conflict in the same way that aggressive patrolling is used to control the physical space. "Aggressive" use of contact skills implies ingenuity, initiative, persistence, and some risk taking. Soldiers on short rotations, without much knowledge of local language, history or culture, are not well placed to use these skills. Offensive operations therefore require specialized teams, civilians, local allies, and careful coordination with the military dimension of the peace force. This coordination itself relies on contact skills and sensitivity to organizational cultures which may be at odds.

Intelligence, psychological operations and public information are tools which can be effectively deployed in support of both offensive and defensive operations. They are susceptible to misinterpretation both by the civilian partners of the peace force and by belligerents. They are appropriately considered as "actions targeted on ending the conflict," only if they are part of a comprehensive campaign plan which includes the contact skills necessary to build trust and de-escalate tensions between the belligerents. Coercion needs to be balanced by communication with the parties; so, too, does the use of public information and psychological operations to shape the operational environment. In doing so, the civilian agencies and nongovernmental organizations collaborating with the peace force must be included in the coordination plan, to avoid undermining unity of effort. As the offensive against violence progresses, intelligence, psychological operations, and public information may become increasingly important to the civilian components of a mission., and the distinction between military and nonmilitary skills may become blurred. Transferring these functions from military to civilian and from international to local staff are important transitions in the progress of a peace operation. In Bosnia, for example, "intelligence" about human rights abuses is collected less by military intelligence teams, and more by OSCE human rights observers, who eventually enlist the aid of local partners, who continue the work after the monitors leave. Militarily strong forces without the contact skills or sophistication to manage such a transition will be poorly equipped to win the savage wars of peace.

Conclusion

The case studies in this book and the paradigm which has been used to examine them are relevant for evolving military doctrine. It has not been my purpose to revise principles or propose new ones. Various principles are widely accepted as a result of common experience of peacekeeping. Consent, impartiality, minimum use of force, and a clear objective (or unity of effort) are the most widely accepted of these principles. They correspond to legitimacy, military actions of the peace force, and unity of effort as dimensions within the Manwaring paradigm. The consensus, however, was built up over forty years of Cold War peacekeeping missions. Wider peacekeeping and peace enforcement missions, both during and after the Cold War, have shown up a divergence of national approaches to use of force. If doctrine is to evolve, it should evolve towards an internationally accepted standard for the use of force in peace operations. Ideas about war fighting in the interests of states, and pursuit of the just society cannot be separated from evolving military doctrine: as long as the inadequacies of society are used to legitimize violence, the potential for violence might spur us to redress these inadequacies. If peace operations become a vehicle for controlling violence without addressing its causes, they will become progressively more coercive and less effective. Doctrine for effective peace restoration needs to take account of the social, political and economic factors which contributed to the violence. We therefore need to frame our doctrine in the understanding that the enemy is violent conflict, the belligerents are our allies, and victory lies in defeating both physical and structural violence, while building a sustainable economy and a civil society.

Notes

[1] International Peace Academy, *Peacekeeper's Handbook*, Third Edition, (New York: Pergamon Press, 1974). Col Johan Hederstedt, LCol Jorn Hee, Maj Nils W. Orum, Maj Simo Saari, and Capt Olli Viljaranta, *Nordic UN Tactical Manual*, Volume One (Jyvaskyla, Finland, 1992). UK Army Field Manual, *Wider Peacekeeping*, Fifth Draft (Revised). B-GL-301-303/FP-001 First Draft. US FM 100-23, *Peace Operations* (Draft).

[2] Richard Smith, "The Requirement for the United Nations to Develop an Internationally Recognized Doctrine for the Use of Force in Intra-State Conflict," *The Occasional*, Number 10, Strategic and Combat Studies Institute, Camberley, Surrey, (1994) pp. 14-15.

[3] F.T. Liu, *United Nations Peacekeeping and the Non-Use of Force*, International Peace Academy, Occasional Paper Series, (1992), describes a two-tier model in which a deterrent force might be held outside the mission area.

[4] John Mackinlay, "Powerful Peacekeepers," *Survival*, Volume XXXII No. 3, (May/June 1990).

[5] Boutros Boutros-Ghali, *An Agenda for Peace: Preventive Diplomacy, Peacemaking and Peacekeeping*, Report of the Secretary-General Pursuant to the statement adopted by the Summit Meeting of the Security Council on 31 January 1992 (New York: United Nations, 1992), 25.

[6] Kofi A. Annan, "Peace Operations and the United Nations: Preparing for the Next Century," unpublished paper, (New York: United Nations, February 1996). Annan writes of "inducing consent" and the limits of coercion.

[7] The mixed messages from the US and USSR during the Congo Crisis reflects this superpower ambivalence. See Indar Jit Rikhye, *Military Adviser to the Secretary General: UN Peacekeeping and the Congo Crisis*, (London: Hurst and Company, in association with the International Peace Academy, 1993).

[8] *Moltke on the Art of War: Selected Writings*, Chapter 1, "The Nature of War," edited by Daniel J. Hughes, Translated by Harry Bell and Daniel J. Hughes, (Novato, CA: Presidio, 1993).

[9] Arthur T. Coumbe, "Operational Command in the Franco-Prussian War," *Parameters*, Vol 21, No. 2 (Summer, 1991), pp. 86-99.

[10] Charles Breunig, *The Age of Revolution and Reaction, 1789-1850*, Second Edition, (New York: Norton and Company, 1977).

[11] Karl Marx and Friedrich Engels, *The Communist Manifesto*, translation by Samuel Moore (New York: Washington Square Press, 1964), original text 1848. V.I. Lenin, "What is to be Done? Burning Questions of our Movement," in *The Lenin Anthology*, edited by Robert C. Tucker (New York: W.W. Norton and Company, 1975), 112-114, advocating revolutionary party organization. Gérard Chaliand, *Revolution in the Third World* (Harmondsworth: Penguin, 1978). Gianfranco Sanguinetti, *On Terrorism and the State: The theory and practice of terrorism divulged for the first time*, translated by Lucy Forsyth and Michel Prigent (London: *Infida Societas*, 1982). Régis Debray, *Revolution in the Revolution? Armed Struggle and Political Struggle in Latin America*, translation by Bobbye Ortiz (New York: Grove Press, 1967).

[12] Breunig, pp. 74-76.

[13] L.S. Stavrianos, *Global Rift: The Third World Comes of Age* (New York: William Morrow, 1981), 44-52.

[14] Stephen H. Roberts, *History of French Colonial Policy* (1870-1925) Volume IV (London: P.S. King and Son, 1929), 438-9.

[15] Paul Wilkinson, *Political Terrorism* (New York: John Wiley, 1974), 45.

[16] R. Tanter, "Dimensions of Conflict Behavior Within and Between Nations, 1958-1960," *Journal of Conflict Resolution*, No. 10 (March 1966), 41-64. T. Gurr and C. Ruttenburg, *The Conditions of Civil Violence: First Tests of a Causal Model* (Princeton, NJ: Center for International Studies, 1967).

[17] Johan Galtung, *The True Worlds: A Transnational Perspective* (New York: Free Press, 1980), 107-112.

[18] Richard A. Higgott, *Political Development Theory*, (London: Croom Helm, 1983), pp. 47-48.

[19] In this, it echoed the international dualism of orthodox development theory, H.W. Singer, "Poverty, Income Distribution, and Levels of Living: Thirty years of Changing Thought on Development Problems," in C.H. Hanumantha Rao and P.C. Joshi, editors, *Reflections on Economic Development and Social Change* (New Delhi: Allied Publishers Private Limited, 1979), p. 33.

[20] International Peace Academy, *The Peacekeeper's Handbook*. (New York: International Peace Academy, 1978), pp. I/6 (definitions) and III/7 (quote).

[21] Gerald Schneider and Patricia A. Weitsman, "Eliciting Collaboration from Risky States," in *Enforcing Cooperation: Risky States and Intergovernmental Management of Conflict*, edited by Gerald Schneider and Patricia A. Weitsman (New York: St Martin's Press, 1997), 4-10.

[22] Breunig, 226-7.

[23] Douglas Porch, "Bugeaud, Galliéni and Lyautey: The Development of French Colonial Warfare,"in Peter Paret, Editor, *Makers of Modern Strategy* (Princeton, NJ: Princeton University Press, 1986), 378-382. Stephen H. Roberts, *History of French Colonial Policy (1870-1925)* Volume IV, (London: P.S. King and Son, 1929), 438-9. These ideas are developed in an unpublished paper, Major D.M. Last, "The Importance of Peripheral Conflicts to Military Thinking: The Case of French Colonialism," US Army Command and General Staff College, January 1995.

[24] Druckman and Diehl have used delphic surveys to distinguish empirically between first-party and third-party roles in peacekeeping-related missions.

[25] Thomas J. Daze and John T. Fishel, "Peace Enforcement in Somalia: UNOSOM II," 5 and 8.

[26] J. Mathew Vaccaro, "The UN Peacekeeping Operation in the Congo, 1960-1964: The Nexus of Decolonialism and Superpower Conflict in the Guise of UN Peacekeeping".

[27] David Last, "Peacekeeping in Divided Societies: Limits to Success," forthcoming, *Low Intensity Conflict and Law Enforcement.*

[28] "Cypriot Youth the Only Losers," *Manchester Guardian Weekly,* 27 June 1997, 4

[29] Other examples are found in David Last, "Peacekeeping Doctrine and Conflict Resolution Techniques," *Armed Forces and Society*, Vol 22 No. 2 (Winter 1995/96), 187-210.

[30] Alija Izetbegovic, *The Islamic Declaration*, 1972. Translation provided by IFOR Information staff, page 23.

[31] For a case study of the dynamics in northwest Bosnia, see David Last, "Defeating Fear and Hatred: Multiplying the Peacebuilding Impact of a Military Contribution," forthcoming in *Canadian Foreign Policy*.

[32] Colonel P.G. Williams, OBE, "Bosnia as a `NATO Safe Area'- A Post-SFOR Solution?" unpublished paper provided by author, 11 June 1997.

[33] Stephen C. Fee, "Peacekeeping on the Ecuador-Peru Border: The Military Observer Mission - Ecuador/Peru (MOMEP)".

[34] Stephen John Stedman, "Spoiler Problems in Peace Processes," in *Synergy in Early Warning*, Conference Proceedings, March 15-18, 1997, edited by Susanne Schmeidl and Howard Adelman (Toronto: Prevention and Early Warning Unit, Centre for International and Security Studies, Forum on Early Warning and Early Response, 1997), 333-374.

[35] According to a Canadian officer on the Operations staff at the time, interviewed at the Pearson Peacekeeping Centre, May 1997.

[36] UK Army Field Manual, *Wider Peacekeeping*, (London: Her Majesty's Stationer, 1995), 2-10. See also Charles Dobbie, "A Concept for Post-Cold War Peacekeeping," *Survival*, Vol. 36, No. 3 (Autumn, 1994), 121, for a more detailed explanation of the ideas in this section of the manual, by the same author.

[37] Use of contact and combat skills is discussed in greater detail in David Last, *Theory, Doctrine and Practice of Conflict De-Escalation in Peacekeeping Operations* (Clementsport, NS: The Canadian Peacekeeping Press, 1997), 43-64.

[38] *COMMARC's Policy Guidance No 8 - Civil Tasks*, 23 March 1996, paragraph 10.

[39] Private communication with author.

[40] Vaccaro. See also Michael S. Lund, *Preventing Violent Conflicts: A Strategy for Preventive Diplomacy* (Washington, DC: USIP, 1996), 32-49. Institution building is appropriate to post-conflict peacebuilding; other techniques are appropriate to different stages in the life cycle of a conflict, 38.

[41] Examples from Bosnia are provided in David Last, "Implementing the Dayton Accords: The Challenge of Inter-Agency Coordination," in Cornwallis Group Seminar Procedings, forthcoming Canadian PK Press.

[42] Eric A. Nordlinger, *Conflict Regulation in Divided Societies* (Cambridge, Ma: Harvard University Center for International Affairs, 1977) 117.

[43] Fee.

[44] Fen Osler Hampson, *Nurturing Peace: Why Peace Settlements Succeed or Fail* (Washington, DC: United States Institute of Peace Press, 1996), 205-208.

[45] Michel Chossudovsky, "Dismantling Former Yugoslavia, Recolonizing Bosnia," paper presented at the *International Conference on Lessons of Yugoslavia*, sponsored by Science for Peace, University of Toronto, 20-23 March 1997.

[46] Gideon Rose, Council on Foreign Relations, "The Exit Strategy Delusion." Paper presented at the 92nd Annual Meeting of the American Policital Science Association, San Francisco, 28-31 August, 1996.

[47] Lawrence A. Yates, "Intervention in the Dominican Republic, 1965-1966".

[48] Fishel and Daze.

[49] NATO *Peace Support Operations* [see Baxter review, C44 file]

[50] Larry Minear and Thomas G. Weiss, *Humanitarian Action in Times of War: A Handbook for Practitioners*, (Boulder, Colorado: Lynne Rienner, 1993). Sadako Ogata, "The Interface Between Peacekeeping and Humanitarian Action," in D. Warner (Editor), *New Dimensions of Peacekeeping*, (Netherlands: Kluwer Academic Publishers, 1995), pp. 119-127.International Committee of the Red Cross, *Symposium on Humanitarian Action and Peace-Keeping Operations: Report*. Editor Umesh Palwankar, Legal Division of the ICRC (Geneva: ICRC, June 1994). Andrew S. Natsios, "Commander's Guidance: A Challenge of Complex Humanitarian Emergencies," *Parameters*, XXVI:2 (Summer 1996), pp. 50-66.

[51] Neil Wright, *Working with the UNHCR* (Geneva: United Nations High Commission for Refugees, 1995). See also *A UNHCR Handbook for the Military on Humanitarian Operations*, (New York: United Nations High Commission for Refugees, January 1995).

[52] John Mackinlay, editor, *A Guide to Peace Support Operations* (Providence, RI: Thomas J. Watson Jr. Institute for International Studies, 1996).

[53] See Combined Press Information Centre (CPIC) Daily Press Briefing transcripts, 4 March 1997, for a description of events at Gajevi. Available on internet from scheurwe@hq.nato.int, or http://www.nato.int

[54] Swan.

[55] Last, 1995, 193-4.

[56] I have personal experience with both Muslim police of the Federation and Serb police of Republic of Srpska doing so at Otoka, 19 April 1996. Other examples can be found in the Combined Press Information Centre briefings, November 1996 to March 1997.

[57] Interview with a UN Civil Affairs officer from UNTAES at Pearson Peacekeeping Centre, 21 June 1997.

[58] Vaccaro.

[59] See Dana Priest, "Army Training Manuals Urged Executions, Torture as Coercion: Manuals Used 1982-91, Pentagon Reveals," *Washington Post*, Saturday, September 21, 1996, page A9, for an alleged example.

[60] Robert Axelrod, *The Evolution of Cooperation* (New York: Basic Books, 1984), 73-87. See also Last, 1997, 81-83 on cooperation in buffer zones.

[61] *Establishing A Canadian Capability in Peace-Building*, Background Paper for the National Forum on Foreign Policy (Ottawa: Canadian Centre for Foreign Policy Development, 1997).

[62] Fee.

[63] David Last, "Peacekeeping in Divided Societies: Limits to Success," forthcoming in *Low Intensity Conflict and Law Enforcement*.

[64] This relationship was described by Dana Eyre, a US Civil Affairs officer and professor at the Naval Post-Graduate School, Monterey, in 1996. It implies a different relationship from that described by a similar figure showing force, impartiality and consent in FM 100-23, *Peace Operations*, Final Draft, 1995, page 1-6.

[65] Vaccaro.

[66] FM 100-23, *Peace Operations*,(Washington, DC: Headquarters, Department of the Army, December 1994), 13.

[67] United Kingdom Army Field Manual, *Wider Peacekeeping*, (London: Her Majesty's Stationary Office, 1995), page 3-17.

[68] Charles Dobbie, "A Concept for Post-Cold War Peacekeeping,"*Survival*, 36:3 (Autumn, 1994) 121. Charles Dobbie was one of the principle authors of the manual, *Wider Peacekeeping*.

[69] The distinction was drawn by A.B. Fetherston, *Toward a Theory of UN Peacekeeping*, and is elaborated in David Last, *Theory, Doctrine and Practice of Conflict De-escalation*.

About the Editor

Dr. John T. Fishel is Professor of National Security Affairs at the US Army Command and General Staff College, Fort Leavenworth, Kansas. He received the PhD in political science from Indiana University. As a reserve officer on active duty, Lieutenant Colonel Fishel was assigned to the United States Southern Command where he was responsible for organizing civic action operations associated with exercises in Peru and Honduras, civic action seminars in Bolivia, conducting assessments in Peru, Bolivia, and El Salvador, and organizing a major assessment of the El Salvadoran Armed Forces in combination with the Salvadorans. After Operation JUST CAUSE, he was responsible for developing the post conflict civil-military operations plan for Panama and establishing and training the Panama National Police. Dr. Fishel has authored numerous articles and book chapters on military and security issues. His publications include *The Fog Of Peace: Planning and Executing the Restoration of Panama*, and *Liberation, Occupation and Rescue: War Termination and Desert Storm*. His latest book is *Civil Military Operations In The New World*. Dr. Fishel is currently a member of the Board of the Visitors for the School of the Americas.

About the Contributors

Thomas K. Adams is a Lieutenant Colonel currently assigned to the US Army War College's Peacekeeping Institute. Before taking his current post, he served as an author and instructor at the US Army Command and General Staff College where he specialized in Peace Operations. In September 1993 he was the UN specialist on a team requested by the US MilGroup El Salvador and the Armed Forces of El Salvador to assist in creating a new national military strategy for El Salvador and an accompanying officer training program. From 1990-1992, he was assigned to the headquarters of USSOUTHCOM in Panama. He holds a PhD in Political Science from the Maxwell School of Syracuse University.

Joseph G.D. Babb LTC, USA (Ret) currently serves as an instructor at the US Army Command and Staff College at Fort Leavenworth, Kansas. A China Foreign Area Officer, LTC Babb has held a variety of joint and service assignments in intelligence and special operations billets in Asia and in the continental United States including China ground forces analyst at the Defense Intelligence Agency at the Pentagon in Washington, DC, and Senior China Analyst and Deputy Director of Current Intelligence, United States Pacific Command in Hawaii. LTC Babb's last military assignment was as the Chief of the Strategic Studies Division at CGSC. He is currently a PhD student in History at the University of Kansas specializing in East Asian history.

Ambassador Edwin G. Corr is the Director of the Energy Institute of the Americas and the Associate Director of the International Programs Center at the University of

Oklahoma. His diplomatic career under both Republican and Democratic administrations includes ambassadorships to Bolivia, El Salvador, and Peru. He has served as the Deputy Assistant Secretary of State for International Narcotics Matters. Ambassador Corr has also served in Thailand, Mexico, and Ecuador, as a Peace Corps Director in Colombia, and as an infantry officer in the US Marine Corps. He received the BS degree from the University of Oklahoma and also holds Masters degrees from both the University of Oklahoma and the University of Texas at Austin. Ambassador Corr is the recipient of several US and foreign awards, and has written and edited various articles and books including *Low-Intensity Conflict: Old Threats In A New World*.

Lieutenant Colonel Thomas J. Daze is currently an instructor at the US Army Command and General Staff College. He received a BS from the US Military Academy and an MMAS from US Army CGSC. He has held a variety of staff positions throughout his military career, including two years on the Department of the Army staff in the Directorate for Strategy Plans and Policy. From April 1993 to January 1994, he served as the military assistant to the Force Commander of the United Nations Operations in Somalia (UNOSOM) II. In May 1994, he served on the Montgomery Board, formed by the Chief of Staff of the Army and chartered to write the US Army after action review for UNOSOM II operations.

Colonel Stephen C. Fee commanded the US Contingent to MOMEP (US Observers and Joint Task Force Safe Border) from August 1995 through February 1996. In September 1996, COL Fee completed a tour as the Commander, US Military Group in San Salvador, El Salvador and is now assigned to the Defense Intelligence Agency in Washington DC. Colonel Fee is a US Army Foreign Area Officer with extensive experience in Latin America. He is a graduate of the Inter-American Defense College (Ft. McNair, Washington DC) and has served overseas tours in Japan, Uruguay, Panamá and El Salvador. He holds a Masters Degree in Latin American Studies from the University of Kansas.

Kimbra L. Fishel is a political scientist specializing in military and security issues. She received the MA in political science from the University of Oklahoma where she worked as a research assistant on El Salvador for Ambassador Edwin G. Corr. In the summer of 1997, she served on the support staff of a US team making a series of presentations to the College of High Strategic Studies in El Salvador. She teaches International Relations and American Government and has published numerous articles on US foreign policy, conflict and warfare under her previous name of Krueger. Her present research focuses on the peace process in Central America, and she is currently pursuing a Ph.D.

Major David Last, CD, PhD has served with the Royal Canadian Artillery since 1975. He is a graduate of the Royal Military College of Canada, Carleton University, London School of Economics, and the US Army Command and General Staff College. He has served in Canada and Germany, on UN duty in Cyprus, Croatia, and Bosnia, and with NATO's Implementation Force as a civil affairs officer. He is the author of *Theory, Doctrine and Practice of Conflict De-escalation in Peacekeeping Operations* (The Canadian Peacekeeper's Press) and is currently seconded to the Pearson Peacekeeping Centre in Cornwallis, Nova Scotia.

Major General John Arch MacInnis, CD, CMM served with the Royal Canadian Artillery from 1961 to 1995. He is a graduate of Queen's University, the Canadian Army Staff College, and the National Defence College. His military appointments included unit and base commands in Canada and senior staff appointments in National Defence Headquarters. He served as Chief of Staff and the Canadian Contingent Commander for the United Nations Force in Cyprus (1986) and was the Deputy Force Commander, United Nations Protection Force in Former Yugoslavia from July 1993 to June 1994, before resuming command of Land Force Atlantic Area in Canada. Since 1995 he has served as Chief of the Mine Clearance and Policy Unit in United Nations Headquarters, New York, and is a member of the Board of International Advisors for the International Committee of the Red Cross.

Dr. Max G. Manwaring is an Adjunct Professor of Political Science at Dickenson College, an Adjunct Professor at the US Army Peacekeeping Institute, and a political-military affairs consultant based in Carlisle, Pennsylvania. He received the PhD in Political Science from the University of Illinois. He has served in various civilian and military positions including the United States Southern Command's Small Wars Operations Research Directorate, the Defense Intelligence Agency, and the United States Southern Command's Directorate for Plans, Policy and Political-Military Affairs. Dr. Manwaring is the author of several articles dealing with politcal-military affairs and is editor of numerous books including *Managing Contemporary Conflict:Pillars Of Success*. Dr. Manwaring retired from the US Army with the rank of Colonel.

Lieutenant Colonel George W. Steuber currently commands 1st Battalion, 19th Field Artillery at Fort Sill, Oklahoma. He is a Southeast Asian Foreign Area Officer and is a graduate of the Thai Command and General Staff College. He was selected as one of three US officers to participate in UNAMIC and was selected by the UNTAC Force Commander, Lieutenant General Sanderson, as his personal representative to Kampong Thom Province. LTC Steuber also served as the Joint Operations Center Chief, JTF Somalia, and Chief of Staff for Task Force Mountain, Multinational Force Haiti. His most recent assignment was as the Asia Branch Chief, Crisis Support Division, Directorate of Intelligence (J-2), on the Joint Staff.

Lieutenant Colonel Murray Swan is an infantry officer in the Royal Canadian Regiment of the Canadian Armed Forces. He has served in a variety of field and staff positions at Battalion, Brigade and National levels. He has been directly involved in Peacekeeping missions serving with an infantry battalion in Cyprus (1978), on the UNFICYP staff as the Force Operations Officer (1986/87), as the UNFICYP Chief Humanitarian Officer and Commander Canadian Contingent (1991/93) and as the Staff Assistant/Chief of Staff in the Multinational Force and Observers (in the Sinai 1987/88). He spent several years in the operations and planning Directorates of the Canadian National Defence Headquarters (NDHQ) where he was directly involved in the staffing of deployments and maintenance of all post 1980 Canadian Peacekeeping missions. Following his command in Cyprus, he was posted to the US Army Command and General Staff College where he initiated the "Peace Operations" curriculum and for two years was the Chief, Military Operations Other Than War Division. Lt. Col. Swan is currently serving as the Assistant Army Adviser at the Canadian Defence Liaison Staff in London, United Kingdom.

J. Matthew Vaccaro serves in the Office of Peacekeeping and Humanitarian Assistance in the Office of the Secretary of Defense. He is responsible for policy issues relating to the planning, fielding, managing, and financing of peace operations. He leads the political-military planning team for on-going operations and contingencies. Prior to joining the Defense Department, Mr. Vaccaro was a Senior Analyst at DFI

International, a research and consulting firm in Washington DC, where he managed studies on conflict resolution. He is a graduate of Stanford University.

Lawrence A. Yates received his BA and MA in history from the University of Missouri-Kansas City and his Ph.D. in history from the University of Kansas, specializing in American diplomatic history, specifically the foreign policy of the Truman Administration. In 1981, Dr. Yates joined the faculty of the Combat Studies Institute, the history department at the US Army Command & General Staff College in Fort Leavenworth, Kansas. There he teaches military history and manages the department's research and publication programs. He is the author of several articles on US contingency operations since World War II and has written a monograph on the 1965 US intervention in the Dominican Republic entitled *Power Pack*. In 1989, he was in Panama during the US invasion of that country. He is currently working on the Army's official history of US military operations in Panama, 1989-1990.

About the Book

This book integrates peace operations into the paradigm first articulated in *Uncomfortable Wars,* edited by Max Manwaring. It not only addresses social science theory of conflict and conflict resolution but it links that theory to military doctrine by way of a series of nine case studies which range from traditional peacekeeping to peace enforcement. The book brings together a group of authors who all combine practical experience with academic insight. With three Canadian peacekeepers among its authors, the book is not limited to the American point of view. Their insights, nonetheless, reinforce the theory as well as expand upon it.